VEDIC EQUALITY AND HINDUISM
Focussing on Dalit Emancipation

The author of the book was a lecturer in Mathematics at the Banaras Hindu University before joining the Indian Foreign Service. He has given expression to his understanding of the original and genuine caste system, the Vedic way and approach to human life; the tradition of Sati, its misunderstanding and misrepresentation, wrong notions spread by the Manusmriti. He feels concerned about the Dalits and their emancipation as also about the ills that beset the Hindu society today and is deeply committed to their removal.

VEDIC EQUALITY

and

HINDUISM

A Reformist Agenda : Dalit Emancipation and Return To Vedic Brotherhood

O.P. Gupta

New Age Books

ISBN: 81-7822-285-x

First Edition: Delhi, 2006

Published by
NEW AGE BOOKS
A-44 Naraina Phase-I
New Delhi-110 028 (INDIA)
Email: nab@vsnl.in
Website: www.newagebooksindia.com

Printed in India
at Shri Jainendra Press
A-45 Naraina Phase-I, New Delhi-110 028

Dedicated to my parents,

LATE SHRI KANHAIYALAL JAISWAL

(Jaitpura, Varanasi)

&

LATE SMT. RAJKUMARI DEVI

(Barhaj Bazar, Deoria)

who inspired me to be dedicated to

Vedic Equality of ALL HINDUS

&

to the welfare of the poor and downtrodden.

PREFACE

During my postings in India and abroad, I met a number of Indian academics, Indian journalists, and religious leaders of almost all faiths, and also interacted with a number of such diplomats, foreign academics and foreign journalists who were either trained Indologists or had first hand experience of the Indian sub-continent. During lively discussions with such foreigners at social gatherings or at diplomatic receptions and dinners, I initially found myself at some disadvantage in replying to often asked questions such as Why proportion of Hindus is declining in India,Why Hindus used to burn alive their widows, What is Sati, Is there any Vedic sanction for Sati, Status of women in Vedas and in Hinduism, Who are *dalit* Hindus, Whether Vedas sanction birth–based casteism, Why Hindus do not take beef, How old are Vedas and Sanskrit, Why so many Gods (330million?) in Hinduism, Who are Aryans, Who are Dravidians, Why Dalit Hindus are opting out etc.

Having largely been ignorant of basics of my own religion, I, from my Tanzania days (1994–98), started studying Holy Vedas, Holy Qur'an, and Holy Bible, the primary sources, so as to understand what primary sources command rather than being guided by secondary sources or by opinions of other learned authors. In my search for replies to the above questions, I have relied exclusively upon the Holy Vedas, as these are the undisputed Supreme Scriptures of all Hindus, superseding anything and everything to the contrary. I have relied basically upon English translation of Rigveda by HH Wilson, Arya & Joshi. To my surprise, I found that many currently held beliefs, principles and practices of Hinduism are not consistent with Vedas, Gita and the two examples (para 3.4) set by Lord Rama.

The basic strategy adopted by the lobby advocating caste by birth is to supersede canonical scripture (Holy Veda) by non-canonical literature composed largely during the Christian era (Anno Domino) while paying handsome obeisance to Vedas. It is the same strategy adopted by the pro–beef lobby and the pro–sati lobby. This is the reason why I have given the full texts of the concerned Vedic richas in Sanskrit so that readers themselves may see how the original teachings were distorted.

Authors after authors universally quote the Purusha–Sukta of Rigveda (X.90) (90th Sukta of the tenth chapter of Rigveda) as the Vedic authority sanctifying birth based casteism among Hindus. But, as per my humble analysis, it preaches just the opposite i.e., it preaches total equality, perfect unity and complementarity of all the four professions or the four classes (brahamana, rajnya, vaishya and shudra). It is my belief that Dalit emancipation and annihilation of casteism is both possible and feasible but only with the assistance of Vedas. Healthy combination of Vedic richas and the Constitutional provisions of equality will succeed where Gandhi and Ambedkar did not fully succeed in annihilating casteism. Gandhi and Ambedkar etc. did succeed in diluting the rigours of casteism.

Some authors quote Rigvedic richas (X.18.7) (the seventh richas of the 18th sukta of the tenth chapter of Rigveda) as the sanction for Sati or widow burning. My studies show that Rigveda does not prescribe widow burning at all but sanctions their remarriages. RV (X.18) describes burial of the corpse of husband; it is really a burial hymn, so, there is no funeral pyre for the corpse of husband in this hymn, which a Hindu widow, as desired by pro–sati lobby, may mount. If there is no funeral pyre in RV (X.18) it is obvious that at least this sukta can't be quoted to justify sati ritual.

Some people say that Hindu women are prohibited to read Vedas and recite the Gayatri mantra. There is no such gender prohibition in Vedas. There are at least twenty–nine lady rishies who were revealed Rigvedic richas confirming Vedic sanction for gender equality. It may come as another surprise to many that Rigveda does sanction institution of female priests.

How old are Vedas? What is their antiquity? Who are Aryans & Dravidians? Whether Hinduism is a missionary religion or not? Vedas use the word 'dravida' to imply wealth, opulence etc., but the East India Company historians misused it to imply dark skinned people.

Some people misquote Vedic richas to claim that Vedas sanction slaughter of cows and beef eating. They do so by translating the word *ghrit* (clarified butter) into 'fat implying tallow of cattle' and *mahisa* (buffalo) into cow. They also invoke 'funeral fire' richas and 'forest fire' richas in their kitchens to justify cow–slaughter in Vedas.

In the Indian political lexicon, the word *manuwadi* implies the one who supports birth–based casteism. It is based on the blind belief that the Manusmriti (composed around 200 AD) supports birth based casteism whereas there are many shlokas in Manusmriti itself which command that social stratification is not birth based, but based on skills and qualifications acquired in this life. (Para 3.5)

Religion, in my humble opinion, does play an important role in nation building. Systems, which initially denounced religion as "opium of people", have now softened their attitudes toward religion. On the positive side, religion reduces internal social tensions, raises levels of peace & stability with less expenditure on policing and saves energy of society for productive sectors. BIMARU states of India (Bihar, Madhya Pradesh, Rajasthan and Uttar Pradesh) have predominance of casteism, so, not surprisingly, are economically backward. I believe that spread of Vedic commandments for equality by birth and gender equality will reduce incidences of caste and gender conflicts releasing our social energy for even faster economic growth. An analytical article which recently appeared in the Financial Times of the UK has also identified the Hindu caste system, among other factors, as responsible for the slower economic growth of India compared to that of the People's Republic of China (para 4.3).

Let us jettison the "excess baggage" of casteism. Let us liberate Hinduism from the shackles of ignorance created by secondary sources by setting into motion this reformist agenda: equality by birth & gender equality.

Most of us, working class English speaking Hindus, rarely get an exposure to the basics of our religion. Our exposure is oftenly limited to certain rituals and recitations of some bhajans and mantras, which we learn from our parents. So, whenever there is a serious discussion on Hinduism, we generally end up either being on the defensive pleading ignorance, or, at the worst, denouncing or denigrating Hinduism, without knowing its basics. This book attempts to plug this vital gap.

Being the Indian Ambassador/High Commissioner, I got invitations to attend religious functions of almost all the communities in temples, mosques, churches, synagogues, gurudwaras, etc. where I was expected to make speeches too. I also had opportunities to have personal interactions with religious leaders of many faiths. This encouraged me to acquaint myself with a few basics of many religions.

In Finland, I had the pleasure of interacting with Prof. Asko Parpola of the University of Helsinki. Gist of our discussions has also been included in this book.

Views expressed in this book are my personal and not that of the Govt. of India. I would like to express my thanks and gratitude to all those who encouraged and assisted me in bringing out this book, especially, my wife Nirupama who in the freezing sub–zero temperature of Helsinki was a constant companion and a source of encouragement.

August 02, 2005
Helsinki, Finland

O.P.GUPTA (IFS: 71)
opg4444@yahoo.co.in
aprgupta@yahoo.com

CONTENTS

Preface *vii*

One
HOLY VEDAS 1

1.1 *Rigveda* 8
1.2 *Samaveda* 11
1.3 *Yajurveda* 11
1.4 *Atharvaveda* 12
1.5 *Single Divine Source* 13
1.6 *Vedic river Saraswati* 14
1.7 *Antiquity of the Vedas* 20

Two
VEDIC EQUALITY AND CASTEISM 35

2.1 *Declining Percentage of Hindus & Its Reasons* 35
2.2 *Supremacy of Vedas* 40
2.3 *Non–Canonical Literature* 43
2.4 *Purusha–Sukta: Reappraised* 44
2.5 *Professions–not–hereditary Richas* 50
2.6 *Equality and Unity Richas* 54
2.7 *Conclusion* 61

Three
GITA AND CASTEISM 63

3.1 *Shlokas Prohibiting Birth Based Castes* 63
3.2 *Common origin of all and Dalit Emancipation in Gita Too* 67
3.3 *Three Gunas Too: Not Hereditary* 71
3.4 *Valmiki Ramayan and Two Examples Set By Lord Rama* 72
3.5 *Manusmriti: Skill Based Social Stratification, Not Birth Based* 73
3.6 *Some Good Questions* 75

3.7 *Hindusim: A Missionary Religion* 76
3.8 *New Roles for The Hindu Priests* 77
3.9 *Dalit Contributions to Vedic and Other-Scriptures* 78
3.10 *Conclusion* 80

Four
DALIT EMANCIPATION AND INTER–RELIGION CONVERSIONS 81

4.1 *Need for Second Generation Social Reforms in Hinduism* 82
4.2 *Ambedkar on Castes* 83
4.3 *Manusmriti: The Root Cause of Hindu Defeats* 86
4.4 *Gandhi Opposes Untouchability* 100
4.5 *Gandhi Opposes Conversions* 103
4.6 *Supreme Court of India on Conversions* 104
4.7 *Shortcomings of Inter-religion Conversions* 105
4.8 *Modus Operandi for Second Generation Reforms* 108
4.9 *Return to Vedic Brotherhood* 111

Five
INTRA–RELIGION CONVERSIONS 113

5.1 *Sects in Islam* 114
5.2 *Holy Qur'an on Lord Jesus Christ* 123
5.3 *Some Convergences between Buddhism, Christianity, Hinduism & Islam.* 124
5.4 *Christ in India?* 127
5.5 *Sects in Christianity* 128
5.6 *Dates of X–mas* 137
5.7 *Anti–ageing DHEA & Murti–pooja* 138
5.8 *Conclusions* 144

Six
GENDER EQUALITY IN THE VEDAS 146

Seven
SATI AND WIDOW–REMARRIAGE 151

7.1 *Vedic Command to separate Living Beings from the Dead* 153
7.2 *Reappraisal of RV (X.18.7) and (X.18.8)* 154
7.3 *Practices in Other Civilizations* 159
7.4 *Nine Vedic Richas sanctioning Widow Remarriages* 161

7.5 *Sati not mandatory in Ramayana and Mahabharata too* 164
7.6 *Vedic Rights of Hindu Women* 165
7.7 *Conclusions* 167

Eight

VEDAS, BEEF AND MEDICAL SCIENCES 168

8.1 *Constitutional Position* 168
8.2 *Diplomatic Dinners & Beef* 168
8.3 *Vedic ban on cow Slaughter* 169
8.4 *Similies and metaphors in the Vedas* 173
8.5 *Scholarly manipulations and Genuine translation difficulties* 177
8.6 *Vedic Richas Mis-Quoted to support cow slaughter* 179
8.7 *Charak Samhita* 190
8.8 *Mughal Emperors on Cow slaughter* 190
8.9 *Views of the Supreme Court of India and Others* 191
8.10 *Vedas supersede all secondary Sources* 194
8.11 *Animal Fat and Rheumatism* 195
8.12 *Bovine Spongiform Encephalopathy (BSE)* 196
8.13 *Cancer, Cholesterol* 200
8.14 *Cardiologists' advice* 201
8.15 *Option is truly yours* 203

Nine

MYTHS OF ARYAN–DRAVIDA DIVIDE 205

9.1 *Meaning of Arya and Dravida in Vedas* 205
9.2 *Confusion about word 'Aryans'* 207
9.3 *Aryan–Dravida Divide: Myths and Realities* 208
9.4 *Aryan Invasion Theory: Now Discarded* 214
9.5 *Ambedkar on Dasas, Dasyus, AIT and his Single Race Theory* 230
9.6 *Dasas, Dasyus; Aryans from the same Racial Stock* 231
9.7 *Some Points* 235
9.8 *Migrations: Eastward or Westward* 236
9.9 *Westward Migration of Rroma People: From India to Europe* 241

Appendix I

VEDIC BROTHERHOOD 246

Appendix II

XIITH WORLD SANSKRIT CONFERENCE, HELSINKI 261

Appendix III
QUESTIONS & ANSWERS 266

Appendix IV
FURTHER RESOURCES 298

A SELECT BIBLIOGRAPHY 304

Index 314

One

HOLY VEDAS

'Veda', literally means divine knowledge. It is the Hindu belief that the richas (also called mantras or shlokas) of the Vedas are eternal (*shashwat*) and that, these were revealed to the blessed ones from time to time by God. When the number of richas became numerous, it is believed that rishi Vedvyas arranged or, redacted all the Vedic richas subjectwise into four books called Rigveda, Yajurveda, Samaveda and Atharvaveda. These are the Supreme scriptures of Hinduism. These are in a way the 'canonical' scriptures. These are written in Sanskrit in the Devanagari script with the same meanings and similar/ same pronunciations as in vogue today. In ancient times there were eighteen ways/styles (*swara*) to pronounce but now there are only three (*udatta, unudatta and swarit*) in vogue, so, our pronunciations of today may not always exactly match with pronunciations of our Vedic ancestors. The famous Gayatri mantra is a Rigvedic mantra RV (III.62.10) i.e., the tenth richa of the 62nd sukta of the third chapter of the Rigveda. We still chant it in our daily lives as was being done during the times of our Vedic forefathers. This shows the unbroken continuity of Vedic traditions among Hindus.

The Vedic rishis explored all the aspects of science including anthropological, metaphysical, psychological, physiological and ethical aspects. Vedas contain richas not only on worshipping and spirituality but also on Agriculture, Algebra, Art, Astrology,

Astronomy, Cosmology, Economy, Family Relationships, Geometry, Geology, Geography, Herbal Medicine, Linguistics, Literature, Logic, Long Life(immortality), Magic, Mathematics, Meteorology, Politics, Psychology, Space Science, Social Sciences, War, etc. About one third of the Rigveda deals with War & Weaponry. RV (V.13.6) mentions the circum–ference of a wheel. Rigvedic sukta RV (X.90) (90th sukta of the tenth chapter) is popularly called the Purusha–sukta. Purusha–Sukta mentions one fourth, three fourth, thousand (*sahasra*), distance measuring ten fingers, etc. The solar eclipse is described in RV (V.40.5–9). Rigveda (I.84.13) mentions multiplication of numbers. In Atharvaveda, AV (XIII.5.2–6) each number from one to ten is enumerated. In AV(V.15 & 16), we find two, three, four digit numbers with specific mention of numbers like ten, twenty, thirty, forty,..... hundred, thousand, etc. The concept of zero and place value of digits or numbers were, thus, known to our Vedic ancestors. RV (X.97), Yajurveda (XII.75–101) and many richas of Atharvaveda describe herbal medicines. The Rigveda mentions 67 medicinal herbs. Similarly, the Yajurveda mentions 82 and the Atharvaveda mentions 288 medicinal herbs.

In various branches of scientific literature, in Phonetics, Grammar, Mathematics, Astronomy, Medicine and Law, Arthur A. MacDonell, in his book 'A History of Sanskrit Literature'(1899AD) (page8) says, "the Indians (i.e., Hindus) achieved notable results. In some of these subjects their attainments are, indeed, far in advance of Greek attainments." He opines (page 4) that Sanskrit literature exceeds in volume that of Greece and Rome put together. The Indians (i.e., Hindus) are the only division of the Indo–European family that has created a great national religion – Hinduism – and a great world religion , Buddhism, while all the rest, far from displaying originality in this sphere, have long since adopted foreign faith (page 5).

The importance of ancient Indian (Hindu) literature as a whole, MacDonell opines, largely consists in its originality. When the Greeks, towards the end of the fourth century B.C. invaded the Northwest, the Indians (i.e., Hindus) had already fully worked out a national culture of their own, unaffected by foreign influences. And, in spite of successive waves of invasion and conquest by the Persians, Greeks, Scythians, Muhammadans, the national development of the life and literature of the Indo–Aryan race remained practically unchecked and unmodified from without down to the era of British occupation. No other branch of the Indo–European stock has experienced an isolated evolution like this. No other country except China can trace back its language and literature, its religious beliefs and rites, its domestic and social customs, through an uninterrupted development of more than three thousand years (MacDonell, page 6).

In Yajurveda (XVII.2) specific words for numerals starting from ten to *parardhana* (i.e., ten raised to the power seventeen) have been mentioned. No wonder, La Place, a famous French mathematician wrote: "It was India that gave us the ingenious method of expressing all numbers by means of ten symbols (Decimal System)...a profound and important idea which escaped the genius of Archimedes and Apollonius, two of the greatest men produced by antiquity." Albert Einstein, inventor of the Theory of Special Relatively and the Theory of General Relatively said: "We owe a lot to the Indians who taught us how to count, without which no worthwhile, scientific discovery could have been made." Lancelot Hogben in his book "Mathematics for Millions" wrote: "There has been no more revolutionary contribution than the one which the Hindus (Indians) made when they invented Zero."

Emmelin Plunret has written in her book 'Calendars and Constellation': "There were very advanced Hindu astronomers in 600 BC. The Vedas contain an account of the dimension of Earth, Sun, Moon, Planets and Galaxies." RV (I.84.15) informs that moon shines by reflecting the light of the sun. RV (VIII.12.30) reads: "O God! When thou upholdest this powerful sun in the heaven, all globes like earth are held by its attraction." Yaj (23.9) asks: "Who does move on its own axis? Who does move round the other?" Yaj (23.10) replies: "The Sun moves on its own axis and the moon moves round the sun and the earth." Yaj (23.62) suggests that the earth is spherical. It says, "This altar is the earth's extremest limit". As we know, any point on the surface of a sphere is the fartherest point from the diagonally opposite point on the sphere.Therefore, this richa clearly implies that the earth is spherical. (See reply to question No. 41 in Appendix III)

Wheeler Wilcox writes: "India – the land of Vedas, the remarkable works contain not only religious ideas for a perfect life, but also facts which science has proved true. Electricity, radium, electronics, airship, all were known to the seers who founded the Vedas." The word electricity (*vidyuta*) appears in AV (I.13). Prof. W. Heisenberg, famous for his Principle of Uncertainty in the Quantum Mechanics, has written: "After the conversations about Indian Philosophy, some of the ideas of Quantum Physics that had seemed so crazy suddenly made much more sense." Erwin Schrodinger, after whom there is the famous Schrodinger equation in the Quatum Wave Mechanics, was also directly influenced by Vedanta. Dr. Robert Oppenheimer, Physicist who supervised explosion of the first US atomic bomb (the Manhattan Project) was familiar with Hindu books and is quoted saying that he recalled shloka (XI.12) of Gita when he saw 'thousands of sun's bursting on the horizon at the time of detonation.On the day of the nuclear test, Oppenheimer fully realized the enormity of what he had just accomplished. As he stood watching the mushroom cloud, he recalled later, a phrase from the Bhagwadgita (XI.32), the Hindu scripture, floated through his mind, "I am become death, the destroyer of worlds." (www.nuclearfiles.org).

So, the top scientists of the world, even when Hindus were under subjugation, took pride in reading Hindu scriptures and publicly,without feeling any inferiority or hesitation, accepted deriving inspiration therefrom.They were not afraid of being labelled 'obscurantists' for going through Hindu scriptures as seekers of knowledge are not afraid of such comments.

In RV (X.129), called the Creation Hymn (*nasadiya* sukta), uncertainties about creation of cosmos have been expressed. RV (X.129.6) reads: "Who really knows? Who in this world may declare it! Whence was this Creation, whence was it engendered? The gods (were) subsequent to the (world's Creation), so, who knows whence it arose?" Yajurveda (III.59) asks, "Who knows this world's central point? Who knows the heaven, the earth, and the wide air between them? Who knows the birthplace of the mighty Surya (sun)?" Steve Weinberg, a Nobel Laureate and a Particle Physicist from the University of Texas, USA, wrote in his 1977 book, 'The First Three Minutes', "The more the universe seems comprehensive, the more it seems pointless." British astrophysicist Stephan Hawking told (BBC, Newsnight, 15th July 2004) that we can never be sure of the past or predict the future. The question whether any information escaped from 'black holes' has philosophical and practical consequences for the question of whether the universe itself is knowable and for the laws of cause and effect (International Herald Tribune, July 17–18 2004). Abhas Mitra of the Bhabha Atomic Research Centre of India has questioned the 'black hole' theory of Hawking. So, uncertainties about the origin of universe as expressed in RV (X.129) still remain.

Europeans call numerals from one to ten 'Arabic numerals' as these went from Arabia to Europe, and, Arabs call these numerals "rukam–al–hindia" or 'hindsa' as these went to Arabs from India (al–hind). Jawaharlal Nehru in his book 'Discovery of India' (page 216) has written: "Highly intellectual and given to abstract thinking as they were, one would expect the ancient Indians to excel in mathematics. Europe got its early arithmetic and algebra from the Arabs–hence the 'Arabic numerals'– but the Arabs themselves had previously taken them from India. The astonishing progress that the Indians had made in mathematics is now well known and it is recognized that the foundations of modern arithmetic and algebra were laid long ago in India." On page 220, Nehru has further elaborated: "In the eighth century, during the reign of the Khalif Al–Mansur (753–774), a number of Indian scholars went to Baghdad, and among the books they took with them were works on Mathematics and Astronomy. Probably even earlier than this, Indian numerals had reached Baghdad, but this was the first systematic approach, and Aryabhata's and other books were translated into Arabic. They influenced the development of Mathematics and Astronomy in the Arab world, and Indian numerals were introduced. Baghdad was then a great centre of learning and Greek and Jewish scholars had gathered there bringing with them Greek Philosophy, Geometry, and Science. The cultural influence of Baghdad was felt throughout the Moslem world from central Asia to Spain, and a knowledge of Indian mathematics in their Arabic translations spread all over this vast area. The numerals were called by the Arabs 'figures of Hind' (or India), and the Arabic word for a number is 'Hindsah' meaning 'from Hind.' From the Arab world, the new Mathematics travelled to European countries, probably through the Moorish Universities of Spain, and became the foundation for European mathematics. There was opposition in Europe to the use of the new numbers, as they were considered infidel symbols, and it took several hundred years before they were in common use. The earliest known use is in a Sicilian coin of 1134; in Britain the first use is in 1490." What Arabs call 'Indian numerals', we Indians are reluctant to call 'Indian numerals.'

Srinivas Ramanujan (1887–1920) is among history's greatest Number mathematicians.Recognising his genius; mathematician G.H. Hardy had invited him to the Cambridge University. 'Lost Notebook' has about 600 plus Ramanujan's formulas written one or two years before his death.George Andrews of the Pennsylvania State University, U.S.A found the manuscript of 'Lost Notebook' at the Trinity College library in 1976 while looking at papers of G.N. Watson. Ramanujan's other note books are at the University of Madras. Andrews and Bruce Bernt, a distinguished research professor at the University of Illinois are jointly working to produce volume two on the "Lost Notebook".

Bill Clinton, the then President of U.S.A, during his official visit to India in March, 2000, at the State banquet, said: "The whole world has been influenced by Indian culture. Indian thinkers have enriched every science known to humanity. And, I welcome the presence of so many Indian scientists in the U.S.A. However, I must confess there are many American High School students who wish that Aryabhatta had kept his work on Trignometry to himself. The computer age would hardly be possible at all without the decimal system invented in India. And, appropriately enough 30 per cent of world's software engineers today are Indians."

Gayatri, *Anushtubha*, *Brhati*, *Trishtubh* and *Jagati Chhandas* are metres having 6, 8, 9, 11 and 12 syllables respectively. From these metres, different combinations were produced showing that Rigvedic people were well versed in permutations & combinations.

1.1. THE RIGVEDA

The Rigveda has 10552 richas (also called shlokas or mantras) revealed to over 414 rishis including 29 female rishis (called rishikas). Rigveda is divided into ten mandalas (chapters/books). A group of richas devoted to one deity (devata or subject) is called Sukta. There are 1028 suktas in the Rigveda. According to Satapath Brahman book, the number of syllables in the Rigveda is 432,000.

RV (X.85.2) denotes the second richa of 85th Sukta of the tenth mandala (chapter) of Rigveda. RV (X.85.2, 3, 7) denotes the second, the third and the seventh richas of the 85th Sukta of the tenth mandala of Rigveda. RV (X.85.3–6) denotes from the third to the sixth richa of the 85th Sukta of the tenth mandala of Rigveda.

The most prominent god in the Rigveda is Indra—the War God who destroys enemies and always leads to victory in wars. About one fourth of the Rigveda (250 suktas) is in praise of Indra. Maximum numbers of rishis, one hundred twenty eight—have praised Indra in Rigveda. RV (I.74.3) talks about the winner of the booty in a battle. RV (X.83 & 84) are war making suktas. Atharvaveda (V.8.4) commands to attack with speed & force: "Shake your enemy as a wolf shakes a sheep, let him not be released from you alive; shut up his breath." Atharvaveda (X.1.20) specifically commands that there be swords of best quality metal/iron in our homes. So, it will not be correct to presume that the Veda is only about worship or spirituality or that its followers were pacifists. The Rigveda preaches war as a justified means to achieve goals. Each deity in Hinduism, including the female deities, is armed; and, in the Vedas, Indra is described as armed with vajra which in English has been translated by Wilson into "thunderbolt" (fire balls, lead balls, grenades). Incidently, initially Manusmriti disarmed half of Hindu Samaj (Vaishya and Shudra) and later, medieval rulers and the British disarmed the entire Hindu Samaj, so as to keep the majority under subjugation and slavery.

The Vedas are composed in a very archaic Sanskrit, generally in verse form with abundant use of similies, metaphors etc. and with the utmost brevity like algebraic formulae. Over thousands of years, Vedic richas are believed to have been passed on verbally from one generation to another, from teacher (*guru)* to disciples (*shishyas*) later on these were reduced to writing as Samhitas on *bhojpatras* (bark leaves) when script for written Sanskrit had been standardised. It seems that in order to maintain correctness of pronunciation, for thousands of years richas were not reduced to written form. It is also believed that a script was invented or standardised much after Vedic richas were revealed. Later on, explanatory notes were composed to explain detailed meanings, background, context of the Vedic richas which are called Brahmana, Aranyak, Upanishad and Purana etc. Even at present, there are many languages which are spoken but have no regular script or written literature of their own such as many local dialects.

In the second half of fourteenth century, Sayana, a Prime Minister of King Bukka Rai of Vijay Nagar Kingdom, wrote detailed commentaries on Vedas, which are taken as reference material for further study. In 1850, Dr. H.H. Wilson translated Rigveda into English based on Sayana's commentary. In 1876–77, H. Grassmann attempted poetic translation of RV into German. Ludwig also brought out his six volumes of translation of RV between 1876 and 1888. R.T.H. Griffith brought his poetical translation into English during 1889–92 from Kasi (Varanasi, UP, India, my home town). During 1909–12, another German scholar H. Oldenberg published his translation of RV into German from Berlin.

There are 191 Suktas in the first mandal of the Rigveda

comprising revelations to 27 rishis including two female rishis. The tenth mandal also has 191 suktas revealed to 181 rishis including 20 female rishis. Ninth mandal has richas devoted to Soma Rasa (Soma Juice soma has many meanings including moon, gravitation etc.) comprising 114 suktas revealed to a number of rishis. Second to eighth mandalas are called family mandalas as these were revealed to members of one rishi family.

Second Mandal	Grits Mandal	43 suktas
Third Mandal	Vaiswamitra Mandal	62 suktas
Fourth Mandal	Vamdeva Mandal	58 suktas
Fifth Mandal	Atreya Mandal	87 suktas
Sixth Mandal	Bhardwaj Mandal	75 suktas
Seventh Mandal	Maitravarunavasista Mandal	104 suktas
Eighth Mandal	Kanva Mandal	103 suktas

Internal sequencing of mandalas on a time–scale has not yet been universally agreed upon among Vedic experts i.e., it is not yet certain which mandala was revealed earlier and which one later. Also, one does not yet know correct sequential order of composition of Vedic richas on a time scale. One safe way to work out sequential order would be by determining family lineage of RV rishis presuming the son/daughter composing after father. Father and son composing simultaneously will add to difficulty in sequencing. In linguistic and philology sciences, experts study changes in literary styles, changes in words & grammar etc. and try to link these changes to a time scale; and, based on it, they guess which work is 'earlier' and which one is 'latter'. But, such studies have at least two fatal structural weaknesses. Firstly, all rishis (or most of them) of one (time) period are presumed to have adopted one and the same literary style, which may not always be true. Secondly, one rishi may have composed his richas in more than one literary style at any given point of time, or, at different stages of his life. A poet is at his liberty to compose his poems in literary styles different from other contemporary poets; and, in different literary styles at different stages of his life. So, sequencing of Vedic richas is a difficult exercise. But, let hundred flowers bloom without any acrimony, imparting forward momentum to academic efforts.

1.2. THE SAMAVEDA

It has 1875 richas (mantras/shlokas) composed by 184 rishis out of which about 1800 are there in the Rigveda. Some writers put the number of Samaveda richas borrowed from Rigveda at 1783. Two Samaveda richas (1832 and 1833) can be located in the Yajurveda. Rest of Samaveda richas cannot be located in Rigveda as available these days. It is presumed that the 73 Samaveda richas might have belonged to some other recensions of the Rigveda which is now lost. According to Acharya Shri Ram Sharma, except 69 richas, the rest are from the Rigveda; and, 17 from Yajurveda and Atharvaveda. Samaveda richa 588 occurs at AV (VI.33.1).

When richas for the Samaveda were borrowed from the Rigveda, in order to set them to musical tone, 106 of them underwent some changes. Also, 264 richas appearing in the first part (Purvaracika) of Samaveda have been repeated word for word in the second part (Uttararacika) of Samaveda. There are four richas of the first part, which are repeated, twice in the second part. These are (487,762,1335) (552,1329,1681) (553,774,1386) and (627,1464,1518).

It is believed that 1875 Samaveda richas were set in musical tones by 285 seers, all of whom not necessarily being the original composers.

1.3. THE YAJURVEDA

It has 40 Adhyayas (chapters) and 1975 richas (mantras/ shlokas). The 40th Adhyaya of Yajurveda is known as Eshavasyopanisad. Richas of the Yajurveda are more in the prose, devoted to performing Yajnas (karma–kand). About 794 richas of Rigveda appear in the Yajurveda. Such as, RV (X.155.5) appears at Yaj (35.18). The Purusha–Sukta of Rigveda appears at Yaj (31.1–16). Richas of RV (X.121) are there in Yajurveda such as RV (X.121.1) at Yaj (25.10), RV (X.121.2) at Yaj (25.13), RV (X.121.3) at Yaj (25.11), RV (X.121.4) at Yaj (25.12) etc. The famous Gayatri mantra of RV (III.62.10) appears in Yajurveda at (3.35), (12.9) and (30.2) and in Samaveda (1462). Mahamrityunjaya mantra of Rigveda (VII.59.12) appears at Yaj (3.60).

1.4. THE ATHARVAVEDA

It is divided into twenty Kandas (chapters) and has 5977 richas (Whitney & Joshi) out of which about 1200 richas are from the Rigveda. Other recensions of the Atharvaveda are said to contain upto 6031 richas. Major contributors of mantras to Atharvaveda are Atharva and Angira rishi families. Lady rishi Surya Savitri who was revealed RV (X.85) has also been revealed the whole XIVth Kanda (chapter) of the Atharvaveda. Rishi Narayan who was revealed the famous Purusha–Sukta RV (X.90) has also been revealed AV (XIX.6) and AV (X.2). Angirasas and Atharvas rishis are mentioned as recent progenitors (piter navagva) who are entitled to the Soma in RV (X.14.6). So, Rigvedic rishis were aware of Angiras and Atharva rishis. Rishi Atharvan is mentioned in RV (X.21.9) also. Atharvaveda covers spiritual prayers, herbal medicine, war, magic, how to achieve immortality & prosperity, etc.

AV (IV.31 & 32) are war making suktas. For example: AV (IV.31.3) prays: "Overpower for us, O fury (Agni), the hostile plotter; go forward breaking, killing, slaughtering the foes; your formidable rush (pajas) surely they have not impeded; you, controlling, shall bring them under control, O sole–born one." (Whitney & Joshi). AV (IV.31.6) prays: "Born together with efficacy, O missile (sayaka) thunderbolt, you bear superior power, O associate; be you allied with our energy, O fury, much–invoked one, in the mingling of great riches." AV (IV.32.3) reads: "Attack, O fury, being mightier than a mighty one; with fervour as ally smite apart the foes; slayer of enemies, slayer of Vrtra, and slayer of barbarians, do you bring to us all (their) good things." And, AV (IV.33.6) reads: "Here I am for you; come hitherward unto us, meeting (us), O powerful, all–giving one; O thunderbolt–bearing fury, turn hither to us; let us slay the barbarians; and do you know your partner."

Thus, in addition to spirituality and worship, Vedas do preach bravery, valour (*purusharth*) and war, not passivity nor impotence.

1.5 SINGLE DIVINE SOURCE

Rigvedic richas are there in other three Vedas but it does not mean that other three Vedas were composed or revealed later than Rigveda as there are specific references to Yajurveda, Samaveda and Atharvaveda in the Rigveda itself.

The Purusha–Sukta of the Rigveda (X.90.9) itself states that Riks (i.e., Rigveda), the Sama–hymns (i.e., Samaveda), Chhandasi (i.e., Atharvaveda) and the Yajus–hymns (i.e., Yajurveda) were born from the same great intellectual efforts (*manasik yajna*).

तस्माद्यज्ञात्सर्वहुत ऋचः सामानि जज्ञिरे।
छन्दांसि जज्ञिरे तस्माद्यजुस्तस्मादजायत॥ RV (X.90.9)

HH Wilson translates: "From that victim, in whom the universal oblation was offered, the Rcas and Samans were produced; from him the metres (chhandasi) were born; from him the Yajus was born." Universal oblation means efforts by all, common efforts.

Ralph T.H. Griffith translates this richa: "From that great

general sacrifice Rcas and Sama–hymns were born: Therefrom were spells and charms produced; the Yajus had its birth from it."

Shri Ram Sharma Acharya translates: "*Un Sarvatmak Purusha ke yajna se Rigveda aur Samaveda ki utpatti huyee. Unse Yajurveda ki tatha Gayatri chhando ki bhi utpatti huyee.*"

Dr. Ganga Sahai Sharma translates: "*Uus sarvatmak Purusha ke kalpnik hom wale yajna se Rik aur Sama utpanna huye. Usi se chhanda utpanna huye aur Yajus ki utpatti huuyee.*"

Specific references to Samaveda appear in RV (I.7.1), RV (I.164.24, 25), RV (II.43.1, 2), RV (VIII.38.10), RV (X.85.11) and in RV (X.114.6), etc. HH Wilson translates RV (I.7.1): "The chanters of the Soma extol Indra with songs, the reciters of Rik with prayers, the priests of the Yajus with texts." Dr. Ganga Sahay Sharma, translates: "*Samaveda ka gaan karane walo ne Samagaan ke dwara, Rigveda ka path karane walo ne richao dwara aur Yajurveda ka path karane walo ne mantro dwara Indra ki stuti ki.*"

So, the source of all the four Vedas is one and the same. Therefore, none is superior or inferior to the other. It is, therefore, totally incorrect to say that this Veda is superior to that Veda. Since many richas from Rigveda appear verbatim in the other three Vedas, it can't be said that the languages of the four Vedas are totally different from each other.

1.6 VEDIC RIVER SARASWATI

Saraswati is a very prominent river in the Rigveda. The word Saraswati is mentioned in about 71 richas and appears in all the mandalas (chapters) of the Rigveda except the fourth mandala. This word has been used in the sense of a Goddess as well as a specific river.Goddess Saraswati is one of the three most worshipped Goddesses in Rigveda. But, in our modern times, there is no trace of this river.

The Vedic river Saraswati is believed to have dried up during

2600–1900 BC; and, if it is so, the implication would be that the Rigvedic richas were composed much before 2600–1900 BC as it has been described, in the present tense, as a mighty flowing river. As regards its geographical location, some opine that it was actually there in Afghanistan under the name Harhvati, not in Punjab/India. But, this contention does not appear to be correct as in RV (X.75), Saraswati is mentioned between rivers Yamuna and Suturdi (Sutlej). So, the Rigvedic Saraswati must have been geographically located between Yamuna and Sutlej.

The school which opines that the Rigveda was composed during 1500–1200 BC also suggests that Rigvedic people carried the the name of Afghan river Harhvati when they crossed over into Punjab (eastward migration) and gave this name to a river channel in Punjab. But, the channel in Punjab region which fits into description of Rigvedic Saraswati had dried up in 2600–1900 BC, much before the Rigveda, as per this school of thought, was composed. So, there is no logic or justification for Rigvedic people to carry the name of a river from Afghanistan to Punjab, give this name to a channel which had dried up hundreds of years ago, and, then compose richas in present tense form in praise of that dried–up–river as the 'mighty river', 'the best of rivers' etc..

AA MacDonell, in his book 'A History of Sanskrit Literature' has written (page 77): "Saraswati is, however, the most important river goddess, being lauded in three entire hymns as well as in many detached verses. The personification here goes much further than in the case of other streams, but the poets never lose sight of the connection of the goddess with the river. She is the best of mothers, of rivers, and of goddesses. Her unfailing breast yields richas of every kind, and she bestows wealth, plenty, nourishment and offspring. One poet prays that he may not be removed from her to fields, which are strange.

She is invoked to descend from the sky, from the great mountain, to the sacrifice."

RV(VII.95.1) reads: "This Saraswati, firm as a city made of iron, flows rapidly with all sustaining water, sweeping away in its might all other waters, as a charioteer (clears the roads)." RV(VII.95.2) reads: "Saraswati, chief and pure of rivers, flowing from the mountains to the ocean...." RV(VII.96.1) reads: "Thou chauntest, Vasistha a powerful hymn to her who is the most mighty of river, worship, Vasistha with well selected praises, Saraswati, who is both in heaven (as goddess) and earth (as river)." RV(VII.96.5) reads: "With those your waves Saraswati, which are sweet–tasted, the distributors of water, be our protector."

RV (II.41.16) reads: "Saraswati, best of mothers, best of rivers, best of goddesses, we are, as it were, of no repute; grant us, mother, distinction:"

अम्बितमे नदीतमे देवितमे सरस्वति।
अप्रशस्ता इव स्मसि प्रशस्तिमम्ब नस्कृधि ॥16॥ RV (II.41.16)

Immediately thereafter in RV (II.41.17), Saraswati is addressed as divine and goddess. In RV (II.41.18), it is again said: "Saraswati, abounding in food, abounding in water....." In RV (III.24.4) banks of Drsadvati, Apaya and Saraswati rivers have been referred. This is another richa proving that Vedic river Saraswati was not in Afghanistan. In RV (V.42.12) and (V.43.11) Saraswati in river form (showerer of water) has been mentioned. Readers may kindly note that in these translations by HH Wilson, descriptions about river Saraswati are in present tense clearly implying that it was a live/flowing river at the time of composition of these richas, not a dead / dried up river.

Dr. Naresh K. Gupta in his article "Legend Saraswati: Legend History" explains that chance discovery of Harappa and

Mohenjodaro in 1920s, as a result of the railroad building activity, revealed a lost but mature civilization which has been named as the Indus Valley Civilization, or, Harappan Civilization, because these two initially discovered ruined cities were located on the banks of the Indus river and its tributary, Ravi. Subsequent discoveries of Harappa type ruins at Ropar in the Indian side of Punjab proved that the Indus Valley Civilization was more extensive than originally thought to be. By now, more than 1400 sites containing the Harappa like artefacts have been discovered spread over more than one million square kilometre area and more are still being discovered. Two third of these sites are located on the Indian side and the remaining one third are located on the Pakistani side of the border. Prominent among these sites are Guneriwala in Pakistan, Manda in Jammu & Kashmir, Ropar in Punjab, Banawali and Rakhigarhi in Haryana, Alamgirpur near Meerut, Kalibangan in Rajasthan, Lothal, Dholavira and Surkotada in Gujarat and Daimabad in Maharashtra. When plotted on the map, these sites seem to crowd around the dry bed of river Ghaggar in Punjab, Haryana and Rajasthan, and rivers Hakra and Nara in Bahawalpur and Sindh in Pakistan, and ending in the Rann of Kutch in Gujarat. Ghaggar is called Hakra when it enters Bahawalpur in Pakistan and continues as Nara in the Sindh province. At the Lothal site, a huge dock capable of handling ocean going and river navigation ships has been excavated. Some donut shaped stone anchors have also been found at Lothal and other sites indicating internal and external maritime trade.

Dr. B.P. Radhakrishna has suggested that circa 7000 BC was a wet spell with the break up of the Himalayan glaciers, the release of Sapta–Sindhu, the mighty Himalayan rivers and the emergence of Saraswati as a major river of NW India; that circa 6000 BC saw the Saraswati and its tributaries flowing with full majestic splendour with village communities settling on banks of rivers; that circa 5000 BC was a wet climate with abundant water highlighting the flowering of the Vedic civilization (6000–4000 BC) along lakes with high water levels; that circa 3000 BC saw the drying up of river Saraswati (Ghaggar–Hakra–Nara–Wahind) while the Indus Valley Civilization emerged (3100–1900 BC) with expansion of agriculture and urbanisation, tectonic disturbance resulting in the capture of upper waters of Saraswati by Yamuna (eastward flow) and westward migration of Sutlej; that circa 2000 BC saw increasing aridity. Dr. Radhakrishna is, thus, suggesting that river Saraswati started drying up by 3000 BC, and that, the Indus civilization followed the Vedic civilization.

By carbon dating, it is seen that North–West India became arid near about 2100 BC, so, river Saraswati should have dried up near about this time.

R.D. Oldham (1886) was the first geologist to suggest changes in drainage pattern of rivers in Northwest India converting once fertile land into arid/desert. C.F. Oldham (1893) also suggested that bulk of waters of the ancient Saraswati was contributed by Sutlej, which later changed its course and became a tributary of the Indus. Herbert Wilhemy (1969) in his paper argues that a mighty river like Saraswati with course extending for over 1300 km and having a breadth of 3 to 6 kms must have been fed by Himalayan glaciers; and that Yamuna would have been its tributary.

In 1980, Professor Yashpal and others recognised the palaeo–channels of the erstwhile Saraswati using Landsat imagery. In 1996, Professor Valdiya traced the course of river Saraswati from West Garhwal in the Himalayas to the Gulf of Khambat in Gujarat using hydro–geological studies. There is a remarkable similarity in the course of the river Saraswati identified from these two different sources. According to this, the Vedic

Saraswati followed the course of contemporary rivers Ghaggar, Hakra and Nara where most of the Indus Valley sites are also located. In 1997, Drs. S.M. Rao and K.M. Kulkarni of the Bhaba Atomic Research Center tracked the old course of river Saraswati from its source in Himalayas and its flow through Rajasthan, Bhawalpur and Sindh to the Rann of Kutch in Gujarat, again using Landsat imagery. Using low levels of tritium, a naturally occurring radioactive isotope, they also collected evidence to prove that waters trapped in the underground channels below the ancient course of the river Saraswati belonged to that river. Other scientists have used Indian Remote Sensing (IRS – 1 series) satellites to track the bed of the lost river Saraswati, confirming the results reached by the scientists mentioned above.

R. Nair, S.V. Navada and S.M. Rao's paper, 'Isotope Study to investigate the origin and age of groundwater along palaeochannels in Jaisalmer and Ganganagar Districts of Rajasthan' echoes an earlier monograph in 'Current Science' demonstrating the use of nuclear physics in groundwater dating and tracing palaeodrainage systems. The Saraswati River palaeochannels were dated to between 2000 to 8400 years BC based on tritium isotope studies applied to water samples taken from deep wells and shown to be qualitatively comparable to the Himalayan glacier waters.

It is now known that a major drought spread over 300 years occurred during 2200 BC to 1900 BC in an immense belt from Aegean to China. It is supposed to have uprooted Harappan Civilization in India; Saraswati dried up. Ancient Eygptian and Mesopotamian Civilizations also suffered.

The main reasons contributing to the drying up of the river Saraswati, thus, appear to be the loss of its important tributaries due to changes in courses of tributaries, climate changes like long periods of drought and water seepage through earth faults and fissures combined with the obstruction of river flow by shifting of sand due to high winds. The whole of northwest India, upto the Rann of Kutch, was subject to earthquake activity resulting in raising of the ground here and there affecting direction of flow of rivers, and creation of earth faults, which contributed to the loss of water of this river Saraswati. When the Aravallis range is traced north to the Himalayas, there is evidence of rise in the ground level on the line of Aravallis. This rise in the ground level appears to have caused the turning of the river Yamuna eastwards at Paontasahib to join the Ganges at Allahabad. This river turning denied the waters of Yamuna to Saraswati. Another blow to the river Saraswati is believed to have struck when Sutlej took a sharp U–turn at Ropar moving to flow parallel to the river Beas, the Vedic Vipasa. Having lost both of its perennial tributaries, i.e., rivers Yamuna and Sutlej, river Saraswati would have been a drying river in around 2000 BC. It is probable that desertification of Rajasthan would have taken place at that time. As supported by the hydro–geological evidence, the ground faults and sand movement would have caused the seepage of the remaining waters of river Saraswati to underground channels, leaving a dry riverbed.

In short, Vedic river Saraswati definitely dried up during 2600 BC to 1900 BC.

1.7 ANTIQUITY OF THE VEDAS

No one is definite how old are the Vedas, the Ramayana and the Gita. What is their real antiquity? "Your guess about antiquity is better than my guess," in my humble opinion, appears to be the polite & correct answer at this point of time.

Some scholars believe that Rigveda was mostly composed in the Punjab region during 1500 to 1200 BC (Before Christ); and, some others believe that Rigveda was composed during

1300–900 BC. The focus of Mahabharata is said by this school to be in the Upper Ganges Valley during 900–700 BC ;and, that old core of Valmiki Ramayan is believed to have been composed during 750–500 BC (Goldman: 1984) or 500–300 BC (BrocKington: 1998). This school believes that as no horse seal has been found in Harappa/Mohen–jo–daro remains, and, as horse is the often referred animal in the Rigveda, the Rigvedic period must follow the Harappan period; and, as (according to this school) horse is not archaeologically attested to in the Indian subcontinent prior to 2000 BC, Rigvedic richas cannot be older than 2000 BC. Another argument of this school is that as Rigveda mentions iron (**आयस**), see for example RV (VII.95.1), Rigveda cannot be much older than the Iron Age. But, what is the correct time of the commencement of the Iron Age particularly when we know that iron ore has all along been there over millions of years right from the birth of earth?

The Vedic period is presumed by some scholars to be spread over from 1500 BC to 200 BC. MacDonell advises (page 9): "The chronology of the Vedic period is almost **conjectural** being based entirely on internal evidence. Three main literary strata can be clearly distinguished in it by differences in language and style, as well as in religious and social views. For the development of each of these strata a reasonable length of time must be allowed; but all we can here hope to do is to approximate to the truth by centuries. The lower limit of the second Vedic stratum cannot, however, be fixed later than 500 BC, because its latest doctrines are presupposed by Buddhism, and the date of the death of the Buddha has been, with a high degree of probability, calculated, from the recorded dates of the various Buddhist councils, to be 480 BC."

Prof. Max Müller's earlier estimate of 1200 BC, for the commencement of Vedic age, MacDonell says, appears to be much nearer the mark. A lapse of three centuries, say from 1300–1000 BC, would amply account for the difference between what is the oldest and the latest in Vedic hymn poetry. One may ask why not a lapse of five centuries, or, lapse of only two centuries should account for this so called 'literary differences' in Rigvedic richas.What is so sacrosanct about 'three centuries'?

Prof. Jacobi of Bonn brought out a paper suggesting the commencement of Vedic period at least from 4000 BC, if not earlier. His theory is based on astronomical calculations connected with a change in the beginning of the seasons, which Prof. Jacobi thinks has taken place since the time of the Rigveda. Meanwhile, MacDonell advises, we must rest content with the certainty that Vedic literature in any case is of considerably greater antiquity than that of Greece.

Prof. Michael Witzel, a reputed Indologist from the U.S.A, suggests Early Rigvedic period(1700–1500BC), Middle Rigvedic period(1500–1350BC),and, Late Rigvedic period(1350–1200 BC). Prof. Parpola, a reputed Indologist from Helsinki, also thinks that the Rigvedic hymns date from the second millennium BC, but he does not endorse some of Witzels' proposals concerning the compositional chronology of the Rigvedic Hymns. In Parpola's view, the oldest preserved hymns (Chapter II to VII) date from 1300–1200 BC and represent the second wave of Indo Aryan Speakers in the Indian Subcontinent but the later hymns of the Rigveda continue partly the tradition of the first wave of the Indo–Aryan Speakers, who (in Parpola's view) entered the Indian Subcontinent around 1600 BC. Shrikant G. Talageri, an Indian expert, has given a different compositional chronology of Rigveda chapters.

The Holy Bible is said to assign the date 23 October 4004 BC for the 'Creation' and 2448 BC for the 'Great Flood.' In this time constraint devout Christian scholars had to assign, in those days of Christian orthodoxy, when many did not dare differ publicly from principles of the Church lest he be declared a heretic, a date to books of pagans. So, Max Müller initially assigned a date of 1500 BC for the Aryan invasion and 1200 BC for composition of the Rigveda. Later, Max Müller himself said: 'Whether Vedic hymns were written in 1000, 1500 or 2000 BC or 3000 BC, no power on earth will ever be able to determine.' Max Müller in his book 'In History of Ancient Sanskrit Literature' (page 557) has written: 'In Rigveda we shall have before us more real antiquity than in all inscriptions of Egypt or Ninevah....the Veda is the oldest book in existence...'

Motilal Banarasidass Newsletter (November 1995) reported that gold coins belonging to the year 1570 BC were found at Palpara village in Patashpur area of Midnapore district of West Bengal; and, coins were embossed with figures of Lord Rama, Sita, Lakshaman and Shatrughan with Hanuman at their feet. This means that Lord Rama was being worshipped in 1570 BC. As such the Vedas must be much older than 1570 BC; further, that Vedic people & their descendants were already there in the Bengal region in 1600 BC period, much beyond the Punjab region. Stone tablet of Narmer, Egypt (3200 BC) and wall panel No 3 of the temple 0–13 at Piedras Negras, Guatemala (Maya Civilization) depict stories similar to those in Ramayana.

Hittites are mentioned in the Old Testament of the Bible. They are supposed to have destroyed Cappadocia (Central Turkey) in 1950 BC. Hittite tablets discovered in Boghaz–koi (Turkey) were deciphered in 1917 establishing their Indo–European origin. One of their gods is pronounced as *Inar* i.e., Indra of Rigveda suggesting their Indo–Aryan origin.

Kassites invaded and conquered Babylon (in Iraq) in 1760

BC and ruled upto 1170 BC. They bore names with components recalling Rigvedic deities such as *su–ri–ya–as (Surya)*, *Indas (Indra)*, *maruttash (marutah) and shimaliya (Queen of mountains, Himalaya)*. Some say that the term Kassites comes from warrior class of Kshatriya from India; and, others say from the Rigvedic word Kasi (Varanasi). Kassites also used the term Indabugas (Indra plus bhaga i.e., bhagavan: God Indra). Bhaga is a divine protector God in many richas such as RV (I.89.3), RV (IV.55.5), etc.

Mitanni kingdom rose in the northern Syria (1500 BC–1300 BC). Prof. Asko Parpola in his famous book 'Deciphering the Indus Script' (page 147) concludes that it is now generally agreed that Mitanni Aryan is related to Indo–Aryan as evidenced by oath deities mentioned in the Mitanni treaties. In the treaty between Hittite King Shuppiluliuma and the Mittani ruler Sativaza (Mattivaza) son of Tushratta (Dusratta), the latter invokes his gods as witnesses to the treaty: "*DINGIR–MESH mi–it–tra–ash–shi–el DINGIR–in–dar DINGER–Mesh na–sha–at–ti–ya–an–na*. This corresponds to Rigvedic gods Mitra–Varuna–Indra–Nasatya. Mitanni cuneiform writings correspond to Vedic gods Mitra–Varuna; and, Indra–Nasatya. All these Gods are invoked in Rigveda and in RV (I.2.7–9), (I.153), (I.162.1), (X.93.4) and (X.125.1) etc., they appear together and in the same order Mitra & Varuna (मित्रावरुणा). Nasatya god is referred in RV (I.116) etc. According to Parpola (page 150) both Indra and Varuna were invoked in the Mitanni oath (1380 BC) and the joint mention of Varuna and Indra in Mittani texts suggests that Rigvedic Aryans were there in Southern Central Asia during 1700–1600 BC.

Dr. Mohan Gupta (IAS: MP) is reported to have calculated that the Mahabharata war started on 17th October 1952 BC. On this account, Vedas must be much much older than 1952

BC.

The Rigveda repeatedly mentions Saraswati River as a live or flowing river, which dried up by 2600 BC or latest by 1900 BC, so, Rigveda should have been composed before Saraswati dried up.

Many authors advise that the Mahabharata war took place in 3137 BC, so, Rigveda must be much older.

Some scholars calculate that the solar eclipse mentioned in RV (V.40.5–9) took place on 26th July 3928 BC.

Some scholars estimate that Rigveda was composed much before 5000 BC, as it does not mention cotton (kapas,karpasa) whereas the oldest cottonseeds found in (Mehrgarh) Baluchistan have been carbon dated to 5000 BC (Scientific American Journal, August 1980). At page 9 of 'Deciphering of Indus Script' by Parpola, it is stated that a small amount of woven cotton cloth dyed red with madder has been found in Harappan civilization, and, at page 15 it is stated that in Phase (II B–III) (5000–3600 BC) of Mehrgarh some sort of irrigation undoubtedly existed required by cotton cultivation evidenced by large amounts of cotton seeds. In a discussion in Helsinki in May 2004, Dr. Asko Parpola told me that there is no mention of cotton (karpasa) in Rigveda. Later in Sept 2004, Prof Parpola reconfirmed to me, "there is no reference to cotton in the Samhitaa or Braahmana texts of any of the four Vedas, but the first reference is in the Srautasuutras of Laatyaayana and Draahyaayana". If 'invading' Rigvedic people came into contact with cotton cultivating Harappan people, how is it that Rigveda (which was composed over a span of hundreds of years) remained unknown to cotton and cottonseeds? How it is that Rigvedic people did not start using cotton cloths so well known to Harappan people, whom they are supposed to have defeated and dispossessed, in warmer climate of India, in any case warmer than their (Aryans') supposed original home in Russian steppes? In the hypothesis of Rigvedic people coming into India from Russian steppes, they are supposed to be familiar only with woolen and hide & skin garments; and, if it was so, how and why Rigvedic people remained stuck to their woolen and hide & skin garments in warmer climate of India, and did not opt for cooler cotton cloths. Reasonable explanation appears to be that there was no cotton cultivation during the times of the Rigvedic people. So, Rigvedic period should be anterior to 5000 BC. (It would be fair to mention that in Parpola's opinion this late attestation of cotton in Vedas does not prevent dating the Rigveda in the second millennium BC)

MacDonell informs that Panini lived around 300 BC; and, that in his writings, Panini mentions no fewer than sixty four predecessors. Taking an average life span of one hundred years for each generation, Panini takes us back to 6700 BC if all predecessors mentioned by him are taken vertically. Panini was a post–Vedic writer.

Astronomical data, some zodiac configurations and references about equinoxes etc. in Veda also support antiquity of Rigveda beyond 5000 BC. Vedas have references to vernal equinox in the Pleiades (2500 BC); to Gemini–Orion era (vernal eqninox in Mrigashira 4000 BC); and to the Cancer era (equinox in Punarvasu 6000 BC) and earlier. Some authors opine that Rigvedic hymns (I.112.13) and (VII.69.3) indicate that the *Aswin–s* (that is the *Aswini* Constellation) were visible at the solstitial points. This solstice could only be the winter solstice, and the winter solstice recurred in the *aswins* in 7000BC. RV hymns (I.161.13) and (IV.33.7) relating to *rbhu–s* (seasons), according to these authors, support this interpretation.

Shri Satya Swarup Misra in his book 'The Aryan Problem– A Linguistic Approach' has proposed the following time–scale:

1.	RV (II to VIII Mandalas)	5000 BC – 4700 BC
2.	RV (I Mandala)	4700 BC – 4550 BC
3.	RV (IX Mandala)	4550 BC – 4400 BC
4.	RV (X Mandala)	4400 BC – 4250 BC
5.	Late Samhita Period	4250 BC – 4100 BC
6.	Vedic prose of Yajurveda	4100 BC – 3950 BC
7.	Vedic prose of Brahamanas	3950 BC – 3800 BC
8.	Vedic prose of Aranyakas	3800 BC – 3650 BC
9.	Vedic prose of Upanisads	3650 BC – 3500 BC

Shri Misra further writes that classical Sanskrit starts with Epic Sanskrit. The date of Epic Sanskrit as midpoint between Vedic Sanskrit and Middle Indo–Aryan should be roughly 3500 BC. The Kali era, which was considered to be fictitious, now can easily be taken as authentic, since the date of RV is placed at an earlier stage on linguistic grounds. On astronomical grounds Kaliyuga started on 17–18 February 3102 BC. This is normally not accepted by Western scholars as authentic. But the description of the positions of planets etc., by Indian tradition is found to be correct on that day by the western scholars, through back calculation. They consider that this day was also fixed later on by back calculation in Indian tradition. But John Playfair has thoroughly discussed this issue and has shown that it was an observation at the period by the astrologers and not a back calculation. Therefore, the period of early classical Sanskrit, i.e., Epic Sanskrit may easily be placed roughly in 3500 BC from linguistic point of view. The language of Ramayana has been often considered by Western scholars to be later than the language of Mahabharata, simply because it is ornate poetry. This is not a sufficient basis. Both share common epic characteristics. There is also no appreciable difference in the language. Since tradition puts Ramayana before Mahabharata, it is safer to follow it unless we get strong evidence against the same. Also, in Gita (X.31) Lord Krishna says that He is Lord Rama among warriors so Ramayana must precede Mahabharata. Therefore, tentatively the language of Ramayana may be placed in 3500 BC. The language of the Mahabharata may be placed a bit later, about 3000 BC, a time very close to Kali era, and the time almost traditionally ascribed to the composition of Mahabharata.

Newsweek (Nov 24, 2003, page–59) carried a report that geneticists in Leipzig, Germany studied maize samples from the Balsas river in Mexico and found that modern maize appeared on the world scene as early as 7000BC, almost 3000 years before the time archaeological evidences available till then had suggested. These studies also give clear evidence of genetic alterations by human selection showing that our forefathers were equally wise, and; that agricultural technique was well developed in 7000BC. So, how old are Vedas especially when agriculture is mentioned in many richas, such as, RV (I.116.6), (I.179.6), (II.14.11), (II.15), (IV.57), (VIII.78.10) and (X.71.2), and; irrigation canal (kulya) in (III.45.3) and (X.43.7)?

Hindustan Times (19th Dec, 2003) reports that three small figurines carved of ivory from mammoth tusks were found in a cave in southwestern Germany, providing stronger evidence that human ancestors were already adept at figurative art more than 30,000 years ago. One of the pieces is the oldest known representation of a bird, which resembles a cormorant or a duck. The others appear to be the head of a horse and a figure of half–man, half–animal. None is longer than an inch. The discoverer, Dr. Nicholas J. Conard, an archaeologist at the University of Tubingen in Germany, said the sculptures "belong to one of the oldest traditions of figurative art known world–wide;" and, that, they point to the region of the Upper Danube River as "an important center of cultural innovation" during the Late Stone Age, also known as the Upper Paleolithic.

The discovery, reported in the Nature, was made at Hohle Fels Cave, in the Swabian Mountains southwest of Ulm. In the report, Dr. Conard said the find complements the collection of more than 20 similar ivory figurines over recent years, all found at Swabian sites. Precise dates for the objects are unknown, he said, but an analysis of related deposits indicates that the artists lived from 30,000 to 33,000 years ago. It was a time when painting on cave walls had also begun to flourish. Colourful drawings discovered at the Grotte Chauvet in France have been dated to 32,400 years ago. Therefore, can it be said that human beings did not inhabit India in those years, particularly when Indian sub–continent has been endowed with hospitable warm and sunny climate? It is neither fair nor reasonable to argue that human beings were there in snow covered Europe some 30000 years ago but not in warm and sunny India.

One billion–year–old fossils recently found in India prove life began in India. AFP Washington reports a Science magazine to the effect that German Scientist Adolf Seilachar and Indian Scientist P.K. Bose have unearthed fossil in Churhat, a town in Madhya Pradesh, India which is 1.1 billion years old and this discovery has rolled back the evolutionary clock by more than 500 million years.

On the evolution of human beings, Newsweek (July 22, 2000) reported that a skull nicknamed Toumai, found in the Djourab dessert of Chad in Central Africa, was at least 7 million years old. Before this discovery, the oldest available skull was only about 2.5 million years old. Discovery of hominid skull about 2500 km west of the Rift Valley (East Africa) made a big hole in the East Side Theory of Human Evolution. This theory held that pre–humans rose when tectonic forces formed the Rift Valley in the East Africa about 5 million years ago, chimps on the eastern side of the Rift Valley having been subjected to harsher & dry climate evolved into homonid/ homosapiens. The next oldest homonid appears to be 6 million years old Orrorin Tugenensis found in 1919 in Kenya. After it, is Ardipithecus Ramidus, which probably lived 4.4 to 5.8 million years ago in Ethiopia. Lucy species called Austra Lopithecus lived about 3.2 million years ago in Tanzania region. Boundary of human evolution, thus, is not static but has been shifting under the weight of new discoveries of older and older skulls.

As per International Herald Tribune of June 12, 2003, some anthropologists hold the view that anatomically modern Homo sapiens were there on this globe nearly 160,000 years ago when old fossilised skulls of three Ethiopians were found which scientists believed to be the first faces of immediate ancestors of modern humans. Was India, despite hospitable climate, devoid of homosapiens when they were walking in Africa? Theories about evolution of human beings are still evolving under the weight of new anthropological discoveries.

According to other school of anthropologists, about 200,000 years ago (International Herald Tribune, 16th August 2002) genes creating language capability among human species developed and about 100,000 to 50,000 years ago, a gene called FOXP2 developed providing the last perfection of language capability among human beings, making it totally modern. So, if Sanskrit is the oldest language; but is not older than 1500 BC, then, in which language did our forefathers communicate before Sanskrit as they had fully developed language faculty/capability over last fifty to one hundred thousand years? In July 2003, I raised this question while addressing the XIIth World Sanskrit Conference held at the University of Helsinki, Finland. (Proto–Indo–European language is an academically constructed language i.e., it does not exist in the old records.)

In 1991, an immaculately preserved body nicknamed Otzi the Iceman was found in the Alps. It was carbon dated to 3400 BC. He had copper ax (with little tin) and cloth made up of deer skin, stiched piece by piece. He had wheat grains too. Complete skeleton of a man –nicknamed 'Cheddar man' was found in 1903 in the Cheddar caves of Someset, UK. It was about 9000 years old and by DNA test, it was established in 1997 that he was an ancestor of Mr. Adrian Targett, a school teacher in a school in the same place Somerset, UK. Kennewick man, the 9000 year old human skeleton found on the banks of the Columbia river in 1996 shows human habitation in the U.S.A. In 1974 a prehistoric painting was discovered on a rock rising out of the lake near the Vera paper mill, Kuusankoski, Finland showing elk and human figures.It is estimated to be 6,000 years old. So, can it be said that India with much more hospitable climate was void of human beings in pre–history years when human beings were living in cold and snowy Europe, UK and the U.S.A?

Rig Veda (IX.33.6) and RV (X.47.2) talk of four oceans, obviously, one each in four directions of India.There are numerous references to oceans, seas and boats with many oars etc. in Rigveda. Boats propelled by oars are frequently mentioned in RV (I.116.3), (V.59.2) etc. There are explicit or implied references to sea going vessels in RV (I.46.8) etc. RV (I.116.5) mentions hundred–oared ship. The famous Sankalpa mantra, *merodaksina bhage Jambudvipe bhara–tkhande*...., talks of Jambudvipe. The question is, whether India was part of any island (*Jambudvipe*) some time ago, if so, how many million years ago? *Dvipa* means an island.

Contemporary Modern Science believes that about 225 million years ago, all the plates on outermost layer of earth were joined together forming a super continent (PANGAEA) that later on broke into many; and, since then plates have been drifting. Mid–Atlantic ridge is drifting at a rate of 2.5cm per year resulting into mighty Atlantic Ocean of today. Similar drift is taking place in Africa creating the East Africa Rift Valley System, near Tanzania. The Indian plate was formed about 200 million years ago near Australian plate (Triassic age) and, thereafter, it started drifting towards the Eurasian plate in northerly direction. The Tethys Sea between Indian plate and Eurasian plate slowly shrunk and about 40 to 50 million years ago, the rise of the Himalayan range commenced. Presently, the Indian plate is thrusting under the Eurasian plate at a rate of 5 cm in a year causing landslide and seismic activities in the Himalayan region. About 50 million years ago, India was an island. About 135 million years ago (Jurassic Age), Indian plate was about half way in the ocean between the Eurasian plate and the Australian plate. In the Creaceons Age (65 million years ago), the northernmost tip of Indian plate was touching the equator and the whole Indian plate was in the Southern hemisphere below the equator. It was about 50 millions years ago that India was an Island. One should research and find out how and when did this information come into the Sankalpa Mantra?

चत्वारि शृङ्गा त्रयो अस्य पादा द्वे शीर्षे सप्त हस्तासो अस्य।
त्रिधा बद्धो वृषभो रोरवीति महो देवो मर्त्यां आ विवेश॥3॥
RV (IV.58.3)

"Four are his horns; three are his feet; his heads are two, his hands are seven: the triple–bound showerer (of benefits) roars aloud: the mighty deity has entered among men. "RV (IV.58.3) may be interpreted to mean that 4,320,000,000 years ago the Almighty God entered into mortals. The Veda is, thus, suggesting that Sristi (i.e., Creation) on earth started (4.32 billion) years ago.

Modern Astrophysics says that the earth is about 4.6 billion years old. Prof. Carl Sagan, the Cornel University Astronomer told an Indian Ambassador P.P. D'Souza (Hindustan Times, January 26, 1997) that we know earth is about 4.6 billion years old, and, the cosmos about 10 to 12 billion years. And, Hindu tradition has one day and one night of Brahma in this range of 8.6 billion years. Thus, Prof. Sagan said that the Vedic tradition is the only tradition in the world, which talks about right time–scale. It should be a matter of great pride for we Hindus that only the Vedic culture among all the cultures of the world has been aware of precessional rotation of earth completing one circle in 25920 years. Therefore, Vedic astrology and Vedic zodiac always correspond to actual positions of stars and constellations in the sky.

द्वादशारं नहि तज्जराय वर्वर्ति चक्रं परि द्यामृतस्य।
आ पुत्रा अग्ने मिथुनासो अत्र सप्त शतानि विंशतिश्च तस्थुः ॥11॥
RV (I.164.11)

"The twelve–spoked wheel, of the true (sun) revolves round the heavens, and never (tends) to decay: seven hundred and twenty children in pairs, Agni, abide in it." Seven hundred and twenty children in pairs mean three hundred and sixty days and three hundred and sixty nights. This richa implies that the wheel of time having twelve months (spokes) revolves round the heavens (sun) but it does not wear out. O Agni! 720 pairs of sons ride this wheel.

Thus, RV (1.164.11) informs that during the period this richa of Rigveda was composed, one–year comprised 360 days and 360 nights. We know that the earth is slowing down in its motion around sun. As such the length/duration of one year (i.e., time taken by earth to complete one circle around sun on its elliptical orbit) is slowly but steadily increasing. How many years ago earth was completing one circle around sun in 360 days? It is a matter of calculation. Why does this richa talk about one year of 360 days? One may also go through my reply to question number 41 in Appendix III.

To answer the age–old puzzle, 'how old are Vedas,' a multi–disciplinary research involving astronomy, astrophysics, archaeology, anthropology, and meteorology in addition to philological/linguist approach should be initiated. This is what I suggested at the XIIth World Sanskrit Conference held at the University of Helsinki in July, 2003. Parameters suggested by Prof. Michael Witzel, a reputed Indologist, and others should also be kept in view.

Two

VEDIC EQUALITY AND CASTEISM

"Equality by birth and gender equality are the two cardinal Vedic norms"

2.1 Declining Percentage of Hindus and Its Reasons :

Over centuries, percentage of Hindus in the world population has been declining; and, even in independent India, percentage of Hindus in the total population has been declining. Percentage of Hindus in the total population of India was 84.98% in the 1951 Census; 83.5% in the 1961Census; 82.7% in the 1971 Census; 82.6% in the 1981Census; and, 82.41% in the 1991 Census. In the Census Data Online report (tables 23 & 24) (www.censusindia.net), percentage of Hindus in the 1991 census had been revised downwards to 82%. In the 2001 Census Report covering the period from 1991 to 2001, officially released on 6th Sept. 2004, percentage of Hindus in India fell to 80.5% of the total population of India. Population growth of Hindus during 1981–91 was 25.1% but it declined to 20.3% during 1991 and 2001. Thus, according to the Registrar General of India data, percentage of Hindus in the total population of India declined from 84.98% in 1951 to 80.5% in 2001 (See Appendix–IV). Shri Ramesh Chander Dogra–Urmila Dogra at page 34 of their book 'Let us know Hinduism' published by Star Publications (2003) placed percentage of Hindus in India at 79% only. In the areas forming the Islamic Republic of Pakistan, Hindu population declined from 25% in 1941 to 17% in 1948 and thereafter slowly and steadily to only 1.5% by 1991. In the areas forming the Islamic Republic of Bangladesh, population of Hindus has declined from 30% in 1941 to 25% in 1948 and to about 10% by 1991. In 1947 Hindu & Sikh population of what is now called 'Azad Kashmir' was 12.5% which by 1991 dwindled to about zero percent. In the Kashmir valley region in the Indian side of J&K, percentage of Hindus declined from 15% in 1941 to 5% in 1981 and further declined to about 0.1% in 1991.

The *World Christian Encyclopaedia*, vol.1, second edition, 2001, page 366 of OPU, NewYork, states: "Christians and Muslims will probably both find room to grow in the mosaic of India's peoples so that by 2025, Christians account for 7.4 percent and Muslims for 12.2 percent while Hindus decline under 73 percent. With sustained growth over the next few decades, Christianity could grow to nearly 10 percent of India's population by 2050AD. Hindus will potentially decline as a percentage of India's population as other religions continue to win adherents over next few decades."

For this decline, we Hindus, atleast those who are neither myopic nor ostrich–like escapists, should pause and think as to why percentage of Hindu population is declining even when Hindus are no more under subjugation. If not for our own sake, let us think about the future of our grand children! What legacy we are going to leave behind for our grand children? General response to the question of declining percentage of Hindus is either total indifference, or, "*arey yaar*! Do not bother about" as we Hindus are in a numerical majority in India forgetting the basic lesson of history that we Hindus were always in numerical majority in the Indian subcontinent even during times of Mahmud Ghazani, Babur, Aurangzeb and the British. Declining percentage of Hindus does call for serious introspection and reappraisal of our socio–religious norms.

History repeats itself, so, let us take care that our great grand children do not face those problems, which our great grand fathers had to face. Numerical majority did not protect our great grand fathers from falling into misfortune. Majority Hutu tribe in Rwanda, Africa, is scared of the ruling minority Tutsi tribe. Readers may recall that despite numerical majority of Hindus in independent India, a very small number of jehadi Muslims (about a few thousand only) succeeded in engineering mass exodus of Hindus from 1989 onwards from the Kashmir valley, whether he was a Leftist Hindu or a Rightist Hindu, whether he was a high caste Hindu or a low caste Hindu. How did handful jehadi Muslims succeed in ethnic cleansing of a much larger number of Hindus should be analysed and lessons drawn so that the same misfortune does not visit our grand children. It is true that history repeats itself but only for those societies which are lethargic, indifferent and casual and do not learn lessons of history objectively and honestly. Colouring the pages of history with saffron or red or green ,or white–washing history is equally dangerous as for mistakes in assessment of lessons of history made by drawing room intellectuals, common people, sooner or later, pay in blood, tears and rapes. Ansar Hussain Khan in his book 'The Rediscovery of India' (his page–71) has rightly written: "Modern Indian historians, even Hindu, have sought to give Aurangzeb's fanatic excesses a political and socio–economic gloss. They play down the aspect of Islam which Aurangzeb's policy recalled. This may suit official policy to heal wounds and build bridges in the India of today, but it is futile. It is not true and does not heal."

History should be studied not to become prisoners of the past, nor to perpetuate bitterness of the past but to develop the faculty to identify and avoid mistakes committed in the past by older generations. In 1931 Jawahar Lal Nehru also complained that books on Indian history were largely wrong or distorted (page 9, Glimpses of World History). He has written: "The history we learn in school or college is usually not up to much. I do not know very much about others, but about myself I know that I learnt very little in school. I learnt a little – very little– of the history of India, and a little of the history of England. And even the history of India that I learnt was largely wrong or distorted and written by people who looked down upon our country."

Perceptions and lessons of history differ from country to country, and, from people to people. There is nothing like a universally acceptable history. One views or interprets historical events as per his loyalty or allegiance– financial or ideological. For example, Maharana Pratap Singh of Mewar and Chhatrapati Shivaji Maharaj of Satara are national heroes of Hindus but to Mughal emperors and to the Mughal historians, they were not heroes but rebels. 'Shaheed–e–azam' Bhagat Singh is our national hero and a national martyr but for British historians and supporters of the British Raj in India, he was a 'criminal' hanged for his 'crimes' by a British Indian Court of Law. Dominant majority of Indians believe that it is the People's Republic of China which treacherously attacked India in October 1962 but there is a section of Indians who do not fully share this belief.

Estonian, Finnish and Russian historians have different perceptions at least on some events of the Second World War causing diplomatic ripples from time to time in their bilateral relations.

Reflecting differences in the Russian and the Estonian perceptions about certain events of the World War II, Mr

Arnold Ruutel, President of Estonia, in March 2005, publicly declined invitation of the Russian President, Vladimir Putin, to attend the 60th anniversary celebrations of the defeat of Nazism scheduled to be held on 9th May 2005 in Moscow.It is interesting to know that during the Soviet days, Mr Ruutel was the Chairman of the Presidium of the Estonian Soviet Republic.

In April 2005, anti–Japanese demonstrations broke out in China and in the Republic of Korea (South Korea) against the Government of Japan approving such Japanese history books which, in the views of the demonstrators, played down atrocities committed by Imperial Japan in those days of 1930s and 1940s. Japanese Foreign Minister (Nobutaka Machimura) summoned Chinese Ambassador (Wang Yi) and demanded an apology and compensation for Japanese properties damaged in China. Earlier, China had denounced some new Japanese history books that it maintains white–wash Japanese guilt about massacres of Chinese civilians during Japan's occupation of China. Japan, in turn, accuses China of distorting history. Speaking in New Delhi on 12th April 2005 at the end of his state visit to India, Chinese Prime Minister, Wen Jiabao, publicly said, "the core issue in the China–Japan relationship is that Japan needs to face up to history squarely". The Chinese premier said, "Only a country that respects history and takes responsibility for the past history wins over the trust of people." So, history is too serious a matter to be left exclusively in the hands of historians.

National perceptions of history influence the diplomacy of that country, and, diplomacy of today gives birth to history of tomorrow. What diplomats do today, under stress and strain of time, often relying upon information which is either sketchy or not very accurate at the point of time of taking a decision, becomes subject matter of historical research few decades after the event when documents are de–classified. Historians have ample time to study declassified documents at their own pace with the added advantage of hindsight.

Whereas Islamic priests (mullah) and Christian priests have been working overtime with missionary zeal to seek new converts so as to increase their political and demographic weight, Hindu priests (pujaries) unaware of Rigvedic norms of equality by birth and gender equality but armed with mis–interpretations of distorted Manusmriti (composed around 200 AD) have been working very hard over last one thousand years in manners ipso facto resulting into relative reduction in percentage of Hindu population, by making it more and more difficult for a sizeable chunk of Hindus (now called ST/SC/Dalits/Harijans) to let them remain Hindus with honour and dignity by concocting high caste–low caste syndrome; by not enthusiastically sanctifying widow marriages; and, by not seeking new converts to Hinduism.

There are twenty–seven Vedic richas listed in this book, which command equality of all (Hindus) by birth; and, unity & harmony among them. There are atleast eleven Vedic richas, which command that professions are not hereditary, not birth based. Widow marriage is expressly sanctioned under nine Vedic richas, namely, RV (X.40.2), RV (X.18.8), RV (X.18.9), Atharvaveda (IX.5.27–28) and AV (XVIII.3.1–4). Seeking converts into Hinduism is expressly commanded under RV (X.191), AV (III.30), Yaj (26.02), Yaj (36.18), Gita (XVIII.68–69), etc.

2.2 Supremacy Of Vedas

Only Vedas are the Supreme religious scriptures of Hindus. Vedas are our canonical scriptures. All others (Brahamanas, Upanishads, Puranas, Smrities, Sutras etc.) are just commentaries on Vedas by individuals, explanations, and stories mixed with historical accounts and poets' imaginations i.e., these are secondary sources. Many Puranas themselves state that these are stories (*mahatmya*) as narrated by Kakbhisundi, Sukracharya or other sages. All books written in Sanskrit cannot be elevated to the status of religious scriptures. Therefore, the latter day compositions must yield to the supremacy of Vedas. It is not a new assertion as these secondary sources themselves acknowledge the supremacy of Vedas. For example, Manusmriti vide Shloka (II.6) states: "the whole Veda is the primary/first source of the sacred law" (George Buhler). Manusmriti (II.13) reconfirms that the supreme authority of law is the shruti i.e., Vedas. So, it is logical that all such shlokas of Manusmriti etc. which are violative of Veda should stand rejected. Apastamba Dharmasutra (I.1) states that Vedas alone are the authority for law. Gautam Dharmasutra (I.3) also admits that Vedas are the source of sacred law. In fact, Maharishi Ved Vyas, who is credited to have compiled, or, redacted all the four Vedas in the present format and who is the author of Mahabharata and Shrimad Bhagwad Gita has himself laid down (Mahabharata: 1–V–4):

श्रुतिस्मशतिपुराणानां विरोधो यत्र दशश्यते।
तत्र श्रौतं प्रमाणन्तु तयोर्द्वैधे स्मशतिर्त्वरा॥

that, "whenever there is conflict between what is declared in the Vedas and provisions in any of the Smritis, Puranas, etc. what is declared in the Vedas shall prevail".

In fact, Manusmriti (IV.176) itself suggests its own abrogation or modification. Dr. A.S. Altekar in his book 'The Position of Women in Hindu Civilization' has written (page 368) that,: "It is further important to note that even orthodox Smriti writers like Manu have recognized that a time might come when their rules would become obsolete, and have, therefore, declared that if any rules framed by them are found to be not conducive to the welfare of society, or against the spirit of the age, they should be unhesitatingly abrogated or modified."

परित्यजेदर्थकामा यौ स्यातां धर्मवर्जितौ ।
धर्ममण्यसुखोदर्क लोकाविद्विष्टमेव च ॥ (Manusmriti : IV, 176)

Its translation by George Buhler is: "Let him avoid (the acquisition of) wealth and (the gratification of his) desires, if they are opposed to the sacred law, and (avoid) even lawful acts which may cause pain in the future or are offensive to men."

In 1899 AD, Prof. Arthur A. MacDonell in his book "A History of Sanskrit Literature" has written (page 28) "works of Vedic revelation (shruti) were deemed of higher authority in cases of doubt than the later works on Sanskrit Literature". On page 31 MacDonell clarifies, "Dharma sutras are, in general, the oldest sources of Indian law and are closely connected with Veda which they quote and which the later law–books regard as the first and highest source of dharma." Thus, MacDonell also concludes that Vedas supersede every other scripture and stand the Supreme.

Justice A.M. Bhattacharjee in his book "Hindu Law and the Constitution" says (his page 16) that by a rule of interpretation, if the shruti (Vedas) and the smriti differ on any point, the former is to prevail but the British Courts used to rule just the opposite! In practice, Justice Bhattacharjee says (page 18) commentaries & digests (nibandhas) replaced smritis in British Courts. In Atmaram v Bajirao, the Privy Council ruled that opinions of latter day commentators (Bhasyakars) would prevail over Vedas. In view of the Privy Council decision in Ramnad case (1868), it was no more open to Hindus even to inquire whether disputed points were in conformity with Vedas or not (page 37, Bhattacharjee).

Thus, while paying lip services to the Supremacy of Vedas, British Indian Courts, in the name of upholding local/latter day usages & practices, slowly but steadily whittled down, caselaw by caselaw, the supremacy of Vedas; and, thus, promoted divisiveness and diversities among Hindus to meet imperial interests of their political masters of the day to divide & rule.

Let us restore the Supremacy of Vedas to usher in Vedic brotherhood of equality by birth and gender equality.

2.3 Non–Canonical Literature

It is believed that Manusmriti was composed much later during Kushan period, about 100 years after Chanakya/ Kautilya, about five or six hundred years after the death of Gautam Buddha. Arthur A. MacDonell, Principal, Oxford College (born in Patna, Bihar) in his book 'A History of Sanskrit Literature' has given the following estimate about likely time of composition of respective books:

200 AD	Vishnu Smriti in its present form
200 AD	Manusmriti in its present form
350 AD	Yajnavalkya Dharma Sutra
500 AD	Narad Sutra/Narad Smriti
900 AD	Commentry of Medhatithi on Manusmriti
1100 AD	Mitaksara of Vijnaneswara (Commentary on Yajnavalkya)
1300 AD	Parasar Smriti
1300 AD	Chaturvarga Chintamani by Hemadri
1500 AD	Dharma Ratna of Jimutavahana containing Dayabhag School of law.

Above Christian era compositions are obviously non–canonical , therefore, can neither be put on par with canonical Vedas nor be allowed to compete with the Vedas, much less supersede the same. In his book, MacDonell (page 366) also warns that "the smritis are not on the same footings as law books of other nations as these are works of private individuals

(Brahamans); were written by Brahamans for benefit of Brahamans, whose caste pretentions these latter–day books consequently exaggerate. Further, none of these books from Manusmriti onwards were approved by any Dharma Sansad (religious congregation)." Vedas are compilations of richas revealed to hundreds of rishis drawn from all walks of life, they, have the aura & majesty of having been approved by a sort of Dharma Sansad, approved by all sections of society. MacDonell advises it is important to check statements/claims made in smrities by outside sources. But, British Indian Courts neglected this advice of MacDonell. Further, the original text of Manusmriti has been tampered with was acknowledged even by Sir William Jones, an employee of the East India Company but he arbitrarily elevated it as the Law book of Hindus in British Indian Courts.

There are many self–contradictory shlokas in Manusmriti proving manipulation and tampering with therein. For example, some people quote Manusmriti shlokas (V.18, 31, 32, 39) to justify beef eating whereas shlokas (V.45 to 54) of the same Manusmriti prohibits killing of animals and eating their flesh. Manusmriti shloka (XI.96) states that flesh is food of pisachas and rakshasas (demons).

Bertrand Russell in his book, 'Power', has traced from prehistoric times that priestly class used religious beliefs and practices to accumulate power and wealth. In medieval times, kings used to rule in many European countries at pleasure of the Catholic Pope. Papal approval was a must for ascending many thrones in the medieval Europe. So, priestly class acquiring power in the name of religion was there in other societies too.

2.4 Purusha–Sukta : Reappraised

As mentioned earlier, the 90th Sukta of the tenth chapter of the Rigveda is popularly known as the Purusha–sukta. It is denoted as RV (X.90). Purusha generally means a healthy &

strong male human being, or the supreme God. The very concepts of castes by birth, upper & lower castes, superior & inferior castes, outcastes, untouchables, dalits etc. are not sanctioned by Rigveda, Valmiki Ramayana, or by Shrimad Bhagwadgita. Protagonists of castes by birth cite in particular the Purusha–Sukta richa (X.90.12) of Rigveda and shlokas (IV.13) and (XVIII.41) of Shrimad Bhagwadgita. This claim totally fizzles out if one looks closely into these keeping in mind other richas of Rigveda and other shlokas of Gita and the two examples (para 3.4) set by Lord Rama.

That there is no birth based caste in Rigveda is also evident from the simple fact that names of none of Rigvedic rishis carry any present day caste titles like Pandit, Sharma, Tripathi, Chaturvedi, Trivedi, Dvivedi, Singh, Chatterji, Mukherji, Rao, Gupta, Namboodari, Iyer, etc. Jawahar Lal Nehru was of the view the caste among Hindus had developed (i.e., gained rigidity) after the Muslim invasions (Page 431, Glimpses of World History). (See last para of 2.5)

As devil is generally there in the details, readers may closely look at English translations. HH Wilson translates RV (X.90.11):

> **यत्पुरुषं व्यदधुः कतिधा व्यकल्पयन्।**
> **मुखं किमस्य कौ बाहू का ऊरू पादा उच्येत॥11॥**
> **(RV:X.90.11)**

"When they immolated Purusha, into how many portions did they divide him? What was his mouth called what his arms, what his thighs, what were his feet called?" Ralph T.H. Griffith translates: **"When they divided Purusha** how many portions did they make? What do they call his mouth, his arms? What do they call his thighs and feet?" One may note that both translators have used verb' called'. They have not translated as to who was 'born' from mouth, arms, thighs and feet.

ब्राह्मणोऽस्य मुखमासीद् बाहू राजन्यः कृतः ।
ऊरू तदस्य यद्वैश्यः पद्भ्यां शूद्रो अजायत ॥ 12 ॥ (RV: X.90.12)

HH Wilson translates the above richa, "His mouth became the Brahamana, his arms became the Rajnya, his thighs became the Vaishya, and the Shudra was born from his feet." Griffith translates, "The Brahaman was his mouth; of both his arms Rajnya was made. His thighs became Vaishya; from his feet the Shudra was produced." One may again carefully note that these famous translators, strictly speaking, do not state that the first three were 'born' from such and such part of the body of Purusha. To represent something symbolically, and to be born from that thing are not identical matters.

With a view to create hereditary monopoly on easy money of *dakshina* (alms), some greedy priests (many many millennia/ centuries after Vedas were revealed) concocted a hypothesis in Manusmriti that as Brahaman was 'born' from the mouth of Purusha, he was the superior most and as Shudra was 'born' from feet which is supposedly the impure part of body, he (shudra) was impure and the inferior most. How could feet of God be impure for we mortals? Neither Wilson nor Griffith attests this 'birth' concoction.

Shloka (V.132) of Manusmriti is often quoted to claim that organs of human body above navel (*nabhi*) are sacred (*apavitra*) and those below are impure (*apavitra)*. Firstly, there is no sanction for such a hypothesis in the Rigveda. Secondly, even such interpretation of (V.132) is totally false as its translation by George Buhler reads: "All those cavities (of the body) which lie above the navel are pure, (but) those which are below the navel are impure". The point is that there is great difference between a cavity in a body and a part or organ of a body. Mischief by casteist lobby is to equate a cavity in the body with a part/organ of that body. Absurdity of such interpretation of shloka (V.132) becomes clearer if one asks a simple question......are the two cavities of nose sacred being above the navel, if so, whether secretions from these are also sacred? The correct position is that all cavities in human body are **equally** important and **equally** useful to remain healthy. If any cavity in human body, specially the lower ones get blocked that person becomes sick and dies.

Wilson says that the objective of (X.90.11) was 'to immolate Purusha;' and Griffith says that it was 'to divide Purusha.' This context, this background, that division of body of Purusha into four parts was done to immolate, to sacrifice, to kill the Purusha has been totally suppressed and manipulated in Manusmriti. In shloka (I.31), Manusmriti, thus, falsely claims that for growth of people (*lokanbridhi*) Brahama created Brahaman, Kshatriya, Vaishya and Shudra from mouth, arms, thighs and feet respectively. What was revealed by God to Rigvedic rishi to Narain, the original *mantra–drastya rishi* (composer) of RV (X.90) reavealed by God is totally different. He was revealed that the human society is like the human body. Just as the human body is healthy and strong only if all the four parts of body are joined together and function in harmony with each other, similarly a human society will be strong only if all the four professions, classes are joined and function in harmony with each other. The Rishi was conveyed a very simple common sense, that even a most powerful man like the Purusha can be killed or immolated if his mouth, arms, thighs and feet are separated. So,if brahamans (intelligensia), rajnya (government), vaishya (business and agriculture) and shudra (employees and service class) are separated, that *samaj* will also get killed,or,get subjugated. If we kill a person what do we do? We cut his body into pieces; we separate head, arms, thighs and feet. This is what the followers of Manusmriti have been doing over centuries: destroying and immolating the Hinduism from within by dividing, segregating Hindus among different castes by birth and by putting them at perpetual fratricidal war with each other thus, reducing the percentage of Hindu population. One may note that the so called upper caste Hindus (Ranvir Sena) killing lower caste Hindus in Bihar and vice–versa in endless caste conflicts is resulting in declining percentage of Hindus. By throwing Shudras out of villages, the followers of Manusmriti have amputated the feet of Hinduism. Thus they have made Hinduism crippled and invalid, no wonder ripe to be defeated by small numbers of foreign invaders in the medieval period. In 1197 AD, Muhammad bin Bakhtiyar is said to have captured Bihar and Bengal with his advance troop of only eighteen cavalry showing there was no resistance from the peasantry as the Manusmriti had made peasantry neutral to governmental (*rajnya*) affairs.

Another interpretation of (X.90.11 & 12) is creative i.e., a powerful man (virat Purusha) with all his four limbs joined emerges from Yajna (efforts) i.e., a powerful society emerges by combined, joint efforts of all the four classes, professions. We say the child born is healthy only when his mouth, arms, thighs and feet are joined and work in perfect harmony with each other.If any limb is missing or limbs are not working in harmony, we say that the child born is not a healthy one. Acharya Shri Ram Sharma of Bareilly translates (in Hindi) "*Virat Purusha kitne prakaron se utpanna huvey. Unka mukh Brahaman, bhuja kshatriye, janghaye vaishya aur charan shudra huye.*" Acharya also does not attest to the birth of such and such class from this and this body part of Purusha. He translates these two richas on lines of creation, not immolation, so, in his translation, body of Purusha is not divided into four limbs, but, instead, Purusha emerges with all the four parts of body 'united', 'unified' into one single body from yajna (efforts). So, the Rigvedic command is that when all the four professions/classes are joined together into one single unified polity, a strong samaj is created.

As per common sense, a virat Purusha is the one who is healthy; and, a person is healthy only if his mouth, arms, thighs and feet are joined together and work in perfect harmony with each other. Whenever this harmony among different parts of body of any person is disturbed or destroyed, he becomes paralysed or sick and he is no more a virat Purusha (i.e., a healthy person). So, what the Rigvedic rishi Narain is saying is that a society will emerge as the most powerful society like the Virat Purusha only if its intelligentsia (educated people i.e., Brahamans), Government (Rajnya), business community (Vaishya) and professionals & workers (Shudra) join together and work in as close harmony with each other as mouth, arms, thighs and feet of a healthy person work. These two richas, contrary to the traditional Hindu beliefs, thus, emphasise total equality, perfect unity & complementarity of all the four classes of people in order to make a Society strong and powerful. In a healthy person, mouth does not claim to be superior to legs, arms do not claim any superiority over legs, arms do not function independently of head (Parkinsons's disease), as each part of the body is composed of identically same materials and is functionally dependent upon each other. No part of body is inferior or superior to any other part of the body; each dependent on the other; each complementary to the other, each supporting the other.

Thus, the Purusha Sukta commands that none of the four professions in a healthy society is inferior or superior to other, and, each is dependent on the other for its healthy survival. But, the greedy people and the British Indian Courts in order to divide and rule over majority Hindus, created, spread and sustained just the opposite interpretations of Purusha–sukta pushing the entire Hindu samaj into slavery and military defeats.

> **नाभ्या आसीदन्तरिक्षं शीर्ष्णो द्यौः समवर्तत।**
> **पद्भ्यां भूमिर्दिशः श्रोत्रात्तथा लोकाँ अकल्पयन्॥14॥**
> **RV (X.90.14)**

Those who say that as Shudra (professionals/service class) represent the feet of Virat Purusha, and, as feet are impure, so, Shudras are impure should know that the above richa RV (X.90.14) says that the earth was also born from the same feet of Purusha. So, will they (i.e., casteist lobby) leave this earth on the same analogy of earth being an impure place? Based on (X.90.14), Shudras will be justified to claim the entire earth as exclusively theirs.

Also, one may note that whenever we worship, we always place our heads at the feet of God in any temple, so, how can anyone say that Shudra representing the same feet of God is impure and untouchable?

To summarise, RV (X.90.11&12) preach that as a person is called healthy only when his mouth (head), arms, thighs and feet are joined together and function in perfect harmony with each other, similarly, a society will become a healthy, organic and prosperous only if its intelligentsia (Brahaman), Government (Rajnya), business and agriculture class (Vaishya) and professionals & workers (Shudra) join together in perfect harmony; and, that society will become sick or invalid in which these classes are disjointed.

2.5 Professions–Not–Hereditary Richas

Thus, there is no stipulation of high or low by birth in the Rigveda. Many rishis of Rigveda under the current Manusmriti definition would not turn out to be Brahamans by birth. There is no stipulation in the Rigveda that son will necessarily inherit profession of his father i.e., there is no hereditary claim on professions, there are no birth based professions. In RV (I.112.11) Dirghasravas being a son of the Rigvedic rishi Dirghatamas should have been called a rishi or a kaksivat but, no, he has been addressed in this very richa as a *vanik* (merchant) as he followed trade to earn his livelihood. In richas RV (V.23.1) and (V.23.2), rishi Dyumna prays to Agni "Bestow Agni, upon Dyumna, a son, overcoming foes by his prowess; one who may with glory subdue all men in battle" (HH Wilson). This rishi of Rigveda is praying for a warrior son.

In RV (IX.112.3) another rishi says, "I am the singer, papa is the physician, mama throws the corn upon grinding stones." So, father of a Rigvedic rishi is a physician!!! Because in the Manusmriti shlokas (III.152) and (IV.212 & 220), a physician has been called impure (Shudra). English translation of Manusmriti (III.152): "Physicians, temple–priests, sellers of meat, and those who subsist by shop–keeping must be avoided at sacrifices offered to the gods and to the manes (female deities)." But in RV (II.33.4), Rudra (Lord Shiva) is praised being the chief physician amongst all physicians. This again shows that Manusmriti violates the Vedas so, Manusmriti should stand discarded. Manusmriti (III.152) degrades even temple–priests by equating them with meat–sellers!

In richa (X.125.5), a rishi says that by imparting training one can be turned into a warrior, a Brahma, a rishi or a sage. Thus, in Rigveda, profession or 'caste' is not by birth, not hereditary, but by training and education (karma/efforts/prayatna in the present life span).

अहमेव स्वयमिदं वदामि जुष्टं देवेभिरुत मानुषेभिः ।
यं कामये तंतमुग्रं कृणोमि तं ब्रह्माणं तमशषिं तं सुमेधाम्॥15॥
RV(X.125.5)

HH Wilson translates RV (X.125.5), "I verily of myself declare this which is approved by both gods and men; whosoever I will, I render him formidable (warrior), I make him a Brahma, a rishi or a sage." This richa appears in Atharvaveda (IV.30.03) also.

RV (X.98) was revealed to rishi Devapi who was the elder brother of King Shantanu of Mahabharata. In RV (X.98.7) Devapi is functioning as a purohit to his own brother King Shantanu. So, Shantanu being a *khsatriya* under Manusmriti definition, one brother (Devapi) in the Rigveda is functioning as purohit to another brother (King Shantanu). Thus, priesthood was not hereditary as per Rigveda.

Hymns RV (IX.96) and RV (X.179.02) were revealed to rishi Pratardana who was either a King of Kashi or from this family. These two shlokas show that the city of Kashi is as old as the Rigveda itself. Puranas name at least six kings of Kashi preceding Pratardana. This means karma–bhumi of Rigvedic rishis included Kashi region too, far away from the Punjab region. Lady rishi Lopamudra, a daughter of King of Vidarbha–was married to rishi Agastya. As such, the karma–bhumi (residence) of the Vedic rishis extended much beyond Punjab to Maharashtra of today.

The third Mandala of Rigveda was revealed to rishi Vishwamitra (also written as visvamitr) and family. Some interpret RV (III.58.6) to say that his family lineage was to the House of Jahnu who was a King of Kanyakubj, whereas others translate this richa to mean that the principal place of residence of Vishwamitra was on the banks of the river Ganga; implying that the karma–bhumi (abode,residence) of composers of the third mandala was the Gangetic region. Even if it is presumed that (III.58.6) refers only to the House of Jahnu, Puranas say that rishi Vishwamitra was the ninth descendant of King Jahnu; so, rishi's family had been living in this area much before chapter three of Rigveda was composed/revealed. So, the East India Company theory that composers of Rigveda had entered into India on horsebacks from the west stands knocked out. Gayatri mantra RV (III.62.10) was revealed to rishi Vishwamitra Gathin. The Gayatri mantra appears in Yajurveda at (III.35), (XXII.9), & (XXX.2) and in the Samaveda (1462) also. Therefore, by reciting the Gayatri mantra one simultaneously venerates three Vedas.

Richas RV (III.53.22–24) confirm rishi Vishwamitra Gathin himself was a warrior. Hymn RV (VI.75) attests to the fact that rishi Payu Bhardwaj was also a great warrior.In Ramayana days, Parasuram was a great warrior. In Mahabharata days, Dronachraya and Kripacharya were great warriors. Rishis were warriors too. There are twenty–nine rishikas (woman rishi) and eleven king rishis in the Rigveda proving that God chose rishis for revelations not from any particular class or community but from all the walks of society depending upon their excellence and achievements (*karma*, education,*tapas*).

R.C. Majumdar, Raychaudhuri & Datta in their book 'An Advanced History of India' have written (page 31): "But it is important to remember that in the hymns of the Rigveda there is little trace of the rigid restrictions typical of caste in its mature form. There was hardly any taboo on intermarriage, change of occupation or commensality. We have instances of marriages of Brahamanas with Rajanya women, and of the union of Arya and Shudra. Families were not wedded to a particular profession. There was no ban on the taking of food cooked by the Shudras, and there is no evidence in Vedas that impurity was communicated by the touch or contact of the inferior castes."

In 1944, while in the Ahmadnagar Fort prison, Jawaharlal Nehru penned his book 'Discovery of India.' In those days, the Theory of Aryan Invasion and the Arya–Dravida divide was at its peak (which has now been discarded). In this background of his time, Nehru has explained at page 85 of his book: "Caste began with a hard and fast division between

Aryans and non–Aryans, the latter again being divided into the Dravidian races and the aboriginal tribes. The Aryans, to begin with, formed one class and there was hardly any specialization. The word Arya comes from a root word meaning to till, and the Aryans as a whole were agriculturists and agriculture was considered a noble occupation. The tiller of the soil functioned also as priest, soldier, or trader, and there was no privileged order of priests. The caste divisions, originally intended to separate the Aryans from the non–Aryans, reacted on the Aryans themselves, and as division of functions and specialization increased, the new classes took the form of castes." Thus, Nehru also attests that (a) there was no birth based casteism during the Vedic period, (b) Rigvedic people formed one class (c) there was social mobility during Vedic period, and; (d) much later professions took the present day ugly form of castes.

2.6 Equality And Unity Richas

Higher caste & lower caste, untouchability and outcastes etc. are in open and direct contradiction of at least twenty seven Vedic richas viz., RV (V.60.5), (VIII.93.13), (X.93.9), (X.191.2–4), Atharvaveda (III.30.1–7), AV (VI.64.1–3), AV (VI.73.1–3) AV (VI.74.1–3), and (VII.54.1–2) (or VII.52); and Yajurveda (19.46), (26.02) and (36.18).

Unity in diversity is a famous Hindu motto. Cows of different colours like black, red and spotted ones give same white milk in RV (VIII.93.13). It is a metaphor used in Vedas for unity in diversity: the pillar of modern Indian State.

Richa (X.93.9) prays "Unite the strength of us Men here, like the chariot–wheel and reins." Following is the Sanskrit text of this richa:

धी नो अह्वयो देव सवितः स च स्तुषे मघोनाम।
सहो न इन्द्रो वह्निभिर्न्येषां चर्षणीना चक्रं रश्मिं न योयुवे ॥9॥
RV (X.93.9)

* * * * *

HH Wilson translates (X.191.2): "Meet together, talk together, let your minds apprehend alike: in like manner as the ancient gods concurring accepted their portion of the sacrifice:"

सं गच्छध्वं सं वदध्वं सं वो मनांसि जानताम्।
देवा भागं यथा पूर्वे सञ्जानाना उपासते॥2॥
(RV:X.191.2)

* * * * *

RV (X.191.3) "Common be the prayer of these (assembled worshippers), common be the acquirement, common the purpose, associated be the desire. I repeat for you a common prayer; I offer for you a common oblation:"

समानो मन्त्रः समितिः समानी समान मनः सह चित्तमेषाम्।
समानं मन्त्रमभि मन्त्रये वः समानेन वो हविषा जुहोमि॥3॥
(RV: X.191.3)

Readers may note, the Rigveda instructs common prayer, common worship and common oblations for all Hindus without any birth–based discrimination among men, and, without any gender discrimination too.

* * * * *

RV (X.191.4) "Common (worshippers), be your intention; common be (the wishes of) your heart; common be your thoughts, so that there may be thorough union among you:" The Vedas command thorough union among the followers.

समानी व आकूतिः समाना हृदयानि वः।
समानमस्तु वो मनो यथा वः सुसहासति॥ 4॥ (RV:X.191.4)

* * * * *

W.D. Whitney & K.L. Joshi translate Atharvaveda (III.30.1) "like–heartedness, like— mindedness, non–hostility do I make for you; do you show affection the one towards the other, as the inviolable (cow) towards her calf when born:" So, one section of the Hindu Samaj must show non–hostility and affection towards the other sections of the Samaj.

सहृदयं सांमनस्यमविद्वेषं कृणोमि वः।
अन्यो अन्यमभि हर्यत वत्सं जातमिवाघ्न्या ॥1॥ AV(III.30.1)

* * * * *

AV (III.30.2 & 3) command harmony among brothers, sisters, sons, father, mother, husband & wife. AV (III.30.4) commands that we should be united and should not go apart as gods do not go apart.

* * * * *

Atharvaveda (III.30.5): "Having superior intentful, be you not divided, accomplishing together, moving on with joint labour come hither speaking what is agreeable one to another, I make you united, like minded."

ज्यायस्वन्तश्चित्तिनो मा वि यौष्ट संराधयन्तः सधुराश्चरन्त।
अन्यो अन्यस्मै वल्गु वदन्त एत सध्रीचीनान् वः संमनस्कृणोमि ॥5॥
AV (III.30.5)

* * * * *

Atharvaveda (III.30.6): "Your drinking saloon be the same, in common your share of food, in the same harness do I join you together; worship you Agni united, like spokes about a navel. " Thus, SC/ST/Dalit Hindus have Vedic right of equal & free access to water wells, tanks, food–shops, temples, worshipping, etc.

समानी प्रपा सह वोऽन्नभागः समाने योक्त्रे सह वो युनज्मि।
सम्यञ्चोऽग्निं सपर्यतारा नाभिमिवाभितः ॥6॥ AV(III.30.6)

In January 2005, great tidal waves (tsunami) hit the eastern coast of India causing heavy death and destruction, especially in Tamilnadu. About twenty thousand Indians got killed or went missing. Amidst this human tragedy, it was painful to read a report captioned "Tsunami can't wash away hatred for Dalits" in the Indian Express of 7th January, 2005. It reported that Dalit Hindus were thrown out of relief camps, given left–over food or no food, and, were not allowed to take water provided by UNICEF lest they 'polluted' the water. This centuries old hatred, flowing from total ignorance of the Vedas, can be removed only when a common Hindu is made aware of these Vedic richas which command "common be your food, common be your water, common be your prayers and common be your oblations"

The Indian Express editorially (8th January, 2005) called to crack down on those who discriminate against Dalits in relief operations. Hindustan Times also in its editorial captioned "Out Caste!" (8th January, 05) has rightly and forcefully argued: "In Nagapattinam alone, 32 families of Dalits have not only been told to fend for themselves but have also been shooed away from using basic amenities lest they 'contaminate' 'caste Hindus'.....For too long, we have come to accept the 'necessary evil' of casteism in this country.We are told that this is a reality we need to understand if we are to understand India—whether it be our politics or society. As the Nagapattinam phenomenon only highlights–for such a forced division among our own people takes place everyday in various places—caste barriers are also not sociological necessities, but societal evils that need to be dismantled,if need be by force."

This social evil can be permanently dismantled neither by force alone nor by few prosecutions here and there alone but only in conjunction with wider dissemination of these Vedic richas.

* * * * *

Atharvaveda (III.30.7): "United, like minded I make you, of one bunch, all of you, by my conciliation; (be) like the gods defending amrita; late and early be well–willing yours." Thus, all Hindus are of one bunch & one stock, a point always so emphatically and so correctly made by Dr. Ambedkar.

सध्रीचीनान् वः संमनसस्कृणोम्येकश्नुष्टीन्त्संवननेन सर्वान।
देवा इवामश्तं रक्षमाणां: सायंप्रातः सौमनसौ वो अस्तु॥7॥
AV (III.30.7)

* * * * *

The following three shlokas of AV (VI.64) are very similar to RV (X.191.1–3).

Atharvaveda (VI.64.1): "Do you concur; be your closely combined; let your minds be concurrent, as the gods of old sat concurrent about their portion."

सं जानीध्वं सं पश्च्यध्वं सं वो मनांसि जानताम्।
देवा भागं यथा पूर्वे संजानाना उपासते॥1॥ AV(VI.64.1)

* * * * *

Atharvaveda (VI.64.2): "Be their counsel (mantra) the same, their gathering the same, their course (vrata) (religious ceremonies) the same, their intent alike (saha); I offer for you with the same oblation; do you enter together into the same thought (cetas)."

समानो मन्त्रः समितिः समानी समानं व्रतं सह चित्तमेषाम्।
समानेन वो हिवषा जुहोमि समानं चेतो अभिसंविशध्वम्॥2॥
AV(VI.64.2)

* * * * *

Atharvaveda (VI.64.3): "Be your design the same, your hearts the same, your mind the same, that it may be well for you together."

समानी व आकूतिः समाना हृदयामि वः।
समानमस्तु वो मनो यथा वः सुसहासति॥3॥ AV(VI.64.3)

* * * * *

Atharvaveda (VI.73.1): "Let Varuna come here, Soma, Agni; let Brhaspati with the Vasus come here; come you together, [his] fellows, all of you, like–minded, unto the fortune of this stern corrector."

एह यातु वरुणः सोमो अग्निबर्ह्हस्पतिर्वसुभिरेह यातु।
अस्य श्रियमुपसंयात सर्व उग्रस्य चेत्तुः संमनस सजाताः॥1॥
AV (VI.73.1)

* * * * *

Atharvaveda (VI.73.2): "The Vehemence that is within your hearts, the design that has entered into your mind " that I frustrate with the oblation, the ghi, in me, O (my) fellows, be your satisfaction (ramati)."

यो वः शुष्मो हृदयेष्वन्तराकूतिर्या वो मनसि प्रविष्टा।
तान्त्सीवयामि हविषा घश्तेन मयि सजाता रमतिर्वो अस्तु॥2॥
AV (VI.73.2)

* * * * *

Atharvaveda (VI.73.3): "Be you just here; go not away from us; let Pusan make (it) pathless for you in the distance; let the lord of the dwelling call aloud after you; in me, O (my) fellows, be your satisfaction."

इहैव स्त माप याताध्यस्मत् पूषा परस्तादपथं वः कृणोतु।
वस्तोष्पतिरनु वो जोहवीतु मयि सजाता रमतिर्वो अस्तु॥3॥
AV (VI.73.3)

* * * * *

Atharvaveda (VI.74.1): "Together let your bodies be mixed, together your minds, together your courses; together has this Brahamanaspati, together has Bhaga made you come."

सं वः पश्च्यन्तां तन्वः सं मनांसि समु व्रता।
सं वोऽयं बह्मणस्पतिर्भगः सं वो अजीगमत्॥1॥ AV(VI.74.1)

* * * * *

Atharvaveda (VI.74.2): "Concurrence of the mind for you,

also concurrence of the heart, also what of Bhaga is wearied – therewith I make you concur."

संज्ञपनं वो मनसोऽथो संज्ञपनं हृदः।
अथो भगस्य यच्छ्रान्तं तेन संज्ञपयामि वः ॥2॥ AV (VI.74.2)

* * * * *

Atharvaveda (VI.74.3): "As the Adityas, severe, not bearing enmity, united with the Vasus, with the Maruts, so, O three–named one, not bearing enmity, do you make these people here like–minded."

यथादित्या वसुभिः संबभूवुर्मरुद्भिरुग्रा अहृणीयमानाः।
एवा त्रिणामन्नहृणीयमान इमाञ्जनान्त्संमनसस्कृधीह॥3॥
AV (VI.74.3)

* * * * *

Atharvaveda (VII.54.1): "Harmony for us with our own men... May we be harmonious with mind, with knowledge, may we not fight...let the day not come when Indra's arrow fall on us."

संज्ञानं नः स्वेभि संज्ञानमरणेभि।
संज्ञानमश्विना युवमिहास्मासु नि यच्छतम्॥1॥ AV (VII.54.1)

* * * * *

AV (VII.54.2): "May we be harmonious with mind, with knowledge, may we not fight with the mind of the gods; let not noises arise in case of much destruction, let not Indra's arrow (thunderbolt) fall, the day being come."

सं जानामहै मनसा सं चिकित्वा मा युष्महि मनसा दैव्येन।
मा घोषा उत्स्थुर्बहुले विनिर्हते मेषुः पप्तदिन्द्रस्याहन्यागते॥2॥
AV (VII.54.2)

* * * * *

Yajurveda (19.46) (richa 1072) commands: "Equals,

unanimous...." Yajurveda (26.02) (richa No. 1460) prays for well being (kalyan) of all including shudras as under:

यथेमां वाचं कल्याणी मावदानि जनेभ्यः। ब्रह्मराजन्याभ्या शूद्राय चार्याय च स्वाय चारणाय च। प्रियो देवानां दक्षिणायै दातुरिह भूयासमयं मे कामः समश्ध्यतामुप मादो नमतु॥2॥ Yajurveda (26.02).

R.T.H. Griffith & Dr. Ravi Prakash Arya translate "That I to all the people say address this salutary speech, To priest and nobleman, Shudra and Arya to one of our own kin and to strangers". This richa is addressed to strangers also, confirming the missionary command of Vedas.This shloka of Yajurveda reconfirms that shudras belong to the same community, to the same race as that of the priest, rajnya and Arya. Thus, shudras are not a separate race, a point always so emphatically and so correctly made out by Dr BR Ambedkar (page 269, Dr BR Ambedkar Life and Mission by D. Keer) "In Ambedkar's view the caste system is a social division of people of the same race."

Shri Ram Sharma translates this richa Yaj (26.02): "*Kalyan karane wali vani ko Brahaman, raja, shudra, vaishya, apne jano aur samasta jano ke liye kahata hoon.*"

Yaj (36.18): "O Deva, strengthen me. May all beings regard me with eyes of a friend? May I regard all beings with the eye of a friend? With the eye of a friend do we regard one another."

**दृश ते दृश्श्रं ह मा मित्रस्य मा चक्षुषा सर्वाणि भूतानि समीक्षन्ताम्।
मित्रस्याहं चक्षुषा सर्वाणि भूतानि समीक्षे।
मित्रस्य चक्षुषा समीक्षामहे॥18॥ Yajurveda (36.18)**

2.7 Conclusion

The central command of the 27 harmony richas, 11 profession–not–hereditary richas and 13 Gita shlokas (in the next chapter) is that all Hindus, men and women, are totally equal by birth, of one bunch, share same water and food, worship together united in the same temple, common prayers, common be the purpose, common be thoughts, united like spokes of a wheel, common be oblation, friendly towards each others, etc. One becomes a warrior (Rajnya), Brahaman (educated ones) or rishies, not by birth but by his education/efforts/training (karma of this life) vide RV (X.125.5). No one is superior by birth and no one is inferior by birth. Hindi term for communism is *samyavad* i.e., equality of all human beings and this equality is very much there in richas detailed in para 2.6 above. Rigveda clearly attempts to blunt 'class cleavages' by preaching "*samano mantrah*, *samano manah*, common needs, common acquirements, common food, etc..." AV (III.30.5) preaches: "accomplish together moving on, with joint labour." Like Marxism and Socialism, Rigveda also calls for collective progress for all that too with joint labour. In fact RV (V.60.5) reads, "No one is superior (*ajyestasa*) or inferior (*akanishtasa*). All are brothers (*ete bhrataraha*). All should strive for the interests of all and should progress collectively. (*sowbhagaya sam va vridhuhu*)":

अज्योष्ठासो अकनिष्ठास एते सं भ्रातरो वावश्धुः सौभगाय।
युवा पिता स्वपा रूद्र एषां सुदुघा पशश्निः सुदिना मरूद्भयः ॥5॥
RV (V.60.5)

Thus, equality by birth and gender equality are the two cardinal Vedic norms, now enshrined in the Constitution of India. Let us return confidently, equipped with modern Science & Technology, to our roots of Vedic brotherhood discarding 'excess baggage' of birth based casteism. Dr. A.P.J. Abdul Kalam, the Hon'ble President of India, in his book 'India 2000' has rightly observed: "Somewhere down the line in our long history, we appear to have lost faith in ourselves." Let us regain faith in ourselves.

Three

GITA AND CASTEISM

3.1 Shlokas Prohibiting Birth Based Castes

Supporters of caste by birth often selectively quote two shlokas viz., (IV.13) and (XVIII.41) of Shrimad Bhagwadgita. Let us, as usual, examine in detail. In shloka (IV.13) Lord Krishna says: "*Chaturvarnyma mayaa sristam gunkarma vibhagsah*" i.e., four orders of society created by Me according to their Guna (aptitude, qualities, behaviour, temperament) and Karma (performance, actions done, skills acquired, professional competence, efforts put into by the individual). One should carefully note that Lord Krishna does not say guna and karma of the previous life. In shloka (XVIII.41), Lord Krishna says "*Brahamana Kshatriya visham shudranam cha paramtapa, karmani pravibhaktani svabhavaprabhavaigunaih.*" It means people have been grouped into four classes according to their present life karma (skills, education, and competence) and *svabhava* (aptitude, behaviour, person's nature, temperament). "The division of labour into four categories– Brahaman, Kshatriya, Vaishya and Shudra–is also based on the Gunas inherent in peoples' nature". Had this division been based on birth, Lord Krishna would have naturally used the phrase "*Janmani pravibhaktani*" in the same very shloka

(XVIII.41) which He has not done. Svabhava/behavior naturally relates to, and can relate only to the present life. One may note that since about a decade or so for admissions into Business schools holding aptitude tests has started.

In shloka (XVIII.42), Lord Krishna prescribes qualifications or the bar (*karma*) which one must fulfil or, acquire by putting in efforts in order to qualify as a Brahaman i.e., among other qualifications (*karma*); he must have studied the Vedas and must teach (propagate) Vedas to others. Thus, if a person has neither studied the Vedas, nor propagates nor teaches Vedas to others, he does not qualify to be called a Brahaman as per definition laid down by Lord Krishna. Categorisation as a Brahaman is an acquirement through physical efforts of study like the present day university degrees of MA, MBBS, and MBA etc. A teacher's son cannot be called a teacher by birth, a General's son is not a General by birth, and the son of an engineer is not an engineer by birth. My son cannot be called an IFS officer by birth unless and until he has passed the Union Public Service Commission (UPSC) exam like me. Is it not? My reply to question No. 13 in Appendix III may also be seen in the context of an excellently worded query raised about "*chaturvarnam mayaa sristam....*"

ब्राह्मणक्षत्रियविशां शूद्राणां च परंतप।
कर्माणि प्रविभक्तानि स्वभावप्रभवैर गुणैः ॥41॥ Gita (XVIII.41)
brahamana Kshatriya visam shudranam ca paramtapa
karmani pravibhaktani svabhava prabhavair gunaih

The Vedas compare, as explained earlier, human society with a living person who's all the four limbs are joined together, each representing the four broad types of works and workers in the society, and not castes fixed by birth as wrongly being practiced in India. The implication is that as in a living person all the four limbs work together, so also in a dynamic society all the four main professions should work together otherwise the society shall die. The Brahamana represents His mouth, Kshatriya the arms, Vaisya the stomach, and Shudra His feet (RV 10.90.12, YV 31.11, AV 19.06.06). If four limbs of a person are separated, he dies. Similarly, the Vedas preach, if four professional groups are at war with each other, that society will also die. (See para 2.4) The Vedas also state that its words are for all mankind (missionary role) and not limited to any single group. Its words are for all people, including the Shudras, and the foreigners (YV 26.02). The caste system in India is an artificial barrier, a social disgrace, and a blot on the face of Hinduism, according to Swami Vivekananada.

शमो दमस् तपः शौचं क्षान्तिर् आर्जवम् एव च।
च्यानं वियानम् आस्तिक्यं ब्रह्मकर्म स्वभावजम्॥42॥
Gita (XVIII.42)
samo damas tapah sauucam ksantir arjavam eva ca
jnanam vijnanam astikyam brahmakarma svabhavajam

"Those who have serenity, self control, austerity, purity, patience, honesty, knowledge, Self–realisation, and belief in God are labeled as Brahamanas, the intellectuals." (18.42)

A Brahamana is the one who has the above mentioned qualities (MB.3.180.21). Anybody may be called a Brahamana if he or she possesses/acquires the gift of education (and not just by being born in a family of Brahamana) vide RV (10.125.05) and AV (4.30.03). Brahaman was an acquirement in Vedic phraseology (rather than birth based) as in modern era we acquire degrees like MA/MSc/MBBS, etc. by passing university examinations by our efforts/studies (karma). Manu has also said in his Manusmriti that all are Shudra by birth, and become a non–shudra by their deeds (efforts/karma/performance) only.

Whenever a society gives predominance to caste, creed,

race, colour, gender or place of birth over the abilities of an individual; the seeds of downfall and inefficiency of that society are planted and begin to grow. The devil of discrimination knows no national boundaries. It is a human temptation, and a manifestation of superiority complex. The wise should try to overcome all types and shades of bias. All are the children of God, equal in His eyes, and should be treated as such. Wise people say that a person, for the progress of the society, must be judged by his or her ability, and not by any other standard.

शौर्यं तेजो धश्तिर् दाक्ष्यं युद्धे चाप्य् अपलयनम्।
दानम् ईश्वरभावश्च क्षात्रं कर्म स्वभावजम्॥43॥
Gita (XVIII.43)
sauryam tejo dhrtir daksyam yuddhe ca py apalayanm
danam isvarabhavas ca ksatram karma svabhavajam

"Those having the qualities of heroism, vigor, firmness, dexterity, not fleeing from battle, charity, and administrative skills are called Kshatriyas, the protectors." (18.43)

Thus, the qualification, the bar for being called a Kshatriya is uncompromising and unrelenting opposition to the evil doers in society. One who does this can be called a Kshatriya RV (10.174.02), AV (1.29.02). RV (X.174.2) reads: "Having overcome our rivals, and those who are our enemies, do you attack him who assails us, and him who behaves insolently towards us." The duty or Dharma of a Kshatriya is to fight all Adharma and injustice in society. So, a coward cannot be called a Kshatriya. One who has surrendered irreversibly to injustice is not a Kshatriya. In other words, who have fighting qualities till victorious are Kshatriya; it is thus not hereditary.

कृषिगौरक्ष्यवाणिज्यं वैश्यकर्म स्वभावजम्।
परिचर्यात्मक कर्म शूद्रस्यापि स्वभावजम्॥44॥ Gita (XVIII.44)
krsi gauraksya vanijyam vaisyakarma svabhavajam

paricaryatmakam karma shudrasya pi svabhavajam

"Those who are good in cultivation, cattle rearing, business, trade, and industry are known as Vaisyas. Those who do service and labor type work are classed as Shudra (18.44)." So, in Gita too, there is perfect social mobility from one profession to another depending upon what skill one has acquired by his efforts.

3.2 Common Origin Of All and Dalit Emancipation In Gita Too

In shloka (X.20), Lord Krishna says "*ahamatama gudakesa sarvabhutaa sayasthitah*" i.e., "Arjuna! I am the universal self seated in the hearts of all beings." Here, the Lord neither excludes Shudras from "all beings" nor excludes Himself from being in the hearts of Shudras. In shloka (XVIII.61), the Lord says "*eshwarah sarvabh–utaanaam hraddeseaarjuna tisthati*" i.e.,"Arjuna! God abides in the heart of all living beings" Again, Shudras are not excluded. In shloka (XIV.4), Lord Krishna says "of all embodied beings Arjuna, prakrti or nature is the conceiving Mother, while I am the seed giving Father." Thus, Lord Krishna says that he is as much Father of Shudras as he is Father of any other Hindu/devotee.

In shloka (XVI.18), Lord Krishna says: "Given over to egotism, brute force, arrogance, etc. they hate Me dwelling in their own bodies as well as those of others." Thus, Lord Krishna instructs that a Hindu must not hate other Hindus as he is there in bodies of all Hindus so, the Gita prohibits untouchability. In shloka (XVI.19), the Lord says, "These haters, sinful, cruel and vilest among men, I cast (them) again and again into demonical (wombs)." In shloka (XVI.20), The Lord again curses Manusmriti supporters that such Hindus never attain Me (i.e., moksha): "Failing to reach Me, Arjuna, these stupid souls are born life after life in demoniac wombs (asura yoni) and then verily sink down to a still lower plane."

श्रद्धावाननसूयश्च श्रशणुयादपि यो नरः।
सोऽप मुक्त शुभँल्लोकान्प्राप्नुयात्पुण्यकर्मणाम्॥71॥
Gita (XVIII.71)
sraddhavananasuyasca smuyadapi yo narah
so'pi muktah subhallokanprapnuyatpunyakarmanam

In above shloka (XVIII.71), Lord Krishna has opened His gates for all Hindus including shudras as well as non–Hindus when he says "The man who hears the Holy Gita with reverence, he too shall reach happy world (*shreshtha ewam shubh lok*) of the virtuous (*punyatmas*)". There are many such shlokas addressed to all persons without any exclusion, without any discrimination. So, how can the Manusmriti or Gautamsutra or anything else ban Shudras and non–Hindus from listening to Vedas and Gita? After all, the Manusmriti and Gautamsutra etc. cannot over–rule Lord Krishna. It is Gita, being the sermon directly from God that supersedes secondary writings by sages/individuals. One may also see my reply to question no. 47 in Appendix III.

In shloka (V.18), the Lord says: "The wise (who desire to achieve moksha, salvation) look with the same eye (*samadarshi*) on a Brahamana endowed with learning and culture, a cow and pariah (*chandal*) too."

विद्याविनयसम्पन्ने ब्राह्मणे गवि हस्तिनि।
शुनि चैव श्वपाके च पण्डिताः समदर्शिनः॥18॥ Gita (V.18)
vidyavinayasampanne brahamane gavi hastini
Suni caiva svapake ca panditah samadarsinah

In shloka (IX.32), Lord Krishna reiterates **emancipation of Shudra**: "Arjuna, women, Vaisyas, shudras (those belonging to the labouring and artisan classes), as well as those of vile birth (such as pariah), whoever they may be, taking refuge in

Me they too attain the supreme goal (*paramgati*)."

मां हि पार्थ व्यपाश्रित्य येपिस्युः पापयोनयः।
स्त्रियो वैश्यास्तथा शूद्रास्तपि यान्ति परां गतिम्॥32॥
Gita (IX.32)
mam hi partha vyapasritya ye'pi syuh papayonayah
striyo vaisyastatha shudraste'pi yanti param gatim

Therefore, those who look down upon Shudra are neither wise nor can they ever achieve *Moksha* (salvation from life–cycle, peace of mind) as they carry the curse of Gita under (XVI.19–20). There are many shlokas which call for being '*samdarsi*' i.e., social equality, social harmony, and, being equal & fair to all such as (VI.9, 29, 30, 31, 32) (IX.29) (X.20), etc. (XII.13) reads: "He who is free from malice towards all beings, friendly and compassionate is dear to Me." (XII.16) reads: "He who is not a source of annoyance to his fellow creatures, and who in his turn does not feel vexed with fellow creatures is dear to Me." Thus, Gita like the Vedas, demolishes "class cleavages" and aims at creating a classless and friction–free society.

No wonder, HH Sri Ravi Shankarji in his thought provoking article "Lord Krishna, the Father of Communism" (Hindustan Times, June 13, 2004) has beautifully explained that Lord Krishna was a better communist than Karl Marx. Many times in the Gita, Lord Krishna says, "One who sees me in everybody, one who sees oneself in everybody, is the one who sees the truth." This is also the basic principle of Communism–See everyone as yourself.

It may be recalled that the Vedas were being translated into German and English in Germany and in UK at the time Karl Heinrich Marx (1818–1883) was formulating his theories. He was born in a comfortable middle class home in Tier on the river Moselle in Germany on May 5, 1818. The core of Marx's economic analysis found early expression in the *Okonomisch–philosophische Manuskripte aus dem Jahre 1844* (Economic and Political Manuscripts of 1844). In his review of a Bruno Baier book 'On the Jewish Question (1844)', Marx described the lingering influence of religion over politics. In 1844, Marx wrote in his essay 'Towards the Critic of the Hegelian philosophy of the Right' that religion was the opium of the people. Marx and his colleague Friedrich Engels issued the *Manifest der kommunistischen Partei* (Communist Manifesto) (1848). Marx settled down in London in 1849. Marx published his 'Das Kapital' first in 1867 and his *Theorien Uber den Mehrwert* (Theory of Surplus Value) in 1862.

The Gita has also enumerated the equality principles of communism (equality of all human beings) but with a human face and without violence & without class prejudices. Sermons of Gita are excellent in stress management, keeping one's blood pressure (BP) low by mentally preparing him to receive even bad news without getting too shocked or too perturbed. One who does his duty without expecting fruits of his actions is a *sankhyayogi* and a *karmayogi* (VI.1) as such a person shall never suffer depression or anxiety even if he does not get his expectations fulfilled. The Gita preaches to put in one's best and repeated efforts in trying to achieve his goals as only putting efforts is well within the reach of an individual. Fruit of one's own actions/efforts is judged and given by another person or by God. It is always another person who judges whether one is eligible to be rewarded with fruits or not or, not yet eligible to be rewarded. In the very famous shloka (II.47), *karman–yevadhikaraste ma phalesu kadacana, ma karmaphalah–eturbhurma te sango's tvakarmani*, Lord Krishna says, "Your right is to work only, but never to the fruit thereof. Be not instrumental in making your actions bear fruit, nor let your attachment be to inaction". Gita shloka (XVI.2) preaches absence of anger even on provocation which, if practiced properly, will keep blood pressure (BP) from shooting up.

3.3 Three Gunas Too: Not Hereditary

In shlokas (XIV.6), Lord Krishna says that intellectuals are endowed more with *sattva guna*; pro–active people full of actions with ambitions to achieve results are endowed more with *rajat guna* vide (XIV.7) and (XVIII.27); and, people who are lazy, sloth, slow and sleepy are endowed more with *tamoguna* vide (XIV.8) and (XVIII.28). These are qualities by birth which one can improve upon by efforts or lose by non–action. One may notice that one child is quite good in studies (i.e., he has more *sattvik guna*) whereas another child of the same parentage is lazy and not so good in studies (i.e., he has more *tamoguna)*. But by efforts of parents and tutors, he also becomes good in studies (i.e., he raises *sattvik guna* by efforts). The point is that these gunas are not hereditary, otherwise, all children of the same parentage should be equally meritorious or equally sloth which is generally not the case. One brother may be short tempered or hot headed, whereas another brother may be mild and of cool temper. Every person is born with a mix of all the three gunas, some guna being dominant at one point of time and another at another time; one can change the mix of his gunas by his efforts. In (XVIII.40), Lord Krishna says: "There is no being, either on the earth or in the heaven or among the Devas, who is free from these three Gunas of Prakriti, the material nature."

In (XIV.10–13), Lord Krishna says that *sattva guna* predominates *rajas* and *tamas* when one is in intellectual mould; *rajas* predominates the other two gunas when one is in pro–active mould with a desire to achieve material gains; and *tamas* predominates the other two gunas when disinclinations to perform one's obligatory duties, darkness over mind, slumber, *alasya* prevail. So, all the three gunas are present in every person, one dominating the other two at different points of time which can be regulated by *tapas* i.e., by conscious efforts. A lazy person can always become active by action (karma/ efforts) and a pro–active person degenerates into a lazy person by continued non–action or inaction (*alasya*).

3.4 Valmiki Ramayan And Two Examples Set By Lord Rama

Valmiki Ramayan also says that whosoever, including a Shudra, reads it, will achieve greatness and get rid of all sins.

पठन् द्विजो वागशृषभत्वमीयात् स्यात् क्षत्रियो भूमिपतित्वमीयात्।
वणिग्जनः पुण्यफलत्वमीयाज्जनश्च शूद्रोऽपि महत्त्वमीयात्॥
(Valmiki Ramayana: 1.1.98–100)

Thus the Vedas, Ramayana and Gita themselves confer authority on the shudras to possess and read these. In Ramayan, Lord Rama has Himself set the following two examples for all *Rambhakta* Hindus which we witness every year in Ramlilas but never follow in our practical lives. That is why we were defeated time and again by foreigners for not following Lord Rama *manasa, vacha and karmana* (in words and deeds). (For a comparison, see how steadfastly Muslims adhere to and follow examples set by their Prophet, PBUH, in Sunnah).

Ravana was a grandson of rishi Pulatsya. He was an expert in the Vedas too. So, he was a Brahaman by birth under Manusmriti definition as well as a Brahaman (educated) by qualification (*veda–gyata*) but he and most of his family members were killed by Lord Rama for their wrong doing (kidnapping the wife of another). So, the first lesson of Ramayana is that everyone (irrespective of his Manuwadi caste) is equal before law. Lord Rama visited Shabri, called her a mother (*mata*); ate food from her hands and washed the feet of Nisadraj. Lord Rama lived for years among *vanvasi* (tribals). So, the second lesson of Ramayana is that a true *Rambhakta* should never discriminate against SC/ST/Dalit Hindus, should never hesitate to visit and dine with them. See, Mahatma Gandhi always followed *manasa, vacha and karmana* both these two lessons of Ramayana and he became a *Yug Purusha*. Let us follow these two examples set by Lord Rama *manasa, vacha and karmana.*

3.5 Manusmriti: Skill Based Social Stratification, Not Birth Based

Perception among the Hindu masses is that Manusmriti sanctifies birth based casteism. So, it may come as a complete surprise to many people that there are many shlokas in the Manusmriti which lay down that it is the qualification (karma of the present life, acquired knowledge & skills in the present life), which is the basis of categorization into four classes. However, such shlokas have largely been ignored by authors:

> **शूद्रो ब्राहम्णनामेति ब्राहम्णश्चेति शूद्रनाम्।**
> **क्षत्रियाज्जातमेवन्तु विद्याद्वेश्यात्त थैव च॥**
> **Manusmriti (X.65)**

i.e., if a person born of a Shudra possesses the virtues, habits and tendencies of the Brahaman, Kshatriya or Vaisya, he should be classed with them according to his merits. In the like manner, if a person born of a Brahaman, Kshatriya or a Vaisya, possesses the merits, habits and nature like those of a Shudra, he should be regarded as such. In short, men and women should be classed with those varnas whose qualifications they possess. Therefore, this classification is not by birth but only by qualifications. Manusmriti, thus, clearly provides for upward social mobility based on education and qualifications. George Buhler's translation of this shloka (X.65) is: "(Thus) a Shudra attains the rank of a Brahamana, and (in a similar manner) a Brahamana sinks to the level of a Shudra; but know that it is the same with the offspring of a Kshatriya or of a Vaisya."

In shlokas (II.157 &158) Manusmriti has again declared that a brahamana by birth is truly speaking not a brahamana if he did not know the Vedas i.e., one is not a brahamana by birth. George Buhler translates (II.157) "As an elephant made of wood, as an antelope made of leather, such is an unlearned Brahamana; those three have nothing but names (of their kind, their class)". Translation by another writer of this shloka is: "Just as a wooden toy elephant cannot be a real elephant and a stuffed deer cannot be a real deer, so, without studying scriptures and the Vedas and the development of intellect, a brahamana by birth cannot be considered a real brahamana." Translation of (II.158) is "As a eunuch is unproductive with women, as a cow with a cow is unprolific,and as a gift made to an ignorant (unworthy) man yields no reward,even so is a Brahamana useless,who (does) not (know) the rikas." So, even the Manusmriti contemplates that categorisation of people into four classes is based on skills & qualifications acquired in this life, not birth based. Manusmriti has laid down the bar which one must pass to be included into a particular class.

In (IV.190), Manusmriti has laid down that: "A Brahamana who neither performs austerities nor studies the Veda, yet delights in accepting gifts, sinks with the (donor into hell), just as (he who attempts to cross over in) a boat made of stone (is submerged) in the water." In (IV.192), Manusmriti again lays down that:" (A man) who knows the law should not offer even water to a Brahamana who acts like a cat, nor to a Brahamana who acts like a heron (a bird, *bagula*), nor to one who is unacquainted with the Veda."

Thus, the Manusmriti clearly states that a person should be given alms only if he has studied the Vedas. That is, the eligibility to receive alms (*daan or dakshina*) is not by birth but only if qualification to receive such alms has been earned by the receiver in his present life. Similarly in the Holy Gita too, Lord Krishna has commanded in shloka (XVII.22) that alms given to an undeserving person (i.e., to a *kupatra*) is *tamasi* i.e., harmful to alms–giver .That *daan* is not to be given to those who do not deserve to receive it. In Gita (XVII.20), Lord Krishna preaches that *daan* (alms, gift) should be bestowed only upon those who deserve it and, at appropriate place and at an appropriate time. That is, *daan* is not to be given on hereditary basis, but only on eligibility basis.How many of us observe this command of Lord Krishna before giving *alms/daan*? Not many.

3.6 Some Good Questions

Valerian Rodrigues, a learned Professor of Political Science at the Manglore University, in his book 'The Essential Writings of BR Ambedkar', has raised some good questions at page 228:

"The Untouchables can very well ask the protagonists of Hinduism the very questions which Lord Balfour asked the Positivists. Nay the Untouchables can ask many more. They can ask: Does Hinduism recognize their worth as human beings? Does it stand for their equality? Does it extend to them the benefit of liberty? Does it at least help to forge the bond of fraternity between them and the Hindus? Does it teach the Hindus that the Untouchables are their kindred? Does it say to the Hindus it is a sin to treat the Untouchables as being neither man nor beast? Does it tell the Hindus to be righteous to the Untouchables? Does it preach to the Hindus to be just and humane to them? Does it inculcate upon the Hindus the virtue of being friendly to them? Does it tell the Hindus to love them, to respect them and to do them no wrong? In fine, does Hinduism universalize the value of life without distinction? No Hindu can dare give an affirmative answer to any of these questions?"

Well, the above citations from the Vedas, Gita and Valmiki Ramayana give resounding answers in the affirmative to all the above provocative questions. The supreme scriptures of Hinduism, the canonical scriptures of Hinduism do not sanction any discrimination; these Scriptures are all inclusive (covering non–Hindus as well as strangers too).

3.7 Hinduism : A Missionary Religion

Readers may note here that Lord Krishna clearly commands that Hinduism is a missionary religion as shloka (XVIII.42) casts a duty on Brahamans (educated class) to teach & propagate the Vedas to others. Many shlokas in the Gita are addressed to all persons (*sarvabhutanam*). The Vedic richas are addressed to all, to strangers too. Baba Saheb Dr. Bhimrao Ramji Ambedkar is the first author who struck me asserting that Hinduism is a missionary religion (Dr. Ambedkar: Life and Mission, Dhananjay Keer, page 270). In shlokas (XVIII.68) and (XVIII.69) Lord Krishna has again cast missionary duties on his devotees to preach His gospel **all over the globe**. RV (X.191), AV (III.30) and Yaj (XXVI.02) also impose missionary duties on Hindu priests to bring all including strangers under harmony i.e., under one religious flag. Gita shloka (XVIII.71) is addressed to all persons. RV (X.13.1) addresses the entire humanity (*srunvantu viswe amrutsya putrah*). RV (I.38.14) and RV (ix. 63.5) are express commands to spread the Vedic religion.

Following is the sanskrit text of missionary shlokas of Gita:

य इमं परमं गुह्यं मद्भक्तेष्वभिधास्यति।
भक्तिं मयि परां कृत्वा मामेवैष्यत्यसंशयः ॥68॥(Gita: XVIII.68)
ya imam paramam guhyam madbhaktesvabhidhasyati

bhaktim mayi param krtva mamevaisyatyasamsayah

(He who, offering the highest love to Me, preaches the most profound gospel of the Gita among My devotees, shall come to Me alone; there is no doubt about it.)

न च तस्मान्मनुष्येषु कश्चिन्मे प्रियकृत्तमः ।
भविता न च मे तस्मादन्य प्रियतरो भुवि ॥69॥ (XVIII.69)
na ca tasmanmanusyesu kascinme priyakrttamah
bhavita na ca me tasmadanyah priyataro bhuvi

(Among men there is none who does Me a more loving service than he; nor shall anyone be dearer to Me on the entire globe than he.)

Reply to question no. 14 in Appendix III may also be seen.

3.8 New Roles For The Hindu Priests

Under the Islamic law, anyone who attempts to convert a Muslim into a Kafir has to be killed. Feroz Shah Tughlak (1351–88) ordered to burn alive those Brahamans who tried to convert Muslims to Hinduism. In view of this Tughlaki punishment under Islamic rule, it appears that Hindu priests permanently gave up missionary zeal. For survival under Islamic rule, it became necessary for Hindu priests to keep aloof from sufferings & ill treatments inflicted upon Hindu masses by medieval Islamic rulers. Reverse conversion was restarted by the Arya Samaj but only during the British rule as '*suddhi*.' But the problem is that Hindu priestly class, even after the Independence in 1947, is still unconsciously following the same tradition of keeping aloof from welfare of Hindu masses, which their forefathers were forced to adopt during medieval Islamic rules. There are many people who even now keep advising Hindu priests to stick to the same old tradition of silence & detachment from worldly affairs as followed by their forefathers under medieval duress. They want the present day Hindu priests to behave as if they are still under subjugation. They don't want Hindu priests to express themselves on issues facing Hindu Samaj. Vashistha advised Dasharath & Bhagwan Ram; Parasuram, Dronacharya etc. played important roles in society and politics. Islamic mullahs and Christian priests touch upon current affairs in their weekly religious discourses. So why should only Hindu priests keep away from this practice especially after Independence. Therefore, in my humble view, it is high time that Hindu priestly class should break out from the medieval mindset and start making vigorous efforts to eradicate the evil of casteism in the Hindu Samaj, speak in favour of the poor and downtrodden Hindus, and spread the Vedic message of equality by birth and gender equality.

Some people say that unlike the Catholic faith, Hinduism does not have a Pope; but, as per commandment of RV (X.191) we can always create one to fight the curse of excess baggage of casteism and to unify & bring all Hindus under one religious banner especially when, unlike our forefathers, we are no more under subjugation.

In June 2004, the Archbishop of Canterbury, UK, suggested that the Church and other non–governmental organizations should be given a voice in the United Nations Security Council (UNSC), i.e., he has suggested a role for Church in the international politics. In November 1995, Christian priests had organized demonstrations in India demanding reservations for what they call 'Christian Dalits' in government jobs to improve socio–economic conditions of their followers. Similarly, Hindu priests should work tirelessly for socio–economic upliftment of Hindus who these days under British nomenclature are called 'the scheduled castes/scheduled tribes'.

3.9 Dalit Contributions To Vedic And other–Scriptures

Many SC/ST/Dalit Hindus are not even aware of rich

contributions made by their ancestors to the supreme Hindu scriptures. To cite just a few:

(i) Rishi Kavas Ilusu was revealed suktas (X.30) (X.31) (X.32) and (X.33) of Rigveda and shloka 453 of Samaveda. Rishi Ilusu Aksova Mojvan was revealed sukta (X.34) of Rigveda. Both, under current Manusmriti definition, were Shudra.

(ii) In Tandya Brahaman (14.66) rishi Vatsa has been called a Shudra–putra. Revelations to rishi Vatsa are there in Rigveda, (VIII.6), (VIII.11), Samaveda (8, 20,137,143, etc.) and Yaj (IV.16–36), (VII.40), (XXVI.15).

(iii) Rishi Kaksivat was the son of rishi Dirghatamas by a shudra maid servant (Brihaddevata IV.24.25). Rishi Kaksivat was revealed many richas in RV (I.119 to 125).

(iv) Maharishi Vedvyas is believed to have redacted all Vedic richas into four Vedas in the format currently available. He is also believed to have composed the Mahabharata, Shrimad Bhagwadgita and all the Puranas. He was born to Satyawati, daughter of a fisherman by rishi Parasar. Further, Satyawati and rishi Parasar were not formally married so, Vedvyas was an illegitimate son. He was of dark complexion (Krishna Dwaipayan). Thus, as per Manusmriti definition, he was a dalit Hindu, a *Varna–sankar* by birth. But because of his Karma as a writer, he rose to be called a Maharishi. Satyawati was later married to Maharaja Shantanu. As we know, Kauravas and Pandavas were descendants of this very Vedvyasa. Readers may recall from BR Chopra's Mahabharata, that following instructions of his mother Satyawati, rishi Vedvyas as per the then prevailing social norm of *niyoga*, fathered Dhritarastra and Pandu to queens of Vichitravirya. But, Kauravas and Pandavas are accepted as Kshatriyas not on basis of birth but on the basis of their karma/occupations (as rulers/kings/warriors).

(v) Maharishi Mahidasa Aitereya, a Maharastrian Shudra (perhaps a Mahar), composed Aitereya Brahaman and chapters I, II & III of Aitereya Aryanaka. His mother was a maid named Itara.

(vi) Maharishi Valmiki who composed the original Valmiki Ramayan in Sanskrit was not a Brahaman by birth as per the Manusmriti definition. He was a contemporary of Lord Rama as Lav & Kush were born at his ashram.

3.10 Conclusion

Thus, no one has the right to deny free access to SC/ST/ Dalit Hindus to what their ancestors have richly contributed, nor, should they give up or run–away from their ancestral heritage on teasing by others. One does not give up his heritage and ancestral properties on false presentations or forged documents produced by others. Let us stand united armed with the Vedas in one hand and the Constitution of India in the other to defeat the twin demons of casteism and gender inequality. To run away is cowardice, not a solution.

Four

DALIT EMANCIPATION AND INTER–RELIGION CONVERSIONS

'Love thy neighbour' and 'Vasudhaiva Kutumbukam' are the best options

Horrible and brutal lynching of five dalit Hindus in Duliana, Jhajhar (Haryana), India, in Oct.2002, and simmering tensions in Chakwara near Jaipur (Rajasthan) on use of a village pond attracted a number of articles either lamenting or accusing someone. In the wake of these, articles justifying inter–religion conversions of Dalit Hindus also appeared and group conversions into Buddhism, Christianity, and Islam were organised at Jhajhar and at Selaiyur (Chennai, 6th Dec., 2002). But on 28th Nov. 2002, SC/ST Commission of India reported that Duliana lynching was not based on caste considerations demolishing the main plank of the conversion lobby.

Religion and conversion should be private matters like the right to choose partners where State has no role to play but only so far as these private rights are exercised privately at private places. Group conversions organised with fanfare at public places causing heartburn to public at large are not sanctioned by the Constitution of India and are subject to the Indian Penal Code (IPC) provisions on apprehensions of breach of peace and public order.

Issues such as whether conversions from one religion to another, or, from one sect to another sect of the same religion are legal or illegal, or, whether such conversions should be banned or not, have not been taken up in this book. The central theme of this book is to return to the original Vedic norms by raising the social outlook of the Hindu Samaj to such a high level that casteism and such issues become unholy, irrelevant, and futile.

4.1 Need For Second Generation Social Reforms In Hinduism

First generation social reforms in Hinduism (abolitions of untouchability and caste–based disabilities) were successfully led by Swami Dayanand, Swami Vivekanand, Mahatma Gandhi, Jawaharlal Nehru, Dr. B.R. Ambedkar, Saint Phule, Sri Narayana Guru (SNDP: Sree Narayana Dharma Paripalana Sangh), Basaveshwar, Varkari, Loknayak Jai Prakash Narayan, Ram Manohar Lohia etc. and have been codified in the Constitution of India and various Acts.

Sant Nirankari Mission for Universal Brotherhood is also making welcome contributions in dissolving caste barriers and inter–religion barriers.The philosophical teaching of the Sant Nirankari Mission is based upon the Vedic view that all humans are created from the same source, therefore, rationally speaking, all are equal by birth and no difference should exist between fellow human beings (paras 2.6 and 3.2). This Mission bases its belief upon the Vedas (Para 5.8) that there is One God and that all the 'Creation' is manifested from Him. In this way, the whole of humanity is intricately connected and there should be equality among all people irrespective of their nationality, colour, caste, status, position in life etc. This concept is encapsulated beautifully in the second noble pledge, which all devotees of this Mission must observe. This Mission believes that such understanding can only become part and parcel of one's way of life through being blessed by a *Guru* with the knowledge of the 'Nirankara'. With the attainment of such knowledge, one begins to realise his true self and thereupon is able to form and crystallize the view of *Vasudhaiva Kutumbakam*. It can be seen being practiced by followers of the Mission, which of course, breaks down man made barriers and distinctions among human beings.

The Gayatri Pariwar led by HH Dr Pandya is also making rich contributions to promoting harmony.

Second generation social reforms in Hinduism from within for wider social acceptability of Vedic norms of equality by birth and gender equality is the real solution to contemporary problems of the Hindu Samaj. The root cause of conversions, as rightly pointed out by Thiru N. Varadrajan, State Secretary of Communist Party of India (Marxist) (Tamil Nadu) are social ostracism and humiliations of dalits which this Chapter attempts to tackle. NDTV.com in its report captioned "Search for Dignity: TN dalits embrace Islam" dated June3, 2004 has quoted S. Sultan, a new Hindu convert to Islam, saying: "People belonging to upper castes abuse and humiliate us. Even the boys abuse us, When we embrace Islam, they treat us with respect". Why should the Hindu Samaj not treat them with respect when they are within the Hindu fold, and treat them with respect after they embrace Islam is a matter worth introspection and deep analysis. Mohit Sen wrote in the Indian Express (5th August, 1995) that what has aggravated the caste problem is the almost complete lack of any campaign against caste system—that decisive impediment to modernisation of Hindustan—to paraphrase the remarks of Karl Marx written in 1835. Let us deploy Vedic richas to initiate the compaign against casteism.

4.2 Ambedkar On Castes

In Ambedkar's view, the caste system is a social division of people of the same race. [Dr. Ambedkar : Life and Mission by

Dhananjay Keer, page 269]. On this point, another author also quotes Ambedkar: "To hold that distinctions of caste are really distinctions of race and to treat different castes as though they were so many different races is a gross perversion of facts. Caste system does not demarcate racial division. Caste system is a social division of the same people". (Dalits and Democratic Revolution, Gail Omvedt, page 245). Gail Omvedt further advises that this statement in 'The Annihilation of Caste' is as clear as could be made and should stand against all attempts to use Ambedkar's name as a justification for a racial theory of caste differences. This assertion of Ambedkar that all 'castes' of Hindus belong to the one and the same race is in total conformity with the Vedas, especially RV (X.191), AV (III.30) and Yaj (26.02). (See Para 2.6)

Ambedkar was of the view that: "Caste is the bane of Hindus. Caste is the cause of downfall of the Hindus. Owing to caste, the Hindus' life has been a life of continuous defeats. Caste has made Hindus the sick men of India. Caste has ruined the Hindu race and has destroyed, demoralised and devitalised Hindu society." What is more, Dr. Ambedkar said, caste has made *Shuddhi*—conversion back into Hinduism— impractical because one does not know which caste the convert to Hinduism will join. Caste has thus killed, he adds, the missionary spirit of Hindu religion [page 270, Keer].

"Ambedkar rightly diagnosed that caste is a notion, a state of mind. Its destruction means a notional change in mental set up. Hindus observe caste not because they are inhuman and wrong headed. They (Hindus) observe caste chiefly because they believe deeply that it is so ordained in their religion" (page 291, Keer). This was a totally correct analysis by Dr Ambedkar but in my humble opinion, he wrongly concluded that destruction of authority of the Vedas, destruction of sacredness and divinity of Vedas would lead to annihilation of castes; and, failing to thus destroy spiritual authority of Veda, he converted to Buddhism in 1956. Perhaps Ambedkar did not fully recognize that the Vedas themselves did not sanction birth based castes. If he had there was no justification to give a call to destroy the sanctity of the Vedas. Gandhiji also committed the blunder of not wholly rejecting birth–based chaturvarna, perhaps, wrongly believing it to be a part of Hinduism. Perhaps, Gandhiji also wrongly believed that birth based castes were sanctioned by the Vedas. As explained in previous chapters, chaturvarna is not birth–based, it is aptitude and qualifications (acquired in this life) based.

But, Gandhiji rightly rejected untouchability and social segregations among Hindus. As conclusively proved in paras 2.4 to 2.6, the Vedas do not sanction birth based casteism. In his famous 22 vows, Dr. Ambedkar mercifully did not re–include destruction of sacredness of Vedas. If Hindus practised casteism, as Dr. Ambedkar had rightly assessed, in the belief that it is part of their religion, how could Hindus have agreed to the destruction of the Vedas–the fountainhead of their religion?

Some authors opine that unlike other dalit leaders, Ambedkar did not try to reform Hinduism from within but tried to liberate himself and others like him from it. It does not appear to be a fair comment as Ambedkar did try to use his position as the Chairman of the Constitution Drafting Committee to reform Hinduism through his Hindu Code Bill and left the Nehru Cabinet in 1951 when the Hindu Code Bill, as drafted by him, was not accepted. Ambedkar was in favour of a uniform civil code and greater rights to women in his Hindu Code Bill. In 1956, Ambedkar chose Buddhism over Islam and Christianity when he converted to it.

I think the best way to annihilate casteism lock, stock and barrel is, firstly, not to repeat the blunder of placing the

Manusmriti and other subsidiary literature at par with the Holy Vedas, not to place at par canonical scriptures with non–canonical compositions, and secondly, to convince Hindus that casteism, as conclusively proved in the preceding pages, is truly not ordained by the Vedas. Birth based casteism is in fact contrary to Vedas, offensive to real Hinduism. Casteism is rust and dust collected around true Hinduism over centuries. I believe that a much more pragmatic way to annihilate casteism is not engineering of conversions, not mutual acrimony, not cursing the present day 'Brahamans' all the time for mistakes committed by their forefathers; not fraternal caste wars, not violence; but full throated articulation of correct interpretations of 38 richas of the Vedas, the thirteen shlokas of Shrimad Bhagwadgita and the two examples set by Lord Rama. If this is done, it would convince upper caste Hindus that by practising casteism, they are actually committing sins (*paap*) of violating the Vedas, Gita and Ramayana. Such a course of action will loosen the religious grip of casteism on the mindset of 'sawarnas'. No Hindu knowingly prefers to earn the wrath (*shraap*) of Vedas or, of Lord Rama, or that of Lord Krishna by going against their commandments.

4.3 Manusmriti: The Root Cause Of Hindu Defeats

The Rigveda mentions four classes (but not by birth), four professions requiring them to be in as perfect harmony with each other as the four limbs viz., mouth/head, hand, stomach/thighs and feet are in perfect harmony in any healthy person; and with total social mobility. Our head is as dear to us as our legs or feet. No one wants his legs to be amputated for the reason that legs often become dirty with dust. The Manusmriti is a Christian era book composed around 200AD. Some shlokas in it mischievously converted these four professions/classes into four birth based castes and introduced about forty mixed castes (*jaties*) though all related by blood. The

Manusmriti did provide some social mobility from one caste to another but generally through marriages. (It has been pointed out time and again in this book that there are self–contradictory shlokas in the Manusmriti). Subsequent literature composed during the Christian era made these much more rigid and hateful. To keep Hindus divided under British Rule, employees of British Raj invented 2378 main castes among Hindus. In the 1891 census, about 1156 sub–castes of *chamars* alone were recorded. God knows how many castes and sub–castes have so far been invented basically to 'divide and rule over' Hindus.

Intercaste marriages were allowed as per Shatapath Brahaman (4.1.5.9), Parashar Grihya (1.4.8–11) and Baudhyana Dharma (1.8.16.2–5) Sutras but later such marriages were discouraged on the basis of the Manusmriti notions of high & low castes according to the Manusmriti.

Manusmriti's caste system also weakened the Hindus militarily. As per the Manusmriti, and subsequent writers (*smritikars*), shudras (working class, service class) were kept out of villages and, thus, excluded from military, politics and the Government. Vaishyas were supposed to confine themselves to business, agriculture and cattle breeding. As such the Vaishyas were also excluded from military, politics and the Government. The Brahamans took the position that arms and military was not their primary concern. So, under the Manusmriti system, majority of population (say 75%) was mentally conditioned to be militarily impotent & politically neutral towards government formation (*rajnya*). They were not supposed to have any stake in the Government i.e.,who became their king was not supposed to be their primary concern. Only the Kshatriya were supposed to be in military and had the duty to fight wars. If the Kshatriya were 25% (say) of population, 12.5% being female were excluded from military, rest one third of male being children and one third being too old to fight were also not available for active military service. Thus, in the Manusmriti system only about four percent of population had a moral duty to fight for the nation. So, under this system a population of 10,000 Hindus could yield a maximum of only 416 to fight whereas from a population of 10,000 of other religions (Islam and Christianity) about 1700 men or more were mentally ready/prepared and socially eligible, to fight Kafirs and pagans. No wonder, Hindus though larger in numbers, were oftenly defeated by small numbers of Afghan, Mongol, Mughal and Turk invaders, their women raped and molested, their temples destroyed. They & their temple priests were repeatedly butchered en masse being dhimmis/Kafirs, and dragged thousands of miles on foot and auctioned as slaves in Kabul etc.

For details on Hindu slaves, one may like to go through 'Muslim Slave System in Medieval India' by Prof. K. S. Lal (ISBN 81–85689–67–9). Medieval slave trade in India, writes Sandhya Jain (HT 22 July 2003), rivals early Arab and later European slave trade from Africa. Dirk Kolff (Naukar, Rajput and Sepoy: The Ethno History of a Military Labour Market in Hindustan, 1450–1850, Cambridge University Press 1990) is fairly emphatic: "There is irrefutable evidence for the enslavement and deportation of thousands and thousands of Hindu peasants by the Mughal aristocracy. Many of these were sold to countries to the west of India. The trade had flourished before 1400 when Multan was a considerable market, but it was continued after that, with Kabul as the main centre. Anyway, it is clear that in the 1660s Indian supply of and Persian demand for slaves was still considerable." Unlike the African slaves in the USA, Hindu slaves in the West Asian countries got merged without any trace because of similarities of skin colour and similarities of physical features. No wonder,

Tapan Ray Chowdhery and Irfan Habib in their book (the Cambridge Economic History of India, Vol I page 167) inform that annual population growth of India during 1600–1800 was very low at 0.14 percent. What does this low figure show? A portion of population was regularly disappearing into thin air as slaves to West Asia.

Was it a punishment under Gita Shlokas (XVI.18, 29 & 20) that caste practising Hindus were often defeated, periodically butchered en masse and auctioned over centuries as slaves for violating Vedic and Gita's norms of equality by birth? If so, should we not free ourselves from this curse by fully obeying Veda and Gita in our present day real lives? Simply worshipping Veda and Gita by wrapping these in yellow cloth won't do any more. Let us read and practise Veda and Gita.

A Pakistani historian I.H. Qureshi in his book 'The Muslim Community of the Indo–Pakistan' (page 33–34) has written that many Buddhist monks of Sindh actively aided and collaborated with invading Muslim forces of Muhammad bin Qasim. Kaka Kotak, a Buddhist Chief of area near Sehwan advised his followers and Jats not to fight against Muslims because Buddhist priests had told him the area was destined to fall in hands of Muslims and walked into Arab camps to pass on information. It was a Buddhist Chieftan who provided boats which made it possible for Qasim to cross over Indus. Nalanda University and other Buddhist institutions of present day Bihar were destroyed by Muhammed bin Bakhtiyar in 1197 AD. Dr. B.R. Ambedkar adds the sword of Islam fell heavily upon priestly class of Buddhism living in Viharas when its numbers perished or fled away from India, nobody remained in India to keep the flame of Buddhism burning. Some say that Bakhtiyar captured Bihar and Bengal with his advance team of only eighteen (horse) cavalry, showing there was no resistance from the peasantry because Manusmriti had made peasanty neutral to governmental (rajnya) affairs.

Ansar Hussain Khan in his book 'The Rediscovery of India: A New Subcontinent' has written that in Sindh, the Arabs were helped by intelligence supplied to them by Brahaman as well as Buddhist priests, and some renegade Indian chiefs. The Indian rulers had time to assess the strength of the Arab invaders and, in a disposition observed again and again in Indian history, generals and chiefs were prone to change sides if it seemed that fortune would abandon theirs (page–51). He adds that Muhammad bin Qasim was the first to impose jeziya in India in 712 AD on the inhabitants of Sehwan near modern Hyderabad (Sindh) (now in Pakistan). Bihar was an easy prey for one of Aibak's generals, Muhammed bin Bakhtiyar, who deliberately killed thousands of monks, thinking them to be Brahamans, though they were Buddhists. Though by this time Buddhism was no longer a flourishing religion, it now suffered a lethal blow from which it did not recover (page–56). Jawaharlal Nehru in his 'Discovery of India' (page 179) has opined that there was no widespread or violent extermination of Buddhism in India, implying, perhaps, not by local inhabitants of India. Nehru was of the view that Buddhism died a natural death in India.

The Manusmriti and its supporters, thus, created such a rotten social frame in which business community, peasantry and shudras having no stake in their government (rajnya) felt alienated and either remained neutral (as preached by the Manusmriti) or joined invaders against their local (Hindu) oppressors of 'higher caste. This is the secret of continuous defeats of Hindus; Manusmriti had killed the *spirit de corps*, the feeling of *camaraderie* among all sections of Hindus. The concept of patriotic feelings to the nation was, thus, replaced by loyalty of soldiers to local chiefs employing them. Late Shri

Madhu Limaye, a great Socialist leader of India, echoing the same has written in his book 'Indian National Movement' (page 60): "The state in India was never such a focus of loyalty. Perhaps, Shivaji's soldiers, in the early years of Maratha power, were an exception. India as a whole never developed a feeling of citizenship. Despotic and arbitrary rulers prospered in a cultural milieu where the people were not infused by any patriotic sentiment. India's would be conquerors were not slow to understand this weakness of the country's unintegrated society and profit by it. The Indians can be said to have forged their own chains."

Lt. General S.L. Menezes of the Indian Army in his book 'Fidelity and Honour' opines that there is little doubt that the British conquered India on the basis of the prowess of the Presidency Armies comprising Indian soldiers. E.W. Shephard, a British Military historian in his book, 'A Short History of the British Army', has also written (1957): "An Army was built up from the people of India themselves, which, in the end brought its own country under the sway of its foreign masters." In medieval times also, a number of Hindu kings/ princes not only gladly gave their daughters to Mughals in marriages but also worked in Mughal Armies to subdue other fellow Hindu rulers showing total absence of any feelings for *Hindu camaraderie*. The concept of *Hindu camaraderie* was alien to them.

The French made this important discovery that a few disciplined Indian troops, trained, drilled and led by Western officers can defeat large masses of disorganized forces of local Indian rulers. One writer called it the invention of "a new technology of organisation in the form of a *sepoy*, the Indian mercenary solider." In 1676 Francois Martin, French Governor of Pondicherry, had enrolled 300 local Indians as soldiers to supplement his small force of Europeans. In 1740, Benoit

Dumas, Governor of Pondicherry, had a force comprising 4000 to 5000 Indian soldiers. As Britain and France were then at war, they were compelled to augument their forces in India by recruiting locals into their Armies and training them in European warfare. Robert Clive wrote to William Pitt in January 1759 that a small body of thousand Europeans would secure the British against any apprehension and enable British East India Company to take the sovereignty upon them. Since the natives had no attachment to the country or its princes they could always make sure of raising any number of 'black troops' and meet the emergency.

A British officer, Captain Stringer Lawrence, copied the French practice of raising and training a native army, and created 'sepoy' companies officered by British personnel. He led them successfully against both the Indian princes as well as Britian's French rivals in India. Lawrence, not surprisingly, is called the Father of the British Indian Army.

In Sept, 1751, Robert Clive marched to Arcot with only 300 Indian and 200 European soldiers and the Nawab of Arcot ran away without giving a fight. The 940 Madrasi soldiers (mostly *Parias*, untouchables) who had arrived with Robert Clive in Bengal in December 1756, marched from Falta and recaptured Calcutta in January 1757. In the Plassey War of 23rd June 1757, Clive had 2100 Indian troops and only 950 European troops but Nawab Siraj–ud–daula's army of about 60,000 troops with fifty three guns was defeated because of the conspiracy of Mir Jaffar, the chief General of the Nawab. On the advice of Mir Jaffar, Siraj–ud–daula repeatedly asked his another General Mohanlal to stop bombardment of Clive positions and pull back which Gen Mohanlal reluctantly complied with. Mir Jaffar did not militarily intervene at all and advised the Nawab to run away which he did with about 2000 cavalry troops. The battle of Plassey was won by the

British with only 65 casualties primarily because Siraj's camp was deserted by his own Generals. Mir Jaffar reached Murshidabad on 25th June and proclaimed himself Nawab of Bengal. Siraj was killed. Mir Jaffar rewarded the East India Company by the grant of the zamindari of 24 Pargana and personal presents of £234,000 to Clive and another 50 lakh rupees in rewards to other officials of the East India Company.The first instalment of wealth paid to the Company immediately after the Plassey war was a sum of £800,000, all paid in silver coins.According to Macaulay, the fleet which conveyed this treasure to Calcutta consisted of more than hundred boats loaded with silver. By 1760, Mir Jaffar owed a debt of about Rs 25 lakhs, but he refused to cede Burdwan and Nadia in lieu thereof. On 27th September 1760 Mir Kasim, a son–in–law of Mir Jaffar, offered to cede Burdwan, Midnapur and Chittagong to the Company plus five lakh rupees per annum towards financing the Company's war against Hyder Ali and Tipu Sultan in the South. Mir Jaffar was deposed on 14th October 1760 by Governor of Fort William (Vansittart) and Col Caillaud in favour of Mir Kasim. Mir Jaffar was given a pension of Rs 1500 per month by Mir Kasim. Mir Kasim paid a bribe of Rs 5 lakh to Governor Vansittart, Rs 2 lakh to Col. Caillaud etc. for helping him to become the Nawab. Mir Jaffar was paid back in his own coins; he betrayed Siraj–ud–daula in 1757 and was himself betrayed by his own son–in–law in 1760. The point to be noted is that rather than offering resistance to occupation by foreigners, Indians were welcomig, financing and bribing foreigners/outsiders to pull down 'other' fellow Indians. No feelings of brotherhood, no feelings of Indian camaraderie.

At Buxar (1764), Indian component of the East India Company troops was even larger, 6200 out of total troops of 7200. From 1776 to 1875, the Bengal Presidency Army was largely recruited from areas between Ganga and Ghaghara in UP & Bihar comprising mostly Brahamans, Bhumihars and Rajputs which delivered the kingdoms of Awadh, Delhi and Punjab to British. At the time of the Anglo–Maratha war (1803–05), there were about 130,000 Indian and only 24,500 European soldiers in the East India Company. With the help of Dogra Hindus, Rohilla Muslims and Indian sepoys, British defeated the Sikh Army led by General Sher Singh Attariwala at Gujrat on 21st February 1849, though Attariwala had earlier defeated the British at Chillianwala on 13th January 1849. Some Sikh Generals (Teja Singh, Lal Singh and Lehna Singh Majithia etc.) did not fully support Attariwala and collaborated with the British which contributed to the defeat of Sikhs.

On the eve of the 1857 Revolt, the East India Company had 313,500 Indian and only 38,000 European officers & soldiers. So, Madhu Limaye is brutally right in pointing out that Indians forged their own chains of slavery, at the biddings of foreigners.

During the Second World War, according to Limaye, Dr. Ambedkar said: "At one time practically three fourth of the Bombay Army (of East India Company) was drawn from Mahars who fought a great many battles on the side of British, including Koregaon, when the Peshwa was defeated." Limaye (himself a 'Chitapavan Brahaman' from Maharashtra) adds: "We cannot convict the lower castes and depressed classes of unpatriotism on the ground of their willingness to serve foreign masters. Men belonging to higher castes also eagerly offered their services to the British masters for a regular pay. The Brahmin caste, which claimed to be the highest in the social hierarchy, was not averse to sell its services to the highest bidder. The British were good pay masters. They paid their troops regularly. They did not default. If the Brahmins and Kshatriyas were devoid of patriotic feelings, how can anyone blame those who were deliberately put in a servile condition by these upper castes?"

So Manusmriti, flouting the Holy Vedas killed the spirit of Vedic brotherhood, killed the spirit of patriotism among many, paving the way for the eventual downfall and slavery of Hindus.

That the Hindus do not lack in bravery, valour and devotion to duty is amply proved by the number of the Victoria Crosses won by them in the First as well as in the Second World War. In the First World War, about one and half million soldiers from the Indian subcontinent fought for the British. Of these 140,000 saw active service on the Western Front in France and Belgium, about 90,000 were on the front line formations of Indian Corps. On 11th March 1917, the British Indian Army entered into Baghdad. At the end of the war, a total of 47,746 Indian soldiers were reported dead/missing 65,126 were wounded. Participants from the subcontinent won about 13,000 medals including 12 Victoria Crosses.

In the Second World War, over 2.5 million soldiers from the Indian subcontinent fought on the side of the Allies. Most of them served in the Indian Army, 700,000 in the XIVth Army in Burma. Indian soldiers served in North Africa against the Germans, in Eritrea and Abyssinia against the Italians in the Middle East in Iraq and in Iran; in the Far East and in Europe. About 36,092 were reported dead/missing, about 64,354 were wounded and about 80,000 were taken prisioners of war by the Axis Powers. Indian soldiers won about 30 Victoria Crosses, the highest award for bravery and devotion to duty.

During 1985–88, I was posted as Assistant High Commissioner (Consul General) of India at Birmingham, UK. One day I invited at dinner some Britishers who had served in the Govt. of British India; they were then in their 80s/90s; and, after the dinner, I asked them secrets of how the British could manage to rule over India for over two hundred years with number of British in India (civil servants plus Army) never exceeding two hundred thousand. They hesitated to reply but on being pressed again and again, said that they found Hindus to be the most docile race in the world, always willing to crawl in anticipation of being asked to bend; there were among Indians who took pride in justifying and rationalizing their own slavery rather than offering any resistance. I was shocked and dumb founded. But, the above data and Limaye's observations justify this assessment of the retired British civil servants.

In international diplomacy there are atleast two phrases to denote similar mindsets of crawling in anticipation of being asked to bend, 'Chamberlain's worldview' and 'Finlandisation'. Chamberlain's worldview or mentality implies inventing justifications for surrender of one's national interests to a would– be–aggressor on pious hope that the aggressor would not launch the aggression after being appeased without realizing that it is the appeasement that stokes the aggression. The phrase 'finlandisation' implies; silent acquiescence to a foreign power even before any external pressure is applied, to submit in advance to a foreign power in anticipation of being asked to do so. This term was first used in 1966 by a West German professor, Richard Luwenthal, and it soon spread into political vocabulary. A finlandised country's power over formulation of its own foreign policy by way of self–abdication is very limited but the management of its internal affairs is quite independent of external influence.

Lokmanya Bal Gangadhar Tilak tried to change this mindset of Indians by giving his famous call that freedom was our birth right; Gandhiji by inculcating the boldness to offer peaceful resistance & peaceful non–cooperation (*satyagraha*) to foreign rulers. Gandhiji changed the mindset from one of meekness to one that of boldness in asserting political rights of sovereignty. Side by side, Gandhiji successfully broke the Manusmriti code by inculcating the spirit among depressed classes that they too had a legitimate stake in the governance (*rajnya*) of India.

If one looks closely and carefully, he would see that there are many among the Hindus who, consciously or unconsciously, out of their own genetic compulsions or for other considerations, or out of ignorance, are working hard to defeat Hinduism and re–forge chains of slavery. They are suffering with what some call genetically acquired slave syndrome (GASS) or what is popularly called '*slave mentality*.' Let us not hate them who are suffering with GASS virus but let us re–educate them. As Assistant High Commissioner of India at Birmingham, UK (1985–88), I was protected by a posse of four British Special Branch Police officers and my driver also happened to be a white British person. I had moved to Birmingham from Lagos, Nigeria. One Indian diplomat (Ravi Mhatre) posted at Birmingham was kidnapped and killed just before I was posted there, so, this extra security was provided to me by the British Government. To my embarassment and that of my security staff, I noticed that some VIP visitors tended to shake hands first with them before shaking hands with me. Sir David Gore–Booth, a former British High Commissioner to India was quoted in the Outlook (17th Aug., 1998, page 43): "Sir David ruffled feathers when he admitted to lingering arrogance of many British vis–a–vis India perhaps compounded by the obsequiousness shown by many Indians." Obsequious means being promptly obedient or submissive. After all, Sir David, being an Ambassador, was not meeting with the common Indians walking on roads of New Delhi or Mumbai. He would mostly be meeting with the cream of the Indian society. And this is the first hand impression he carried from his few years of diplomatic assignment in New Delhi about our Indian elite. Sir David observed the same behaviour, the same mindset among the top echelon of Indians of independent India which Francois Martin, a Frenchman observed in 1676 and Robert Clive, a British, noted in 1759. Rajeev Shukla, a veteran journalist and a distinguished Member of the Indian Parliament in his Front Foot column (Indian Express, 26th June 2004) has referred to this very mentality. Shukla wrote, "What surprises me is how we happily stomach major inconveniences dished out to us by foreign airlines, but throw tantrums at the slightest snags by the national carriers. This duality can be explained only by a negative mindset reminiscent of the Raj. Sadly, even after a decade of globalization, we are yet to overcome our fascination for anything foreign." Vir Sanghvi, another veteran Indian journalist and a keen observer of Indian society also has commented,: "We Indian are either too off–handed, or, too obsequious; rarely do we stand middleground." (Brunch, May 8, 2005 page 15, a HT publication).

Referring to the June 12, 1947 report of Lord Mountbatten to the British Govt. in which he Mountbatten narrated a Cabinet meeting in the most patronising terms, Ajit Bhattacharjea in his book (Countdown to Partition: The Final Days, page 39) has written, "Mountbatten was prone to exaggerate his role, but the episode underlined once again the subservient attitude of Indian leaders." At page 54, Bhattacharjea has added that Lord Mountbatten, in his another report to London, claimed having publicly reprimanded Nehru at a Cabinet meeting, which Nehru is implied to have taken lying down!!

Jawaharlal Nehru has himself stated that most of Indians had this inferiority complex. In his book 'Glimpses of World History' (page 441), he has written, "The Japanese victory, therefore, was a great pick–me–up for Asia. In India it lessened the feeling of inferiority, from which most of us suffered."

Slave mentality is the one in which people destroy members of their own group at a faster rate than they destroy their enemies. People suffering with slave mentality derive some sort of satisfaction and pleasure in running down, harming, hurting and humiliating their own brethren (other than their immediate family members), members of their own group at biddings of any 'outsider'. They consider themselves as well as other members of their community to be inferior to 'outsiders/foreigners'. They try to mimic/copy 'outsiders' and consider it a great achievement if they succeed in doing so. They love to obey any 'outsider' and love to be patted or, even to be kicked around by 'outsiders'. Their psychological reference group is 'foreigners/outsiders'.It is something like the 'Stockholm syndrome.'Those Hebrews (Jews) who were born in Egypt under Egyptian slavery were unable to disassociate themselves from their slave mentality even after they were got liberated by Moses and brought to Israel. They were always ready to crawl, always ready to please outsiders/others, always ready to let down each other, always running to get certificates of good behaviour from 'outsiders'.

According to the three part analytical article brought out by the Financial Times, London, UK (February 23–25, 2005), both China and India are heirs of great civilizations. But China's civilization is inseparable from its state, while India's is inseparable from its social structure, above all from the role of castes.This difference permeates the two countries' histories and contemporary performances. As Lord Desai of the London School of Economics has noted, "for India, the problem is achieving unity in diversity, China however is a unitary hard state which can pursue a single goal with determination and mobilize maximum resources in its achievement (with less social efforts)" China has accepted both growth and social transformation, India welcomes growth but tries to minimize social dislocations". China's gross national savings in 2002 was 44% of its gross national income while India's was only 22%. In 2002, China's trade in goods was 49% of its GDP while India's was only 21%. In 2003, the stock of inward foreign direct investments in China was US$ 501.8 billion against only US $ 30.8 billion in India. In 2000, India's overall illiteracy rate was 35% against just 6% in China. In 1999–2000, only 47% of all Indian children had passed through five years of primary education against 98% in China. Thus, for faster economic growth of India and for quickly getting rid of poverty, let us first get rid of the germs of casteism.

Let us make conscious efforts by self–control to change our mind set. Atleast from 15th August, 1947 onwards we Indians do not need certificates of good behaviour from foreigners. For the sake of better future of our children and grandchildren, we must identify those among us who are carriers of this deadly virus of self inflicting slavery, self–imposed inferiority complex. Those Hindus who, without knowing the basics of Hinduism keep denouncing Hinduism, those who are concocting justifications to reduce bit by bit employment opportunities of our children; those Indians who enjoy running down India and other fellow Indians just to curry favours, psychological or material, from outsiders/foreigners are definitely suffering with GASS virus. This virus can be killed only by conscious self–efforts, by introspection.

4.4 Gandhi Opposes Untouchability

When Gandhiji started the fight against untouchability, we started our successful march towards our political salvation too. When the Constitution of India restored Vedic norms of equality by birth and gender equality, see, our Armed Forces have never been defeated. Reversing the trend of history, in 1971 under the able leadership of Indira Gandhi, we took hundreds of thousands of prisoners of war (POWs), we Hindus have not again fallen as slaves, we are being accorded respect all over the world; India has become the fourth largest economy (Purchasing Power Parity basis) in the world in a short period of fifty years, a nuclear weapon country with its own missiles, satellites, digital telemetry, etc. India has the fourth largest Army and Air Force in the world. As per the latest World Development Indicators, India's gross national income in 2001 on Purchasing Power Parity (PPP) basis was US$ 2913 billion, the fourth largest after the U.S.A. ($ 9781 billion), China ($ 5027 billion) and Japan ($ 3246 billion). These Big Four were followed by Germany ($ 2580 billion), UK ($ 1431 billion), France ($ 1425 billion), Canada ($ 825 billion) and Pakistan ($ 263 billion). India has been invited to become a member of G–20 countries. In July 2003, India again reversing the history became a net lender country to the International Monetary Fund/World Bank. From being a food deficit country, India over last two decades has become a food surplus country. India is now the largest producer of milk in the world. For more on India's rank in the World, please see Appendix IV. India retained its position as the fourth largest economy in the world on PPP basis in the World Bank's World Development Indicators 2004 released on 23rd April, 2004 which is based on 2002 data.

Mohandas Karamchand Gandhi (Mahatma Gandhi) fought tooth and nail to maintain unity of Hindu Samaj by fighting against untouchability, underwent 21 days fast to retain unity with scheduled caste Hindus by promising them more number of reserved seats in legislatures (Yeravda Agreement) than offered by the then British rulers. Under this agreement, also called the Poona Pact, as against 78 seats allotted to the depressed classes by the British in the state legislatures, 148 seats were reserved for them. On August 17, 1932, Ramsay

MacDonald, the British Prime Minister, announced the Communal Award separating depressed classes from the rest of Hindus as a separate electorate. Announcing the fast, Gandhiji said, "What I want, what I am living for, and what I should delight in dying for, is the eradication of untouchability root and branch". Robert Payne in his book, 'The Life and Death of Mahatma Gandhi,' has written (page 443) that the miracle that Gandhi had hoped for by announcing the fast had already taken place; all over India the untouchables were being welcomed into Hindu temples without any restrictions. Great temples, which had never permitted a single untouchable to enter their precincts suddenly, flung open their doors."

In January 1935, in his reply to Sir S. Radhakrishanan, Gandhiji wrote, "My religion is Hinduism which, for me, is the religion of humanity and includes the best of all the religions known to me". (The Essential Writings of Mahatma Gandhi, page 159, Raghavan Iyer)

Whereas Manu of Manusmriti, after the Rigvedic rishis, was the one who fragmented and divided Hindus creating ground for their eventual slavery, Gandhiji, in my humble opinion, proved himself to be the grand Unifier in that grand chain of Rigvedic rishis who *manasa, vacha and karmana* (by words and deeds) implemented the missionary sukta RV (X.191) to unify the Hindu Samaj and, like Moses delivered Hindu Samaj to its political liberation/freedom. Some may argue at much higher cost in terms of Hindu lives lost, Hindu blood & tears but Gandhiji was not a member of the Government. He had a moral duty to save Hindu lives, but he had no legal/administrative instrument at his hands to do so. It is roughly estimated that during the partition, five million Hindus were murdered, about twenty million were displaced and an unknown number of women were raped/mutilated. It is another thing that Gandhi totally failed in handling and assessing the then Muslim League, a subject not addressed in this book.

4.5 Gandhi Opposes Conversion

Gandhiji was against conversions by Christian missionaries as it created, in his views, social tensions and frictions and was harmful to minorities (Harijan, 11th May and 5th Dec 1935). In Dec 1938, Gandhiji told Christian Missionaries "If you missionaries come as preachers of true gospel to Indian people who are wandering in darkness, so far as I am concerned, you can have no place in India"(Mahatma by DG Tendulkar, vol V, page 4). Similarly, Gandhiji addressing Christian missionaries, wrote in the Harijan (7th January 1939): "If you feel that only you can lead the suffering humanity from darkness to light, then, as far as I know, there is no place for you in India". Gandhiji felt that Christian missionaries spread hatred against Hindus and Hindu religion.

Dom Moraes has described how in his Convent in Bombay Christian students were asked to convert their 'heathen' (a pagan, an unenlightened or barbarous person) class fellows, and, how he was considered half mad for refusing to do so. Triloki Nath Kaul, ICS and a former Foreign Secretary of India has written how a Christian missionary lost interest in teaching Latin to him when he realized that he (Kaul) could not be converted. RK Narain has described how hatred against Brahamans was promoted by his Christian teachers in Madras.

In May 1936, Harilal, the eldest son of Gandhiji, became a Muslim adopting the name of Abdullah. According to Payne's book, both Gandhiji and Kasturba objected to his giving up his ancestral religion. Kasturba wrote "Alas! We, your father and I, have to suffer so much on your account in the evening of our life. What a pity that you, our eldest son, have turned our enemy!" (Page 470) Gandhiji wrote on this conversion

"Surely conversion is a matter between man and his Maker who alone knows His creatures' hearts. And, conversion without a clean heart is a denial of God and religions. Conversion without cleanness of heart can only be a matter for sorrow, not joy, to a godly person" (page 473). Gandhiji opposed 'colourable' conversions. Kasturba cried for days and days for her eldest son, and Gandhiji clearly objected to conversion for motives, hidden or otherwise.

4.6 Supreme Court Of India On Conversions

The Supreme Court of India in 1977 in Rev. Stanislaus vs. the State of Madhya Pradesh ruled that there is no fundamental right to convert another person to one's own religion while upholding constitutional validity of the two State Acts passed by Madhya Pradesh and Orissa which made conversions by force, fraud or allurement an offence. Fali S. Nariman (Times of India, 17th January 99) has justified conversions based on allurements saying "People below certain level of economic well being will always be ready to accept a religion which offers their basic needs. If you can persuade someone to change his religion even by giving some economic benefits, I don't see anything wrong in it .It has been happening and will continue to happen. Hindu missionaries can reconvert them. There is no inviolability of conversions." Some columnists, flying in the face of the Supreme Court, assert that the right to convert others to one's faith is an integral part of the Constitutional right to practice and propagate one's religion. Even if this is so, this so called right is equally available to all Hindu missionaries too, but this line of argument justifies perpetuating conversion war, backward and forward, inter–religion and intra–religion, which diverts the attention of people from focusing on achieving faster socio–economic developments of India.

Congress President, Sonia Gandhi, rightly said at the

Ramakrishna Mission (Jan 12,1999): "India is secular primarily because Hinduism, both as a philosophy and as a way of life has been based on what our wise ancients have said that truth is one, the paths to it many." (Para 5.8). The CWC resolution (16th Jan, 1999) also says: "Hinduism is the most efficient guarantee of secularism in India".

Saeed Naqvi, a reputed Indian journalist, informs that give or take a century, Muslim rule in India and Spain lasted for a similar length of time, over different periods. Today, there are virtually no Muslims in Spain, but there are roughly 150 million Muslims in India, another 300 million in Pakistan and Bangladesh and 50 million in Afghanistan.This would not have been possible, Naqvi argues, had there not been considerable Catholicism in the indigenous society of Indian subcontinent. (Indian Express, October 8, 2004)

If more than 80% population of India were Muslims, it is anybody's guess whether India would be today a secular country or an Islamic country.

4.7 Shortcomings Of Inter–Religion Conversions

Conversion of Dalit Hindus to another religion has not proved to be a satisfactory answer, as even after conversion, converts do not get 'social equality' in their new religions. Conversions have proved to be divisive, raising social tensions and creating law & order problems. Use of phrases like dalit Christians, dalit Muslims, and dalit Buddhists in contemporary Indian media proves the point. These phrases are totally inconsistent with the teachings of Jesus, Prophet Muhammad (Peace Be Upon Him) and that of the Lord Buddha. R. Thirumalvalavam, Head of the Panthers Party of India told rediff.com (Nov. 15, 2002): "that for emancipation of dalits, conversion is not the solution. Converts remain Dalit Muslims or Dalit Christians or Dalit Buddhists." A Dalit writer, told The Week (Nov 18, 2001): "Over the years, when Dalits converted to Islam, Sikhism or Christianity, they did not lose their Dalit identify. They remained primarily Dalits, and, then Christians or Sikhs. Conversion is not the answer to exploitation of Dalits." As I have argued, only the Vedic richas can make them lose their dalit stamp.

Dalits also complain that the Hindu caste system follows them into other religions too, so, a Dalit convert is not treated as well as, say, a Brahaman or a Kshatriya convert.

Some Dalit activists insist that Dalits should try to erase Hinduism's prejudices against them from inside the faith. Says Krishnaswamy: "Religious conversion is not an escape. It's a temporary shelter. We are the original owners of this country, so why should we lose our identity?" (Time, Oct. 20, 1977).

Detlef Kantowasky, a German Professor of Sociology, in his recent book 'Buddhisten in Indien heute' says that Mahars who converted to Buddhism are still not able to shake off their untouchable stigma. In addition, new converts invite ridicule from Dalit Hindus for abandoning old faith generating another ripple of social tensions. Gaining 'social equality' is a two–way process involving two parties, oppressor and the oppressed. Unilateral action (i.e., conversion i.e., running away by oppressed) does not solve the problem as the other party continues to treat converts as before in villages.In addition, converted dalits get socially cut off even from the Hindu dalits. Converts find their social circle in new religion further narrowed, reduced and limited to earlier converts from their old Hindu caste.

The Catholic Bishops Conference of India (Sunday magazine, June 28, 98) estimated that 41% of new Pentecostals in India were former Catholics and 31% from other Christian sects. So, intra–Islamic and intra–Christian conversion wars are realities. (Paras 5.1 and 5.5). In many countries Pentecostals have replaced Catholics as the majority denomination.

Christians of one denomination generally do not attend Church of another denomination. One sect of Muslims generally doesn't and sometimes cannot attend mosques of another sect. But generally there is no such problem in most of the Hindu temples.

Indian Christians are said to still discreetly follow pre–conversion castes of their Hindu forefathers. Syrian Christians (i.e., St. Thomas Christians) are said not to marry Latin Christians or Neo–Christians. 'High caste' Christians allegedly do not mix with 'Dalit Christians'. The Indian Roman Catholic church is divided into three rites–Syro–Malabar, Syro–Malankara and Latino.

As per **www.dalitchristians.com,** Christian Dalits still suffer same oppression, segregation and discrimination at the hands of 'caste Christians' and 80% of jobs in Church and Church related institutions have been monopolised by 'caste' Christians though 'dalit' Christians comprise 75% of Catholic population in India. TK Oommen & Hunter P. Mabry in their book 'The Christian Clergy in India' verify this discrimination. Dalit Christian website further alleges that 'untouchable' Christians are forced to sit separately in many rural churches in India. They must enter through a separate door into rural church and receive communion at a separate altar.

Jat Sikhs generally do not intermix with Ramgarhias (tarkhan) and Mazhabi Sikhs. Strangely, there are separate gurudwaras for each group.

"The structures" says Rev Smith–Cameron, "are not inclusive enough not because anybody is being malicious but because they are organizationally unjust." The Church of England report (Called to Lead: A Challenge to Include Minority Ethnic People) says Christians of Indian origin and blacks and other non–white Christians have felt "stereotyped, unwelcome and undervalued." (Outlook, Dec. 18, 2000, page 37)

One Muslim leader of Bihar (Dr. Ezaz Ali, President, All India Backward Muslim Morcha) was quoted (March 1997) claiming that "social and economic condition of Muslim Dalit (arzal) is same as that of Hindu Dalit. Their conversion to Islam has not helped them acquire social class mobility. While as Hindus they were ridiculed by upper caste Hindus; as Muslim Dalits, they are looked down upon by 'upper caste' Muslims (Ashrafs)". As per The Week (Jan. 31, 1999), Pasmanda Muslim Samaj of Bihar reiterated oppression of Dalit Muslims at the hands of upper caste Muslims pointing out that out of 245 Muslim MLAs produced by Bihar during 1952 to 1995 there has been no Dalit Muslim MLA so far. There are wheels within wheels.

4.8 Modus Operandi For Second Generation Reforms

Articulation of the above 51 richas & shlokas should convince Hindu priests that what they have been preaching is contrary to the Holy Vedas, contrary to Shrimad Bhagwadgita and contrary to Bhagwan Shri Ram's examples (thereby helping other religions to grab converts from among Hindus). For comparison, one may note how steadfastly Muslims follow examples set by their Prophet (PBUH) in Sunnah. And, Muslims never allow any person/book to be placed even on par with their Holy Qur'an. But, we Hindus do not even put into practice what Bhagwan Ram himself practised and which we see every year in Ramlilas.

Managers of Hindu temples must instruct their priests to immediately put into practice these richas and shlokas. Stopping entry of SC/ST/Dalit Hindus into temples is violative of RV (X.191) and AV (III.30). Hindus of Chakwara, Rajsthan violated AV (III.30.6) in denying access to village pond to Bairwa Hindus.

The command of RV (X.191) often came as shock and

pleasant surprise to many Hindu priests whom I personally talked. Many admitted neither knowing Sanskrit nor having ever read the Vedas but only having memorised some mantras and shlokas here and there for conducting rituals and earning their livelihood. Pujaries said that they expect present–day leaders of the Hindu Samaj to re–educate them and make Vedas available to them. They assured that they would be second to none in spreading the correct i.e., unity & harmony message of the Vedas. Pujaries also agreed with me that they should visit SC/ST/Dalit houses for offering religious services to them as, on one hand it will be paying true obeisance to the Holy Vedas and on the other hand, it would also increase their meagre income. However, their main difficulty was jhijhik i.e., who would bell the cat. Let us, we the English speaking middle class Hindus, bell the cat. We will be doing a great service to restoration of true Hinduism if we gift a set of four Vedas to our family pujari (priest) or to our village pujari. Let us, we the members of the Great Indian middle class, take initiative to re–educate our priests with the full set of Vedas.

Simply abusing and cursing Hindu priests or cursing the present generation of Brahamans in general will not lead to annihilation of caste; rather, their re–training along the above lines will certainly. Income of all Hindu temples should be pooled to re–educate pujaries and an All India Hindu Pujari Service (IHPS) should be started in which all Hindus should be eligible for recruitment based on their knowledge of the Holy Vedas and Gita. Salary should not be less than five thousand rupees per month even in villages.The Hon'ble Supreme Court has been faster than our socio–religious leaders in opening recruitments in temples for all Hindus. In March 96, the Supreme Court (JJ K. Ramaswamy and B.L. Hansaria) rightly ruled that the office of temple priest couldn't be hereditary. In October 02, the Supreme Court (JJ S.

Rajendrababu and Doraiswamy Raju) held that non–Brahamns are eligible to perform religious ceremonies and work as temple priests if they are well versed with relevant rituals. These two decisions are consistent with real Hinduism as per RV (X.125.5) and RV (X.98.7) (See Para 2.5) as well as with Manusmriti (X.65) (Para 3.5). At page 271, Keer informs that Dr. Ambedkar had also suggested doing away with the idea of hereditary priesthood and democratisation of the profession of priests by the grant of a *sanad* (certificate) to any Hindu who passed a certain test; now, it has been given full force of law by the Supreme Court. We have already seen priesthood is not hereditary in the Vedas. Female priests are also sanctioned by Holy Vedas vide RV (V.28) (see chapter 6).

Another shocking but real problem is the practice of some sort of hierarchy/ untouchability within SC/ST/Dalit Hindus. Conversion from one religion to another does not address this problem. Some websites espousing emancipation of Dalits publicise only divisive/negative shlokas of Manusmriti (to the exclusion of harmony seeking richas/shlokas of Vedas, etc.) which makes double damage to their own cause as, on one hand, it only further depresses SC/ST/Dalit Hindus to meekly give into submission believing it is too difficult to fight 'Dharma'; on the other hand, it convinces 'caste' Hindus more and more that this is what Hindu Dharma actually ordains. So, they are reluctant to give up casteism i.e., upper caste/ lower caste syndrome.

Various reform movements during freedom struggle made substantial gains, which have got codified in the Constitution of India. But, from 1950s onwards there has been no real social reform movement. It is high time to initiate a second generation reforms of Hinduism from within. SC/ST/Dalit Hindus who are already armed with the Constitutional articles and various Acts should be exposed more and more to above cited 38 Vedic richas, 13 shlokas of Shrimad Bhagwadgita and to the rich contributions of their ancestors to the Supreme Scriptures so as to boost their morale and to convince them that their fight is not against the Holy Vedas, not against 'real' Hindu Dharma but their effort is only to cleanse Hinduism of the rust and dust collected over centuries ; that they are going to wage a mental or ideological (*manasik*) fight to restore original teachings of the three Holy Hindu Scriptures; that ,they are returning to their original and pure roots. Such a strategy will liberate Dalit Hindus from their mindset of being 'lowly born' and empower them mentally and spiritually to take up the fight. Only such a strategy would free them from the 'dalit stamp'. On the other hand, exposure of caste Hindus to these very richas will change their mindset and convince them that practising untouchability and casteism is really a sin (paap). Democratised All India Hindu Priest Service (IHPS) will only accelerate this process. Casteism cannot be annihilated by mutual acrimony, by violence or conversions, or by caste wars as it is a mental state or a mindset. During my foreign service, I have seen educated Indians living in foreign countries for decades but still practicing casteism in foreign countries though in more subtle form!!

4.9 Return To Vedic Brotherhood

Let the Yajna (social movement) assisted by 38 Vedic richas and 13 shlokas of Gita be initiated to permanently destroy both the demons – the demon of intra–Hindu casteism and the demon of intra SC/ST/Dalits Hindu casteism from the Hindu mind. Let us confidently return to our Vedic roots – equality by birth & gender equality— duly equipped with modern Science and Technology. Let us restore the primacy and supremacy of the Holy Vedas. Let us no more place secondary sources on par with the Vedas. Let us no more allow supersession of the Vedas by secondary sources (books composed during the Christian era). It is only Veda, unshackled from the burden of secondary literature which, piercing through darkness created by secondary sources can help a section of Hindus lose their dalit stamp, not the gimmicks of conversions from one religion to another religion. Religious conversion of Dalit Hindus is really futile, as experience shows it does not liberate them from their dalit–stamp.

For initiating this second generation social reform movement, neither any procession on road is required nor any demonstration. This yajna can and should be initiated in each house by discussing the full import of the 51 Vedic richas/Gita shlokas listed above at social gatherings, in drawing rooms after dinner with guests, at tea stalls, at cafes, at village chaupals etc. Let us, the English speaking middle class Hindus, first self–educate ourselves. Let us then acquaint or confront our family pujari with the 51 Vedic richas/Gita shlokas. Let each of us start practicing these richas in our real day to day life without waiting for others. Let us start following Vedas *manasa*, *vacha and karmana* (by words and deeds). This will become the beginning of our Second generation reform led by educated English speaking middle class Hindus.

Thus, restoration of Vedic equality, return to Vedic brotherhood is the only route for Dalit emancipation and wider unity in the Hindu Samaj.

Five

INTRA–RELIGION CONVERSIONS

'sarva dharma sambhava' is the best option.

Within Hinduism, conversion from one sect to another (i.e., conversion, say, from Shaivaite to Vaishnavaite, etc.) has now lost relevance as Hindus of one sect practically face no difficulty or restrictions in attending Hindu temples/festivals of other sects. Followers of one Hindu God are no more hostile to other Hindu Gods, taking all Gods as one. But, in other religions, it is generally not so; intra–religion conversions (i.e., conversions from one sect to another sect of the same religion) do take place. To understand the dynamics of such intra–religion conversions, it is relevant to know, with an open mind and without any bitterness, a few basics of different religions. There are two basic limitations; first, it is obviously not possible to cover all details of each religion in this short book. Second, my own knowledge of religions is not so deep. My own background is university lecturer in mathematcs turned a diplomat.

Sant Nirankari Mandal ably led by HH Baba Hardeo Singhji Maharaj is preaching universal brotherhood.(See para 4.1) Nirankari Mission is also putting into practice the principle of *sarva dharma sambhava* i.e., peaceful co–existence of all religions. The Mission's foundation lies embedded in the view that there is only one religion, which is the religion of humanity. Human values can only exist if one has nurtured love for people of this whole world. HH Baba Hardeo Singh ji teaches that working for the benefit and general upliftment of the society was always one of the primal objectives of every Avtar, prophet, Seer, Sage, Guru who has walked on this earth. The indispensable instruction, therefore, is to express fellow feelings, camaraderie for all and the natural upshot is that there should be peaceful co–existence. Hence, *Sarva Dharma Sambhava* is a path which all devotees of the Mission follow having complete and equal respect for all religious practices. The Mission does not seek to convert but rather teaches that if you are a Christian be a practicing Christian, if you are a Hindu, practice the essence of Hinduism and the same applies to Sikhs, Muslims and the followers of any religious order. The key objective being to actually practice what is inscribed within all religious writings. Devotees of the Mission are not asked to change their culture, way of life or religion. They are invited to acquire knowledge from the *Guru* and apply the said wisdom in their lives. Knowing about the subject is the essential feature as it is this element that allows one to break down inner barriers. The results are observed within their *Satsang's* where an extremely broad outlook is offered and the philosophies and observances of all scriptures are talked about. The innumerable names of God as mentioned in different religions are taken as becoming a knower of His constant presence, no inter–religious disputes arise. Consequently this feeling of oneness allows them the flexibility to practice the concept of *Sarva Dharma Sambhava*, which is essentially a constituent of their third noble pledge.

5.1 Sects In Islam

In the famous NCERT case, the Hon'ble Supreme Court

of India advised (Sept, 2002) that what is required today is not religious education but education about religions, their basics, and the value inherent therein; and also a comparative study of the philosophy of all religions. Let us do so in brief. Let us look at a few basics of other religions with reverence and an open mind. The cardinal rule is that religious beliefs are not subject to judicial or 'rational' scrutiny. Theological differences are found in almost all the religion, for the simple reason that these differences are based on different interpretations of the same sacred texts. Therefore, development of sects within any religion is a natural phenomenon.

There are 73 sects in Islam; major sects being Sunni and Shiite.The five fundamental pillars of Islam, common to almost all the sects are: (i) to bear witness that there is no God but Allah, and, that Muhammad is His (last) Prophet (PBUH)(Peace be upon Him) (ii) to offer prayers (salat or salah) (iii) to give alms (zakah or zakat equal to 2.5% of one's total wealth each year) (iv) to perform hajj, and (v) to keep fast during ramadhan (sawm). (Some authors use the phrase *sallhu alai wa sallam* instead of PBUH.) Ahmadi or Qadiani Muslims do not accept Prophet Muhammad (PBUH) as the last prophet. Therefore, some Muslims do not accept Qadianis as Muslims.

Each sect naturally considers its own theological interpretations to be the 'true' and the 'authentic' giving rise to theological polemics within the Islamic fold. In this context, it is worthwhile to take note of a recent address made by H.E. Mr. Mahathir Bin Mohammad, till recently the Prime Minister of Malaysia, at the Al Azhar University, Cairo on 22nd Jan. 2003. He said, "We all know that Prophet brought only one Islam but today there are many Islamic religions. There are Sunnis and Shiites divided into numerous groups by different

Imams and Orders. Some of these interpretations and teachings are so different that their followers actually accuse each other of not being a Muslim. In fact, they regard many who profess to be Muslims as infidels because of the thousands of different interpretations of Islam and the very many sects and adherents, each claiming to be true followers of Islamic religion, Muslims are thoroughly confused." (International Herald Tribune– Jan. 28, 2003). Incidentally Mahathir has been a very successful Prime Minister of Malaysia.

In order to explain the origin of so many sects, Maulana Wahiduddin Khan, a learned Indian scholar of Islamic studies, in his book 'Islam Rediscovered' says (page 70) that one reason for original Islam becoming alien is that as time went by, self–styled interpreters of the Qur'an and Sunnat gradually placed a veil over the original contents of these texts. He further clarifies at page 71, "They begin to interpret religion according to their own mind–set. The result is that, although they refer to the Qur'an and Sunnah, their interpretations have little bearings on the original texts. They fail to differentiate between God–sent religion and man–made interpretations."

Which interpretation is correct basically depends upon which sect or theological school one belongs to. Which interpretation is correct and which one is not correct is beyond the scope of this book.

As per the Hindustan Times (June 15, 98), the then Census Commissioner of India (Dr. M. Vijaymuni) was quoted as saying that there were caste divisions in Muslims (584), Christians (339), Sikhs (130), Buddhists (93), etc. The 1901 census of Bengal placed Muslims into three groups: Ashraf (better class), Ajlaf (lower castes) and Arzal (Degraded castes). This categorisation was repeated in the Indian Express of March 19, 1997. According to one characterisation, descendants of foreign invaders (Turks, Mughals, Afghans,

Persians and Arabs) are known among Indian Muslims as Ashrafs, meaning the nobility. Converts from the so–called higher Hindu castes like Brahamans and Rajputs are known as Ajlaf. Converts from the so–called lower Hindu castes are known as Arzal meaning the 'mean' fellows. In the Arab World, people of Hashim clan occupy the highest position in the social hierarchy being from the Prophet's (PBUH) own clan. Thereafter, other clans from the Q'oraish tribe take precedence over other Arab tribes.

On 12th February 610 AD (date as per Farida Khanam), Prophet Muhammad (full name: Abual–Qasim Muhammad ibn Abd Allah ibn Abd–Al–Muttalib ibn Hashim) (sallahu alai wa sallam) (PBUH) had a vision from Angel Gabriel that he is the Messenger of God. From this time onwards, at frequent intervals until his death, he received 'revelations'. A compilation of these revelations is called the Holy Qur'an. It is believed that it was compiled into its present form between 644 and 656 A.D. For further details one may visit www.sacred–texts.com. Maulana Wahiduddin Khan in his book 'Islam Rediscovered' informs that (page 161) the present text of the Qur'an does not follow the (datewise) order of revelation that is, the chronological order of revelations. Maulana Khan advises that for grasping the correct meaning of any verse of Qur'an, one must take into account the background/context in which that verse was revealed (pages 165–169).

According to Saiyid Safdar Hosain, Prophet's date of birth reckoned by Shiite as the most authentic one is the seventeenth of Rabi–al–Awwal (June 25, 570), while Sunnis regard the twelfth of Rabi'I as the correct date. Cassin de Perceval put the birth date on 29th August 570 AD. Prophet (PBUH) died in 633 AD (or 632 AD) at sixty–three years of age. Some believe he died on 2nd of Rabi'I, others say on 28th of Safar (May 25, 632) or 12th Rabi'I (June 8, 632 AD). Prophet

(PBUH) left behind no son, all his sons died in their infancy. Ruquaiyyah, Zainab, umm kulthum and Fatima were his daughters from his first wife Khadijah. Hazrat Ali ibn Abu Talib was a cousin as well son–in–law of the Prophet (PBUH) married to Fatima. Lady Ayesha–daughter of Hazrat Abu Bakr and Lady Hafsa–daughter of Hazrat Omar were married to Prophet (PBUH). Some believe that the Prophet (PBUH) was born on a Friday and some believe he was born on a Monday. However, it is unanimously accepted that he breathed his last on a Monday. Some Muslim countries, especially in the Middle East, do not celebrate the birthday of the Prophet (PBUH).

It is said that before the advent of Islam, there were 360 idols in the Kaba, each idol being deity of one Arab tribe or the other with the result that followers of each idol used to visit Kaba every year to worship generating good business for merchants settled around Kaba. These merchants initially opposed Prophet Muhammad (PBUH) when he first gave the call to abolish idolatry fearing that doing so would adversely affect their business.

Sunnis accept Hazrats Abu Bakr (632–634), Omar bin Khattab (634–644), Uthman (644–656) and Ali ibn Abu Talib (656–661) as their first four rightly guided & pious Caliphs (Khalifa i.e., successor to Prophet Mohammad, peace be upon Him) in this sequential order. Hazrats Omar and Uthman were murdered. In November 644–AD, Hazrat Omar was stabbed by an Iranian slave Firuz and later died. In June 656 AD, rebel troops from Egypt, Basra and Kufa killed Hazrat Uthman in his house in Medina. Hazrat Ali was elected the next Caliph but his elevation was questioned by some including the Umayyad tribe led by Muawiya. After the battle between them at Siffien, Ali and Muawiya agreed for an arbitration which annoyed some supporters of Ali and they (kharijiya) attacked him at a mosque in Kufa (Friday 19th ramadhan, 40AH). Hazrat Ali died a few days thereafter and Muawiya from the Umayyad tribe became Caliph in 661 AD. Hazrat Ali's son Hussain and others were killed in a dispute/ war on the 10th of Muharram 61 in Karbala in Iraq (May 681 AD) by the army of new Caliph Yazid, successor of Muawiya. Hazrat Hussain was decapitated and his severed head was presented to Yazid.

Shiat Ali (i.e., followers of Hazrat Ali, shishya of Hazrat Ali, written as Shia or Shiite) believe that Hazrats Abu Bakr, Omar and Uthman improperly became Caliphs against the expressed desire (Khumb Declaration) of the Prophet (PBUH) and that, Hazrat Ali ought to have been accepted as the first Caliph and the first Imam after Prophet (PBUH). This is one of the fundamental differences between Shiites and Sunnis. Sunni authors inform that the Prophet (PBUH) was of the opinion that the task of leadership of Muslims after his death should go to Abu Bakr as the Prophet (PBUH), during his life–time, had made Abu Bakr lead the prayers several times.

Shiite Muslims do not accept Hazrats Abu Bakr, Omar, and Uthman as Caliphs, and Sunni Muslims do not accept Shiite interpretation of the Khumb Declaration. Shiite Muslims treat Hazrat Ali as the first Caliph and the first Imam. Sunnis accept Hazrat Ali only as the fourth Caliph. Consequently, the texts of Shiite Kalama and Shiite Namaz are different from those of Sunnis. Shiite texts directly and indirectly declare and reaffirm that Hazrat Ali is the first Imam and the rightful successor of Prophet (PBUH), which Sunnis do not accept and cannot recite. The text of Sunni Kalama is *La ilaha il Allah, Muhammadan Rasul Allah*, the text of Shiite Kalama (Shahadatah) is *La ilaha il Allah, Muhammadan Rasul Allah, Aliyun Wali–Allah, Wasiyu Rasulillah, wa Khalifa tuhu bila fasl*, which means that, "There is no God but Allah,

Muhammad is the Messenger of Allah, Ali is the Friend of Allah, The Successor of the Messenger of Allah And his first Caliph".

Basic tenets (usul–e–din) of Sunni Muslims are three: (i) Tauhid (unity of God), (ii) Noubouat (Prophethood) and (iii) Maad or Qayamah (day of final judgement). Shiite Muslims have two more basic tenets: (iv) Imamah based on family line from the House of Prophet (Ahlul–Bayt) and (v) Justice of God (ahl). Sunni Muslims do not subsribe to Shiite institution of imamate. Shiite further believe that 'noor' (light, radiance) of Allah passes only through family line from generation to generation. These are matters of faith and belief, which separate Shiites and Sunnis. Shiite and Sunni generally do not inter–marry. They have different mosques, different texts of namaz, different body postures while offering namaz and different timings of namaz. Sunnis generally don't go to Shiite mosques for offering namaz with them, and vice–versa.

Generally Sunni Muslims follow Shariat laws whereas Shiite follow Jafaria laws. Muta marriage is an accepted form of marriage among Shiite but Sunni Muslims consider it illegal/ haraam. Muta marriage is a short–term marriage; the short period is agreed upon before the nikah/marriage. Every year in the month of Muharram, Shiite Muslims observe *ashura* in which Sunni Muslims generally do not participate. In fact in Iraq, ashura processions of Shiite in Karbala were attacked, allegedly by non–shiite Muslim groups killing many Shiite Muslims. Even in India, Shiite–Sunni tensions erupt during ashura processions of Shiite Muslims, especially in Lucknow.

Shiite are mainly divided into Ithna–Asheri (12 imam–wale), Bohras and Ismailies, generally with no inter–marriages without conversion of bride to husband's sect; and, even these Shiite generally do not attend each other's mosques. First six imams of these three main Shiite sects are common. Ismailies or Khojas are also known as Aghakhanies as HH Agha Khan is their living Imam; the present Agha Khan (HH Prince Karim) is said to be the 47th Imam. Shiite Ismailies (about 15 million world wide) believe that HH Agha Khan is a direct descendant of Hazrat Ali. Zaidi Shiite (the fivers) share the first five Imams with the Ithna–asheri shiite and follow a different line of Imams beginning with Imam Zaid, son of Zain–al–abidin. Ismailies share the first six Imams with the Ithna–asheri Shiite and follow a different line beginning with Imam Ismail, older son of Imam Jaafar–al–sadiq. Those who followed Imam Musa–al–kazim, the younger son of Imam Jaafar–al–Sadiq came to be known as Jaafaries, and later, Ithna–Asheri. There are Sunni Khojas too.

The Prophet (PBUH), his daughter Fatima and four Imams (Imams Hassan, Zainul Abedeen, Mohammad Baqr, Jaafar Sadiq) are buried in Medina in Saudi Arabia. Imam Raza is buried in Meshad, Iran. The remaining seven Imams of ithna–asheri Shiite are buried in Iraq viz., Najaf (Hazrat Ali), Karbala (Imam Hussain), Kadhimain in Baghdad (Imams Musa Kazim and Mohammad Taqi) and Samara (Imams Ali Naqi, Hasan Askari, and the Mahdi). Shiite Muslims believe that Imam Mahdi went into seclusion in Samara, Iraq and will reappear on the day of judgement. (Saeed Naqvi, Indian Express, 8th October, 2004)

Bohras believe that from the 21st Imam onwards, all Imams have chosen to remain in seclusion, and their representative called *al–dai–al–mutlaq* heads their mission on the earth. Bohras are also divided into three main groups (i) Dawoodi Bohras with HH Sydena, based in India, as the head (ii) Sulemani Bohras (iii) Alia Bohras. The last two have their own religious heads. Badri vrs Vakili controversy is raging among some sections of Bohras.

Dr.Rafiq Zakaria, a well known Indian intellectual and an Islamic scholar, in his book 'The Man who Divided India' informs that Mohammed Ali Jinnah was born in Karachi into the Ismaeli/Khoja community owing allegiance to the Aga Khan but he later changed his sect and became an Ithna–aseri shiite. At page 2, Dr. Zakaria adds, "Jinnah could neither read the Qur'an, nor did he say his prayers nor fast in Ramadan. He did not perform the Haj." At page 3 of his book, Zakaria says, "Jinnah even toyed with the idea of converting to Christianity." At page 30, quoting MC Chagla, it is stated that Jinnah used to eat pork sausages also!

In many countries, intra–Islamic conversions have been noticed: Shiite and Ahmadias were seeking converts from Sunnis and vice–versa. Ahmadias do accept Prophet Muhammad (PBUH) as a messenger of Allah but not as the last one. (www.alislam.org) (www.thepersecution.org). The Ahmadiya sect was founded in the nineteenth century by HH Mirza Ghulam Ahmad in Quadian near Batala in Punjab, India.

The main sects in Sunni Muslims are Hanafi, Maliki, Shafii and Hanbali. They are followers of HH Maulanas Abu Hanifa Al–Numan (699–767), Malik ibn Anas (714–796), Mohammad ibn Idris Al–Shaffi (767–820) and Ahmad bin Hanbal (780–855) respectively. HH Abu Hanifa al–Numan was an Iranian merchant based at Kufa and Malik ibn Anas was a Medina based lawyer. Other Sunni sects are Wahhabi and Ahle Hadith.

Wahhabis are believed to be the most puritan ones, living mostly in Saudi Arabia. HH Sheikh Mohammed ibn Abd–al Wahhab of Saudi Arabia is believed to be the founder of the Wahhabi sect. Wahhabis call for renewal of original Islamic spirit, moral cleansing and the stripping away of all innovations to Islam since the seventh century. It frowns upon idolatry, tombstones, or, venerations before statues/artwork/mazars. They prohibit smoking, shaving of beards, rosaries and many rights of women. They regard all those who do not practise their form of Islam, including other Muslims, as heathens and enemies.

There are theological differences between Deobandi and Barelvi Sunnis too.

In the Islamic Republic of Pakistan, Ahmadias were declared non–Muslims in 1974 by the Z.A. Bhutto Govt. There is strong pressure on the Islamic Republic of Pakistan to declare Shiite to be non–Muslims. Sunni Muslim groups in Pakistan (Sipah–e–Sahaba–Pakistan, Lashkar–e–Jhangvi, etc.) and Shiite groups (Tehrik–e–Jafaria Pakistan, Sipah–e–Mohammed Pakistan, etc.) keep opening gun–fires at each other's mosques killing namazees and damaging mosques of each other.

5.2 Holy Qur'an On Lord Jesus Christ

The Holy Qur'an (ISBN: 0–940368–56–0) does not accept Lord Jesus Christ as a 'Son of God' or his crucifixion, or his resurrection. It accepts Jesus only as one of the many messengers of God. Surah (IV.157) says that "they did not kill Isa son of Miriam, the apostle of Allah (Jesus Christ) nor did they crucify him;" and Surah (IV.158) says that Allah took him upto Himself (i.e., he was not killed on the Cross). In Surah (IV.171) it is stated that Messiah, Isa son of Miriam is only an apostle of Allah. "Desist, it is better for you; Allah is only one God: far be it from His glory that He should have a son." In Surah (V.116) the concept of Christian trinity has been declared to be false. It reads: "And when Allah will say: O Isa son of Miriam! Did you say to men, Take me and my mother for two gods besides Allah, he will say: Glory be to Thee, it did not befit me that I should say what I had no right to (say)." Surah (XXV.2) again asserts that Allah did not take to Himself a son. Thus, the Holy Qur'an does not accept the basic principles of Christianity i.e., Trinity, Crucifixion and, therefore, the Resurrection.

About two dozen Prophets have been mentioned by name in the Holy Qur'an. In a hadith, the number of these prophets and messengers has been placed at 124,000. It is the Islamic belief that in this long chain of prophets, Prophet Muhammad (PBUH) is the last prophet; and Jesus Christ is the last but one prophet.

5.3 Some Convergences Between Buddhism, Christianity, Hinduism And Islam

On the subject matter of Resurrection, which is an important pillar of the Christian beliefs, there are some doubts prevailing in some Christian sections. For example, in Aug 1999, a section of British press reported that in his book 'Jesus 2000', Dr. George Carey, the then Archbishop of Canterbury had written that unlike birth of Jesus Christ and the crucifixion, Christians cannot say with the same certainty that He was resurrected. The Lambath Palace later denied it. (www.religioustolerance.org). Indian Express (Dec. 28' 99) reported a BBC Radio investigation that a vast majority of British Bishops "Anglican, Catholics and Methodists don't believe the Bible's version of the creation of the world and a quarter of them doubted that Jesus was born to a virgin." Resurrection of dead is an accepted doctrine in Hinduism and in Zoroastrian faith. In Hinduism, Savitri got her dead husband Satyavan resurrected in the same physical body. In the Rigveda, God Savita confers immortality vide (I.110.3, 4). Rebha is raised on 10th day like a buried vessel full of gold under RV (I.117.12). Life is restored to triply mutilated body of Syava under RV (I.117.24). The Christian belief of salvation by faith is also found in Zend Avesta:" happiness and immortality will be lot of the faithful" (Part III, Yasna XXXI). In Gita devotees get salvation by reposing full faith in Lord Krishna and attain happiness, emancipation and the *'baikunthadham'* (bliss & heaven).

The Atharvaveda (XII.2.33) says: "let him not hate us, nor let us (hate) him." The Dhammapada says: "Hatred does not cease hatred at any time, hatred ceases by love, this is its nature. Let us live happily, not hating those who hate us." [1.5]. The New Testament says: "But I say unto you, Love your enemies, bless them that curse you, do good to them that hate you, and pray for them that despitefully use you, and persecute you." [Matthew 5.44]. "But I say unto you which hear, love your enemies, do good to them which hate you" (Luke 6.27). "Bless them that curse you, and pray for them which despitefully use you" (Luke 6.28). "But love ye your enemies, and do good" (Luke 6.35). Gita (XVI.2) commands absence of anger even against those who harm/hurt. Gita (XVI.3): "Sublimity, forbearance, fortitude, external purity, bearing enmity to none and absence of self–esteem these are marks of him, who is born with divine gifts Arjuna." Gita (XII.18): "He who is alike to friend and foe." According to Maulana Wahiduddin Khan (page 85 of his book), the Qur'an also portrays Muslims as individuals who "repel evil with good (28:54)". Similarly, Maulana adds, Prophet Muhammad (PBUH) advised a Muslim to "do good to those who harm you" (al–tirmirdhi) and "do good to others, even if they are not doing good to you" (al–tabarani).These show some convergences among these religions.

Christians acknowledge Holy Trinity of the Father, the Son and the Holy Ghost and at the time of Baptism water is sprinkled. In Buddhism, water is sprinkled while performing '*abhishekam*', and Buddhists acknowledge trinity of Buddha, Dhamma and Sangha. Stars preceded births of Buddha and Christ and both had twelve disciples. Hindus also have Trideva (Brahma, Vishnu & Mahesh), and also sprinkle water at religious ceremonies. The Rigveda (X.17.10) lays down purification by consecrated water i.e., *jal abhishekam.*

Sprinkling of consecrated water is a Rig Vedic ritual, which is being followed in Buddhism and in Christianity. HH Wilson's translation of this Vedic richa is: "May the maternal waters, purify us; may the shedders of water purify us with the effusion; for the divine (waters) bear away all sin; I come away from them purified (to heaven)." RV (I.23.21–23) also describes purification by water. Catholics sprinkle water during baptism but Pentecostals immerse people into water at time of baptism to purify them. RV (I.23.23) says: "I have this day entered into the waters: we have mingled with their essence: Agni, abiding in the waters, approach, and fill me, thus (bathed), with vigour." It appears Pentecostals follow more closely immersion prescribed in RV (I.23.23). Some say that John the Baptist, being an Essene/Buddhist, introduced *"abhishekam"* into Christianity.

Karna was born to unmarried virgin Kunti by blessings of God Sun (Surya Bhagwan); and in the Christian belief, Jesus was born to virgin mother Mary. In the Rigveda, a son (Hiranyahasta) is bestowed by blessings of God upon Vadrimati, wife of an impotent/incapable husband under RV (I.116.13) and (X.39.7). In Luke (1/7), it is said that Elisabeth was barren but in (1/13) she is blessed with a son. There are, thus, many similarities in Hindu and Christian beliefs such as virgins giving births on divine blessings and barren women bearing children.

MacDonell at page 360 of his book 'A History of Sanskrit Literature' has written: "The influence of Indian philosophy on Christian Gnosticism in the second and third centuries seems at any rate undoubted. The Gnostic doctrine of the opposition between soul and matter, of the personal existence of intellect, will, and so forth, the identification of soul and light, are derived from the Samkhya system. The division, peculiar to several Gnostics, of men into the three classes of pneumatikoi, psychikoi and hylikoi, is also based on the Samkhya doctrine of the three gunas. Again, Bardesanes, a Gnostic of the Syrian school, who obtained information about India from Indian philosophers, assumed the existence of a subtle ethereal body which is identical with the heavens of the Gnostics are evidently derived from the fantastic cosmogony of later Buddhism". MacDonell completed his book in 1899 A.D.

5.4 Christ In India?

The Holy Bible is silent about life, whereabouts and activities of Lord Jesus Christ between twelfth to thirtieth years of his age. There is no unanimity on this subject. A German scholar Holger Kersten in his book 'Jesus Lived in India' (ISBN–1–85230–5509) has described in detail His unknown life in India before and after crucifixion. Some scholars believe that Christ after twelfth year of his age had visited many cities in India learning Vedas, Yogas, meditation, etc. before returning to Palestine to preach, and; after surviving crucifixion returned back to India and died in Kashmir. Some scholars suggest that Jesus Christ was an Essene preacher. Philosopher Schoupenhaure in his book 'Religion and other Essays' (page–116) asserts that the Christian faith sprung from the wisdom of India. From Girnar inscriptions of Ashoka the Great, it is observed that Buddhist monks went to Syria to preach Buddhism. Pliny, a Greek historian of first century AD has written that a religious sect Essene lived in Palestine about a century before Christ, which is now accepted as a sect of Buddhism. In Egypt, Essenes were called Therapeuts.

Dead Sea scrolls (about 800 in number) discovered in eleven caves near Qumran during 1947–65 are believed to be Essene literature. Dead Sea scrolls are carbon dated between a span of about 68 BC to 124 AD but despite being contemporary of Jesus, experts advise that these scrolls do not mention Jesus

Christ as the Son of God.

On Internet when one puts 'Jesus Christ in India' into search mode, one gets about 267,000 references on Yahoo. Website www.tombofjesus.com gives graphic details of grave of Yuz Asaf in Srinagar (India) which points east west in keeping with Jewish custom. Some believe it is the grave of Jesus. The second century (AD) Church Father Irenaeus (who lived until about 180 C.E.) in his book 'Against Heresies' has written that Jesus lived to be an old man upto time of the Emperor Trajan (98 AD), before finally dying in Asia. The Acts of Thomas describes the stay of Jesus and Thomas in Taxila (now in the Islamic Republic of Pakistan) at a marriage ceremony at the court of King Gundafor in the twenty– sixth year of his rule (47 C.E.). On this subject of life of Jesus Christ after crucifixion one may see books by Nicolas Notovitch (1894), Maury Lee (Jesus of India), Elizabeth Clare Prophet (Lost Years of Jesus), Paul C. Pappas (Jesus–Tomb in India) and Mark Mason (In Search of the Loving God). Jesus Christ preached in Aramaic language. Modern scholars believe that the Hebrew Bible (Old Testament), or Tanakh, was composed by four or five writers between 1000 to 400 BCE based on much older traditions. The New Testament was composed by a variety of writers between 60 to 110 CE. The contents of the New Testament were formalized about three hundred years after death of Jesus Christ by Athanasius of Alexandria in 367 CE, and finally canonized in 382 CE.

5.5 Sects In Christanity

The News Week of U.S.A (April 16, 2001) at page 45 reported that there are 33,000 different Christian denominations in the world!

In 1378 A.D. there was a split in the College of Cardinals and two Popes were elected, one lived in Rome and the other lived in Avignon, France. For forty years this split continued during which both sides cursed each other and excom–municated each other. In 1417, there was a compromise and a new Pope resident in Rome was elected. (Jawaharlal Nehru, Glimpses of World History, page 231)

There are many disagreements about the order and composition of the Holy Bible among various Christian sects (www.sacred–texts.com). The four Gospels (Matthew, Mark, Luke and John) differ in some aspects at places. What is the correct chronological order of these four Gospels is known as the Synoptic Problem in the Christian theology. Very little has survived about the origins of these Gospels, when, where, why and by whom these were composed. From first few centuries to 18th century, the Augustinian hypothesis that Matthew, Mark, Luke is the correct sequence was the dominant view. In 1783, Johann Jakob Griesbach proposed Matthew–Luke–Mark sequence. In 1820, Johann Gottfried Herder proposed that Mark's Gospel being the shortest should be the earliest document.

Roman Catholics, Protestants, Pentecostals, Orthodox Russian Church, Seventh Day Adventists, Coptic Christians of Egypt, Jehovah's Witnesses, Mormons, etc. have many fiercely contested theological differences among themselves. In the medieval period, one sect of Christians used to kill/ execute Christians of other sects (Catholics vs. Protestants; Inquisitions, Catholics vs. Orthodox, etc.). Basic Pentecostal belief is that Jesus will come again and that year of his advent will be a multiple of 1000. Rev. Charles F. Pariham started it at the beginning of twentieth century in the US city of Topeka, Kansas. Seventh Day Adventists believe that true followers of Jesus will be raised from dead and reign with Him in Heaven for a millennium. It believes that man is the soul. This sect was started by William Miller in 1831 in the U.S.A. Mormons claim to be the only true Christian religion in the world; their church is called the Church of Jesus Christ of Latter–Day–Saints. It is a sect started from U.S.A by Joseph Smith. Jehovah's Witnesses reject many Christian beliefs such as original sin, divinity of Jesus, his resurrection, concept of trinity etc. They are critical of Catholics and Protestants.In February, 2005 a theological difference on the place of homosexuality within the church (i.e., gay and lesbian bishops/pastors), church sanctification of the same sex marriage came into light between the Anglican Church led by the Archbishop of Canterbury and the North America and Canadian Anglican Churches.

The News Week (April, 2001) further reported that in the fall of 2000, the Vatican published *DOMINUS IESUS* in which the Congregation for the Doctrine of Faith reiterated the supremacy and uniqueness of Catholic Church as the (only) privileged path to salvation. 'All religions are not equal', the Congregation insisted. "Catholics must be committed to announcing the necessity of conversion to Jesus Christ." Cardinal Joseph Ratzinger of the Vatican was quoted as saying that those who try to put other religions (including other Christian denominations) at par with Roman Catholics are crossing all the limits of tolerance. Here lies the root cause of inter–denominational conflicts within Christianity.

A Jamaican newspaper (The Gleaner, January 23'99) reported that during his visit to Mexico, Pope John Paul II committed his Church to win back 'straying' Roman Catholics and combat inroads made/being made by evangelical Protestants. Does it not show the fight for inter–denominational conversions within Christianity? The Times of India (Jan. 27' 99) reported that the Pope signed a new strategy for Catholics in Latin America urging them to offer a more vigorous defence of their faith against Protestant sects.

Pope John Paul II visited India twice, in 1986 and in 1999. On his State visit to India in Nov., '99, he said "People of Asia need Jesus Christ and His Gospel. Asia is thirsting for living water that Jesus alone can give.'Ecclesia in Asia hopes that' Just as in the first millennium the– Cross was planted in the soil of Europe, and in the second on that of America and Africa, we can pray that in the third millennium a great harvest of faith will be reaped in this vast and vital continent." The Statesman's headline (an Indian newspaper) was "Conversion is the basic Christian tenet". The Pioneer (another Indian newspaper) in its front–page headline reported "Spread Christianity in Asia". The Indian Express editorially (Nov. 9, 1999) commented, "Motivated dialogue is no dialogue, Your Holiness". Indian Express added that those who expected the Pope to unfold a new doctrine that took into account the religious and cultural diversities that Asian continent represents seem to have been disappointed because he continued to believe that religious values Asian religions teach await their fulfilment in Jesus Christ. In other words, the editorial noted, the dialogue is with a view to furthering the mission of conversion to Catholic faith.

During this 1999 visit, the Pope is also reported to have said, "I begin this visit with sincere interest in all religions of India and my interest is marked by genuine respect by attention to what we have in common, by a desire to promote inter–religious dialogues and fruitful collaboration between people of all different faiths."(Hindustan Times: April 3, 2005)

Johnson Punneliparambil has written in the Hindustan Times (August 26, 1996) "The Christian missionaries propagate their faith only in response to the mandate given to them by Jesus Christ: "Go therefore and make disciples of all the nations, baptizing them in the name of the Father and of the Son and of the Holy Spirit, teaching them to observe all that I have commanded you" (Matthew 28:19–20). This mandate of Jesus finds its meaning only in the context of his entire gospel. In line with the Old Testament prophets, Jesus invited people to conversion (Matthew 4:17; Mark 1:15). Conversion for Jesus was not a mere change of religion, but a change of heart. The Greek words used in the Bible to denote conversion are Metanoia and Epistrophe. Metanoia tends to stress more the processes of thinking and willing that lie behind an action, whereas epistrophe emphasizes more the visible characteristics of an external act." It can be forcefully argued that there is similar a mandate for Hindu priests in RV (X.191), AV (III.30), and Yaj (XXVI.02) and in Shrimad Bhagwadgita (XVIII.68–69) etc. (See paras 2.6 and 3.7) to seek conversion of non–Hindus to Hinduism.

In 1993, under Pope John Paul II, the Vatican established diplomatic relations with the State of Israel. He became the first Pope to have prayed in a synagogue in 1986. Rev. John I. Jenkins, president of the University of Notre Dame and John Cavadini, chairman of its theology department, recalling the legacy of late Pope John Paul II wrote in the International Herald Tribune (April 4, 2005): "His outreach to the Jewish people was remarkable. He spoke of a special relationship between the Church and the Jews and insisted that the Old Convenant had never been revoked."

In his historic and welcome efforts for inter–faith reconciliations, Pope John Paul II became the first Pontiff ever to enter a mosque in Damascus, Syria in May 2001 and urged Christians and Muslims to forgive each other. He said: "For all the times that Muslims and Christians have offended one another, we need to seek forgiveness from the Almighty and to offer each other forgiveness."

Earlier, in March 2000, Pope John Paul II had asked forgiveness for sins of Roman Catholics through the ages, singling out the mistreatment of Jews and violations of rights of ethnic groups (The Gleanor, March 13, 2000, Jamaica). On behalf of the Vatican, five Vatican Cardinals and two bishops made confessions of sins with a response from the Pope. Cardinal Edward Cassidy spoke about sins against Jews. Other confessions touched on treatment of racial and ethnic groups and "contempt for their culture and religious traditions and toward women who are all too often humiliated and emarginated."

In May 2001, the Pope sought forgiveness from the Orthodox Church in Greece. He said: "For the occasions past and present, when sons and daughters of the Catholic Church have sinned by action or omission against this Orthodox brothers and sisters, may the Lord grant us the forgiveness we beg of him." (The Sunday Observer, May 06, 2001, Jamaica)

On 26th August 2004, Pope John Paul II returned Vatican's copy of a Russian Orthodox icon (Kazan) to Russia hoping it would pave the way for reconciliations between the Russian Orthodox Church and the Catholics. Vatican officials had floated the idea of a possible stopover of the Pope (a person of Slav origin from Poland) in Kazan during a proposed trip to Mangolia in August 2003 but the trip was postponed as the Russian Orthodox leaders continued to accuse stridently the Vatican of proselytizing since restraints on religious freedom in Russia were eased. The original icon had appeared in the Russian city of Kazan in 1579 and is credited with working miracles. Patriarch Aleksy II, born in Estonia, is the current head of Russian Orthodox Church. This is another example of irritation caused by intra–religion conversions. Directly addressing his counterpart, Patriarch Aleksy II, Pope John Paul II said: "May it (copy of Kazan icon) speak to him of the desire and the firm will of the Pope of Rome to progress together with them on the path of mutual understanding and reconciliation, to spread the day of full unity of the faithful", before touching the icon to his lips.

The Vatican has been calling upon leaders of the European Union that the proposed Constitution of the European Union should make specific mention of the Christian roots of Europe. The preamble to the draft Constitution, as finalized by Valery Giscard d'Estaing Committee, reads: "Conscious that Europe is a continent that has brought forth civilization; that its inhabitants, arriving in successive waves from earliest times, have gradually developed the values underlying humanism: equality of persons, freedom, and respect for reason. Drawing inspiration from the cultural, religious and humanist inheritance of Europe, the values of which, still present in its heritage, have embedded within the life of society the central role of the human person and his or her inviolable and inalienable rights, and respect for law." The Vatican was not satisfied with this preamble. Poland, Portugal, Italy, Spain, Ireland, etc. were also pushing hard to have some specific reference to Christianity in the EU Constitution. UK, Belgium, France and other countries were opposed to include any more specific reference to Christianity in the EU Constitution. In June, 2004, EU Draft Constitution was accepted without making more specific reference to Christian roots. Visibly upset at the EU's failure to mention Christianity in its newly–agreed Constitution, Pope John Paul II said that Europe's Christian roots cannot be overlooked. The official Vatican spokesman said the Holy See was disappointed that the opposition of some governments had prevented an explicit reference to Christian roots in the Constitution. "It shows a disregard for historical evidence and for the Christian identity of the European population," Joaquin Navarro–Valls said in a statement.

The Indian Express (May 15, 2004) under the caption,

"Vatican warns Catholics marrying Muslims", reported that the Vatican on May 14, 2004 had warned Catholic women to think hard before marrying a Muslim and urged Muslims to show more respect for human rights, gender equality and democracy. The Vatican has advised such Catholic women marrying non–Catholics that they must insist on Church policy that children born of such mixed marriages be baptized and brought up as Catholics. It further advised such Catholic brides not to sign Kalama or Shahada at the time of marriage or subsequently amounting to conversion to Islam (also reported in International Herald Tribune of May 15–16, 2004).

Pope John Paul II (1920–2005) was elected Pope on 16th October 1978. He was the first Slavic person from Eastern Europe and the second non–Italian to become the Pope. Pope Adrian VI was a Dutchman. Pope John Paul II was born on 18th May, 1920 as Karol Jozef Wojtyla in Wadowice town, 50 km southwest of Krakow, Poland. His mother Kaczorowska was of Lithuanian origin. He died on 2nd April 2005 at his official residence in Rome.

Women activists and feminists were not very happy with the pronouncements of Pope John Paul II. "A woman must give priority to her role as mother before any other public or professional activity", he wrote in an exhortation entitled 'Familiaris Consortio' (The Chistian Family in the Modern World). "Her original mission, for which she cannot be replaced, is to stay at home to raise children", this document said. John Paul II's 1998 letter 'Mulieris Dignitatem' (The Dignity of Women) did little to appease those who objected to his stand against abortion, divorce and the ordination of women as priests. Joanna Manning, co–founder of Catholic Organisations for Renewal, for her part, criticized the late Pope JP–II for trying to re–establish humility and subordination as the traditional virtues of women.(sify.com., April 4, 2005,

Pope's ingrained views on women)

According to the International Herald Tribune (April 4, 2005), the encyclical issued in March 1995, "Evangelium Vitae" (Gospel of Life), condemned abortion and euthanasia, called on Catholics to oppose laws that sought to legitimize them, upheld the Church's ban on contraceptions and condemned experimentation with human embryo.Two months later, another encyclical was issued, 'Ut Unum Sint' (That They May Be One), which called for greater unity among Christians asserting that the Pope remained the absolute doctrinal authority, an article of faith among the Catholics, but a claim not accepted by many other Christian sects. It editorially commented that Pope John Paul II was a man who used tools of modernity to struggle against the modern world. He improved the Church's relations with Jews and Muslims.At the dawn of the third millennium, he delivered a solemn apology for errors of the Church, including religious intolerance and injustice towards women and the poor.Under his direction, the Church denounced anti–semitism, although it did not criticize Pope Pius XII for his equivocal response to the Nazi holocaust. For Catholics, the editorial says, he was more complicated, who resisted all attempts to liberalise the Church's teachings on birth–control, abortions, homosexuality, priestly marriages, divorce and the ordination of women. This champion of freedom brooked no dissent in his flock, and his travels sought not only to minister the faithfuls but also to make the Church more disciplined, heirarchical and orthodox. For all his worldwide evangelism, the editorial claims, John Paul II left behind a Church with a dwindling number of priests and nuns and a shrinking percentage of world's population as followers; Islam has overtaken Catholicism as the globe's most popular religion.

Cardinal Joseph Ratzinger, a German born in Bavaria, was

the prefect of the Congregation for the Doctrine of Faith under Pope John Paul II. After the death of Pope John Paul II, he was elected on 19th April 2005 as the new Pope; he assumed the Papacy under the name of Pope Benedict XVI. He is the 265th Roman Catholic Pope.

5.6 Dates Of X-mas

X–mas is globally celebrated on 25th December as the birthday of Lord Jesus Christ but not by all Christian faiths. Armenians celebrate it on 6th January. Russian Orthodox Church also celebrates it on 6th January. In early Christianity, Christ's birthday was celebrated on various dates including 6th January, 21st April, 5th May etc. However, about 300 years after crucifixion, the Pope decided that Christ's birthday be celebrated on 25th December to coincide with the popular Roman festival of celebrating birthday of MITHRA, the Sun God (*natalis solis invicti*) believed to be born on the winter solstice day in December. From the 25th December, duration of daytime starts lengthening/increasing figuratively implying that the Sun has been born and is growing up day–by–day. Therefore, some Christians feel that origin of X–mas is pagan. Some sects of Christians don't celebrate Easter or Christmas. The Catholic encyclopaedia also says "X–mas was not among the earliest festivals of the Church." Roman Emperor Aurelian had chosen Dec. 25th as birthday of Sun god; after conversion of Roman Emperor Constantine to Christianity, the Church of Rome started commemorating the birthday of Christ on the same day viz., 25th December.

Christians in Jerusalem did not accept 25th December as the birthday of Christ until the sixth century AD. The Gospel of Luke (1/26) informs that in the sixth month, the Angel Gabriel was sent from God unto a city of Galilee, named Nazareth, and he appeared unto Mary and said that she would conceive and give birth to the Son of God. So, after nine months, Jesus in normal course ought to have been born in the month of March, if sixth month meant the month of June. Luke (II.8) says that at the time of birth of Jesus: "And there were in the same country (near Bethlehem) shepherds abiding in the field, keeping watch over their flock by night." It is said that in Palestine/Bethlehem, December is the coldest month when shepherds and their flock are not likely to be there in fields by night. Shepherds are out in fields with their flocks in better months of summer. The Holy Qur'an, vide surah (XIX.20) does attest that Mary (Miriam) was a virgin & chaste, untouched by any mortal man before conceiving Jesus. But surah (XIX.23) states that Mary gave birth to child Isa (Jesus) near the trunk of a palm tree, not in a cave/stable. Surah (XIX.25) says that fresh, ripe dates fell upon Mary when shaking trunk of the palm tree. It is said that ripe dates fall only in the summer months in Palestine. Thus, both Holy Qur'an and Luke's Gospel create some doubts about the correctness of the present popular belief that Jesus was born in December. These are great puzzles of religion but could always be explained as miracles of Jesus being the Son of God. In fact, Luke (1/37) informs, 'For with God, nothing shall be impossible.'

5.7 Anti–Ageing DHEA and Murti–Pooja

The primary mode of worship by the Rigvedic people was undoubtedly performing yajna/havan. But some people wrongly presume that Murti–pooja i.e., idol–worship is not sanctioned by Vedas. In fact, the Vedas accept *nirankaar* (without physical features, featureless) as well as *saakaar* (with physical features) forms of deities. During Rigvedic time, yajna/havan was no doubt the dominant form of worship; after the Vedic period, worship of *saakaar* forms of deities slowly became the dominant form.

There are many richas in the Rigveda suggesting *saakaar*

form of deities. In many Vedic richas, Gods are being decorated with ornaments, their forms are being praised (radiant etc.) which proves that *saakaar swaroopa* was accepted. RV (I.79.1) mentions golden–hair Agni and RV (I.79.5) says: "Mouth of Agni glows with many flames." In RV (I.21.2), Indra and Agni are decorated with ornaments meaning that these deities have *saakaar roopa.* RV (III.4.5.) reads: "May the many deities who are engendered in sensible shapes at sacrifices come to this our rite." In RV (II.33.5), Rudra (Lord Shiva) is said to be soft–bellied, of a tawny hue (brownish/wheatish colour) and with handsome chin. In RV (I.9.3), Indra, too, has handsome chin. In RV (X.86.8), Indra's wife has a beautiful body. In RV(I.7.2), Indra is richly decorated. RV (I.8.7) talks of the belly of Indra. RV (I.3.1) says: "Asvins, Cherishers of pious acts, long armed, accept with outstretched hands the sacrificial viands." RV (II.33.9) reads: "Firm with strong limbs, assuming many forms fierce, and tawny coloured, he shines with brilliant golden ornaments, vigour is inseparable from Rudra, the Supreme Ruler and Lord of this world." In RV (II.33.10), Rudra bears arrows and a bow, wears an adorable and omniform necklace. In RV (II.33.11), Rudra is riding his car and is ever youthful. In RV (II.33.14) he is a 'radiant deity'.In RV (I.152.2) trishul (trir–asri) of Lord Shiva is mentioned. In RV (V.53.4): "Maruts are all self–irradiating, splendid in ornaments, in arms, in garlands, in breast–plates, in chariots and in bows." The word Shiva in Sanskrit does occur in RV (X.92.9). Name of Lord Vishnu occurs in RV (I.22.16–21), (I.154–156), (V.3.3), (X.93.11), etc. All these confirm the concept of *saakaar* form right from the Rigvedic times.

The *saakaar roopa* (form) of deity may be seen in the following three richas:

स्थिरेभिरङ्गैः पुरूरूप उग्रो बभ्रुः शुक्रेभिः पिपिशे हिरण्यैः ।
ईशानादस्य भुवनस्य भूरेर्न वा उ योषद्रुद्रादसुर्यम् ॥9॥
RV (II.33.9)

"(Firm) with strong limbs, assuming many forms fierce, and

tawny–coloured, he shines with brilliant golden ornaments; vigour is inseparable from Rudra, the supreme ruler and lord of this world."

अर्हन्बिभर्षि सायकानि धन्वार्हन्निष्कं यजतं विश्वरूपम्।
अर्हन्निदं दयसे विश्वमभ्वं न वा ओजीयो रुद्र त्वदस्ति।10॥
RV (II.33.10)

"Worthy (of reverence), you bear arrows and a bow; worthy (of praise), you wear an adorable and omniform necklace; worthy (of adoration), you preserve all this vast universe: there is no one more powerful than you."

स्तुहि श्रुतं गर्तसदं युवानं मृगं न भीममुपहत्नुमुग्रम्।
मृळा जरित्रे रुद्र स्तवानोऽन्यं ते अस्मन्नि वपन्तु सेनाः॥11॥
RV (II.33.11)

"Glorify the renowned Rudra, riding in his car, ever youthful, destructive, fierce like a formidable wild beast: Rudra, propitiated by praise, grant happiness to him who praises (you), and let your hosts destroy him who is our adversary."

In the Holy Gita too, there are many shlokas such as (IV.5–9), (IX.26) etc. in which Lord Krishna Himself says that He is born in person/ human form i.e., in *saakaar* form.

Our Vedic ancestors were very good at group prayers, collective recitation of mantras and could focus easily on God, whether *nirakaar* or *saakaar*, through meditation and concentration. Different idols were later conceived, for different manifestations of one and the same God to help ordinary people to easily attain *dhyan–magana–pooja* i.e., a state of focused meditation by visualising that idol with their eyes closed. Present day science has discovered that those who do focused meditation everyday enjoy higher levels of DHEA (dehydroepiandrosterone, a 19–carbon steroid), which is anti–ageing and anti–stress. It is secreted by the adrenal glands, which sit on the top of kidneys. It is not found in any food item. DHEA hormone reaches its highest levels at around 25 years of age and, thereafter, declines in almost a straight line year by year till it falls to 5 to 10% of peak levels of youth, in old age.

Dr. Dean Ward, M.D. has written in his web–article that Dehydroepiandrosterone or DHEA, as it is more often called, is a steroid hormone produced in the adrenal gland. It is the most abundant steroid in the bloodstream and is present at even higher levels in brain tissues. DHEA levels are known to fall precipitously with age, falling 90% from age 20 to age 90. DHEA is known to be a precursor to the numerous steroid sex hormones (including estrogen and testosterone) which serve well–known refunctions, but the specific biological role of DHEA itself is not so well understood. It is difficult for researchers to separate the effects of DHEA from those of the primary sex steroids into which it is metabolized. The apparent lack of any direct hormone action for DHEA has prompted the suggestion that it may serve the role of a 'buffering hormone' which would alter the state–dependency of other steroid hormones. Although the specific mechanisms of action for DHEA are only partially understood, supplemental DHEA has been shown to have anti–ageing, anti–obesity and anti–cancer influences. In addition, it is known to stabilize nerve–cell growth and is being tested in Alzheimer's patients. Dr. William Regelson, Dr. Mohammed Kalimi and Dr. Roger Loria, in their introductory remarks have written: "DHEA modulates diabetes, obesity, carcinogenesis, tumor growth, neurite outgrowth, virus and bacterial infection, stress, pregnancy, hypertension, collagen and skin integrity, fatigue, depression, memory and immune responses." (www.ceri.com/dhea.htm)

DHEA (dehydroepiandrosterone) (5–Androstene–

3«beta»–ol–17–one) is called 'mother of hormones', or prohormone because it is further converted to generate 50 other essential hormones. For example, DHEA is converted to androgens (male hormones) or estrogens (female hormones) in the cells. DHEA is the most abundant hormone in our blood, and adequate blood DHEA level is critical for many vital hormonal and metabolic functions of our body. Our bodies produce less and less DHEA as we age, and as a result, our blood DHEA level decreases as we get older, generally falling significantly after the age of 30.

Improved DHEA levels have been correlated with improved sense of well being, reduced body fat, improved skin tone and moisture, sex drive, immunity, memory and bone density. Numerous studies have proven great correlations between DHEA deficiency or insufficiency and a variety of diseases and

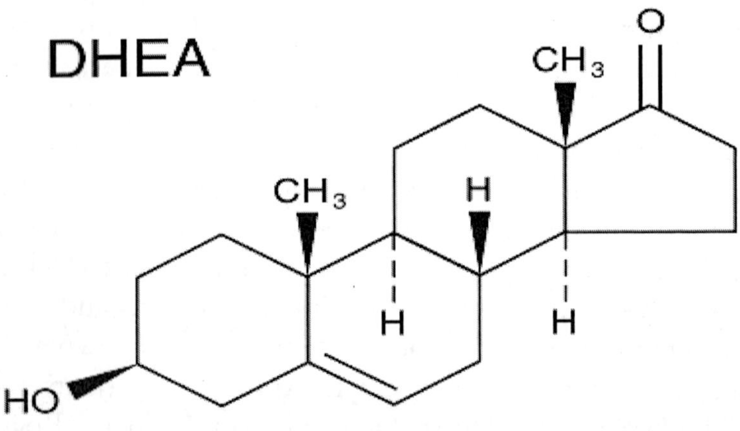

symptoms. For example, decreased levels of DHEA predispose humans and animals to higher probability of breast cancer, autoimmune diseases, osteoporosis, and Alzheimer's diseases, etc. A study reported in the prestigious journal *Science* in August 2002 directly correlates increased blood DHEA level to longevity.

DHEA was first isolated from urine by Adolf Butenandt in

1931, who won Nobel Prize for this. S–DHEA, the sulfate ester of DHEA, was isolated in 1944. In 1960, Etienne–Emile Baulieu discovered that DHEA is produced from adrenal cortex. (http://www.dreampharm.com/zDHEA.asp)

Researchers have found that people with higher DHEA levels tend to live longer, enjoy healthier lives than those with lower levels of DHEA. (www.healthandage.com). In 1978, Dr. R. Keith Wallace found that meditators were biologically younger than their age. In 1986, Dr. Jay Glaser found that DHEA levels were higher in meditators. Wallace studied eighty–four meditators and found that short–term meditators were five years younger than their chronological age, and the long–term meditators were about twelve years younger. Glaser took about 300 experienced meditators and compared their DHEA levels to those of about 1500 non–meditators and found that in all women's groups, DHEA levels were significantly higher for meditators, and the same was true for eight out of eleven men's groups. Glaser found the biggest differences in older people. The meditating men over the age of 45 had 23% more DHEA, the women 47% more. Glaser also noticed that older meditators had the same DHEA levels as people five to ten years younger. Meditation slows or even reverses the ageing process. Especially after menopause, hormone estrogen and progesterone become much reduced in women hastening the ageing effect.

This is the scientific secret of worshipping our *ishta–devata* (family God idol) with focused meditation, as prescribed in Hinduism at least for ten minutes everyday. It keeps one medically fit by elevating his DHEA levels, by reducing his biological age below his actual age. Therefore, to derive full benefits of *murti–pooja,* simple mechanical *namaskar* and flower offerings is not sufficient, one must sit before his *ishta–devata* for five to ten minutes everyday with his eyes closed visualising that very idol. This type of daily *pooja* (worshipping) with meditation causes maximum formation of DHEA. And the body creates it especially in the morning time. That is why Hinduism prescribes doing *pooja* in the morning time. Our Vedic ancestors, by sheer observation, had become aware of this causal relationship between meditation and better health and passed on this knowledge to us in the form of *murti–pooja*.

Hindu religion says that we should offer water to the rising sun in the morning after bath with wet body. Present day science has found out that when rays of morning (still reddish) sun fall on our wet body, there is maximum formation of Vitamin D in that body, which protects that person from osteoporosis in the old age.This is the secret of offering water to Sun while standing in river water.

Contemporary medical science accepts that all health disorders have two components, the mind and the body. A disease affects human body when the first component (also called the subtle component) has been negatively affected by anxiety, stress and emotional swings, self–doubts, uncertainty etc. and consequently the natural immunity of body falls. As the immunity begins to fall, an unhealthy food and unhealthy life–style add to the destructive process resulting into sickness. Hindu rishis had recognized this cycle and tackled the first part first by prescribing yoga and meditation to keep mind healthy and focused.

5.8 Conclusion

So, there are wheels within wheels in matters religious; these are too complicated for a common man, one does not know which is Truth and which is not and the best way out, in my humble opinion, is not to get involved in religious bigotry but to live and let live in peace and harmony with neighbours. Let us avoid the endless futile debate on which religion is the better one, or, is the best one.We should avoid religious extremism. 'Love thy neighbour' should be our motto, more so, as India is a multi–religious country. Let one not question the correctness of religious faith of the other. Let us sort out our problems amicably and peacefully. Matters of faith are not subject to legal scrutiny or tests of rationality. The Supreme Court (JJ MJ Rao and AP Misra) as per Times of India (3rd April 2000) has also rightly decided that faith and belief couldn't be judged through any judicial scrutiny. Let us live happily under the banner of our tricolour reflecting our unity in diversity. Concepts of *Vasudhaiva Kutumbakam* i.e., universal brotherhood and *sarva dharma sambhava* are the best policies for us in India and all over the world. There should be more active inter–faith dialogue to realize these goals.

God is one; all paths (religions) lead to Him, or, all gods are manifestations of one and the same almighty God. This should be our guiding belief. This is what the Vedas also preach: RV (I.89.10), RV (I.164.46), RV (X.114.5) and RV (X.121.10) etc. The often–quoted RV (I.164.46) richa is "*....ekam sad vipra bahudha vadantyagni*"... meaning "He is one Reality; sages call Him by different names". These four Rigvedic richas prove that monotheism is the bed–rock of Hinduism. Atharvaveda (XIII.5.7) says: "Into Him is entered this power, He Himself is one, single, one only." AV (XIII.5.8) reaffirms: "All the gods in Him become single." So, the thirty three crore (a metaphor for multitude, a figurative phrase) deities in Hinduism are actually, the Vedas command, different manifestations of one and only one God. But some people, out of their ignorance, start counting one by one thirty three crore deities in Hinduism and land up no where! (One crore is equal to ten million)

Six

GENDER EQUALITY IN THE VEDAS

The Vedas do not discriminate against women. There is no gender bias against women in the Vedas. Rigvedic richas were revealed to over 414 rishis out of which, as far as I could make out, twenty-nine are ladies (rishikas) implying gender equality. Women were neither discriminated in matters of religion & education nor were prevented from gaining excellence in the society. Presence of so many rishikas in the Rigveda proves that Almighty God Himself considered women fit enough, qualified and eligible to receive divine revelations. Therefore, women have equal access to and equal claim over the Vedas. If God Himself did not discriminate against women in matters of religion, how could any one else or we?

One who closely goes through texts of RV (X.191), AV (III.30), and Yaj (26.02) etc. will notice that there is no gender discrimination. There was no exclusion of women in any field. The Vedic richas talk of *samano mantrah*, *samano manah*, *samanam mantrambhi mantraye* for all, not excluding women. The exclusion, by definition, has to be express and specific which is not there in the Vedas. In fact, sukta RV(V.28) is the express Rigvedic authority sanctioning female priests in Hinduism because in RV (V.28.1), it is rishika Visvavara who, facing the east, bearing the ladle with oblations is proceeding alone to the sacred fire to worship. She is mantra–drastya rishika of (V.28). Yajurveda (26.02) (richa No. 1460) enjoins imparting Vedic education to all, not excluding women:

यथेमां वाचं कल्याणी मावदानि जनेभ्यः। ब्रह्मराजन्याभ्या शूद्राय चार्याय च स्वाय चारणाय च। प्रियो देवानां दक्षिणायै दातुरिह भूयासमयं मे कामः समृध्यतामुप मादो जमतु॥2॥(Yajurveda 26.02)

RTH Griffith & Dr. Ravi Prakash Arya translate, "That I to all the people say address this salutary speech, To priest and nobleman, Sudra and Arya to one of our own kin and to the stranger." One may note that there is no exclusion of women in this Vedic richa.

Atharvaveda AV (XI.5.18) expressly sanctions study of the Vedas by girls/women: "**ब्रह्मचर्येण कन्या, युवानं विन्दते पतिम्।**" Its translation by Whitney & Joshi: "By Vedic-studentship, a girl wins a young husband." In fact, there are some richas like Yaj (III.60) which are to be recited and can be recited only by a girl or unmarried female as in these, girl prays to get good qualified husband.

A list of thirty-one lady rishis (rishikas) who were revealed Vedic richas is given below. Out of these, fourteen rishikas were revealed complete suktas; they composed these independently:

Lady Rishis (Rishika) in Vedas

Sl. No	Name of the Rishika	Richa revealed to/ composed by rishika
1.	Romasaa Brahmavadini	RV (I.126.7)
2.	Lopamudra (wife of rishi Agastya and daughter of King of Vidarbha, Mah–arashtra)	RV (I.179.1–2) Yaj (XVII.11–15) Yaj (36.20)

Continued....

3.	Aditi	RV (IV.18.7)
4.	Visvavara Atreyi HH Wilson & Joshi clarify that this sukta (V.28) attests that a female is discharging the office of a priest worshipping the gods at dawn with hymns and oblations. This Sukta (V.28) is the Rigvedic authority sanctioning women priests in Hinduism because in (V.28.1), it is rishika Visvavara who, facing the east, bearing the ladle with the oblations is proceeding to the scared fire to worship.	RV (V.28) (six shlokas) (Complete Sukta)
5.	Saraswati Angirasi	RV (VIII.1.34)
6.	Apapa Atreyi	RV (VIII.91) (Seven shlokas) (Complete Sukta)
7.	Sikata Nivavari	RV (IX.86.11–20)
8.	Akristabhasadi	RV (IX.86.31–40)
9.	Sikhandini	RV (IX.104) (Six sloka)
10.	Yami Vavasvati	RV (X.10.six shlokas) RV (X.154) (Complete Sukta)
11.	Indrasnusa Vasukra Patni	RV (X.28.1)
12.	Ghosa Kalsvati	RV(X.39) (fourteen Sh–lokas (complete Sukta) (X.40) (fourteen Shlokas complete Sukta)

Continued....

13.	Gaupayana : (One of the composers)	RV (V.24) (X.57) (X.59) (X.60)
14.	Agastya Svasa aisa mata or Agastya Bhagini	RV (X.60.6)
15.	Aditi Daksayani	RV (X.72) (nine shlokas) (Complete sukta)
16.	Surya Savitri	RV (X.85) (47 shlokas) (Complete sukta) AV (XIV.1.....(64 shlokas) AV (XIV.2).....(75 shlokas)
17.	Urvaisi (wife of King Pururavas)	RV (X.95. nine shlokas)
18.	Prajaptya Daksini	RV (X.107 (eleven shlokas) (Complete sukta)
19.	Sarma Devasuni	RV (X.108) (six shlokas)
20.	Juhu Brahmajaya	RV (X.109) (seven shlokas) (Complete sukta)
21.	Vac Ambhrini or Vag–ambhrini	RV (X.125) (eight shlokas) (Complete sukta)
22.	Ratri Bhardvaji	RV (X.127) (eight shlokas) (complete sukta)
23.	Godha	RV (X.134.6–7), Samaveda (176)
24.	Jarita	RV (X.142. 1–2)
25.	Indrani	RV (X.145) (six shlokas) (Complete sukta) (X.86.2-6,9–10 15–18) (eleven shlokas)
26.	Sradha Kamayani	RV (X.151)(five sloka) (complete sukta)
27	Indramatarah Devajani	RV (X.153) (five sloka)

Continued....

		(complete sukta) Sam (120, 175)
28.	Paulomi Sachi	RV (X.159) (six sloka) (complete sukta)
29.	Sarparajni (Kadru)	RV (X.189) (three shlokas) (complete sukta) Sam (630– 632), Yaj (III. 6–8)
30.	Saraswati	Yaj (XXVIII.24–28)
31.	Savitri	AV (II.26) (XIX.31)

Seven

SATI AND WIDOW REMARRIAGE

The Sati or suttee (i.e., widow burning, self–immolation of a widow on the funeral pyre of her deceased husband) was prohibited by many Indian Kings including some Mughals. The Portuguese administration in Goa had forbidden *sati* as early as 1510 AD. The British Govt. also prohibited it by law vide Regulation XVII of 1829 declaring Sati illegal and punishable by the Criminal Courts as culpable homicide for which capital sentence could be awarded. Lord William Bentinck, then Governor General, had shown personal courage to enact and introduce this law. The orthodox Hindus, ignorant of the Veda, had protested this legislation as a violation of their religion and went into an appeal to the Privy Council in England but the Privy Council rightly dismissed their appeal. Thus, widow burning became illegal in India by a law enacted by a foreign power. In Bengal alone, in the nineteenth century, the number of widow burning was about twelve hundred a year implying that all widows were not burnt. After Independence, laws against widow burning have been further tightened.

On this subject, Jawahar Lal Nehru has written in his 'Glimpses of World History' (page 431): "A great deal of credit is taken by the British for the abolition of what is (rather incorrectly) called sati, the practice of a Hindu widow burning herself on the funeral pyre of her husband. They deserve some credit for this, but as a matter of fact the government only took action after many years of agitation by Indian reformers headed by Raja Ram Mohan Roy. Previous to them other rulers, and especially the Marathas, had forbidden it; the Portuguese Albuquerque had abolished the practice in Goa. It was put down by the British as a result of Indian agitation and Christian missionary endeavours. So far as I can remember, this was the only reform of religious significance which was brought about by the British Government."

In August/Sept. 2002, one case of committing *sati* and two failed attempts to commit sati in Madhya Pradesh were reported in the media. Reports also appeared that the Hon'ble Rajasthan High Court allowed prayers within premises of *Rani Sati Mandir* of Jhunjhunu district, but prohibited organising fairs, distribution of pamphlets and performing *chunri* ceremony at the temple till final orders. In August 2003, the Hon'ble Rajsthan High Court asked the State Govt of Rajsthan to prevent *Sati* melas from being held and to strictly enforce the law. The Hindustan Times (20th March, 2004) reported that a 65–year–old woman (Rukia Devi) committed *Sati* by jumping into the funeral pyre of her husband (Raghu Yadav) at Sakardiha village, Samastipur district in Bihar. On his return from this village, the officer–in–charge of Hasnapur Police Station confirmed this incident.

Incidents of committing Sati have generally been reported from the Hindi speaking north Indian states. Some reported incidents are: (i) Saraswati, wife of Todaram, Bhimsar Police Station, Churu, 16th August, 1955, (ii) the wife of Brigadier Jabar Singh, 7th December, 1957 (iii) Sikar, 6th April, 1973 (iv) Sikar, Hathideh, 1978 (v) Omkanwar, Sikar, Jharali, 1979 (vi) Sonkanwar, Nagore, Neemari Kotihari, 29th February, 1980

(vii) Savitri, Kotadi, Sikar (viii) Roopkanwar, Devarala, 4th September, 1987 (ix) failed attempt by Jaswant Kaur, Devipura, Jaipur, 12th March, 1983 and (x) failed attempt by Gokul Bai of Jaipur, 27th January, 1987.

Some people assert that the Rigveda, vide richa, (X.18.7) commands a Hindu widow to mount funeral pyre of her deceased husband. Pro–sati lobby quotes this richa to claim the Vedic sanction for committing *sati.* Let us, as usual, examine this claim also in depth. One website (www.dalistan.com) attributes this translation of RV (X.18.7) to PV Kane: "Let these women, whose husbands are worthy and living enter the house with *ghee* applied as *corrylium* (to their eyes). Let these wives first step into the pyre, tearless without any affliction and well adorned." One may note that even this English translation does not categorically state that let these widows first step into the pyre. This translation simply says, "Let these wives first step into pyre." As per common sense, from the very moment of the death of her husband, a Hindu woman is no more called 'a wife' but a widow (*vidhava*). As we will see, the word *vidhava* has been used in many richas of the Rigveda, so, it cannot be argued that the Rigveda was not aware of the term *vidhava.* Therefore, the phrase 'these wives' in the above the translation attributed to Kane cannot be linked to 'widows.'

7.1 Vedic Command To Separate Living Beings From The Dead

In fact *Sukta* (X.18) commands a Hindu widow to return to the world of living beings; to return to her house to live with her children and grand children and the Rigveda confers on her all the properties of her deceased husband. The Rigveda and the Atharva Vedas command immediate re–marriage of a widow to another person, not necessarily limited to her brother–in–law (*devar*).

One should go through all the fourteen richas of this 18th Sukta (revealed to Rishi Sunkusuk Yamayan) to understand the true and correct meaning of (X.18.7).

The third richa (X.18.3) commands, "May those who are living remain separate from dead...." (Rigveda Samhita by HH Wilson, Arya and Joshi). Dr. Wendy D. Flaherty, in her book the *Rigveda* (Penguin Classics) (page 52) translates: "Those who are alive have now parted from those who are dead....." Ralph T.H. Griffith translates....."Divided from the dead are these, the living:....." Shri Ram Sharma Acharya of Bareilly in his *Rigveda* (in Hindi) translates: *"mritak ke pass se jeevit manushya laut aavey......"* Dr. Ganga Sahay Sharma, in his *Rigveda* (Delhi Pocket Books) translates: "*ye jite huve log marey huve vyaktiyo ke pass se laut aavey......*" This command of the *Rigveda* to leave behind the dead; to separate from the dead is equally applicable to Hindu widows too, as they are also living (*jeevit*) persons.

इमा नारीरविधवाः सुपत्नीराञ्जनेन सर्पिषा सं विशन्तु।
अनश्रवोऽनमीवाः सुरत्ना आ रोहन्तु जनयो योनिमग्रे॥7॥
(RV: X.18.7)

7.2 Reappraisal Of RV (X.18.7) And (X.18.8)

English translation of the above quoted seventh richa (X.18.7) as given by HH Wilson is: "Let these women who are not widows, who have good husbands, enter (anointed) with unguent and butter. Let women without tears, without sorrow, and decorated with jewels, first proceed to the house." There is no stepping into pyre in this translation by Wilson.

Dr. Wendy O'Flaherty, translates this seventh richa thus: "These women who are not widows, who have good husbands let them take their places using butter to anoint their eyes. Without tears, without sickness, well dressed let them first climb into the marriage bed."

Shri Ram Sharma Acharya translates "*yeh sunder patiwaali sadhawa naariya ghrit yukta kaajal lagaati hui apne grih ko prapta ho. Yeh naariya aasuuon ko tyag kar manoovikaaroo ko duur karati hui sundar aishwarya waali ho kar sabase aage chalati hui apne gharo ko prapt ho.*"

Dr. Ganga Sahay Sharma, translates it thus: "*Ye sadhawa ewam shobhan patniya naariya ghrit aur anna ke sath apne ghar mey pravesh kare. Ye streeya aasuuon ke bina roga rahit aur shobhan dhan waali ban kar apne ghar mey sabse pehle pahuche.*"

Shri Radhakrishna Shrimali & Smt. Ashalata Upadhyaya of Jodhpur in their Hindi book *Rigveda* (Diamond Pocket books) (page 156), give similar translation of (X.18.7).

Thus, six different authors, from different places and different periods, vouch that the richa (X.18.7) does not refer to widows at all, it does not ask a 'widow' to step into funeral pyre. What this richa says in a nutshell is that married women should be the first (among others) to return to their homes. In fact, a widowed woman is being instructed to return to society from the burial ground after getting remarried then and there itself to a second husband, just after burying the corpse of her previous husband, yes burying. After getting remarried, she (the widow) is being told to return "without tears, without sorrow (for the dead husband), and decorated with jewels (on being remarried)". The sukta (X.18) is really a **burial** sukta. Readers may see that as per these authors, this richa does not say that first these women (widows) step into pyres.There is no funeral pyre in (X.18) as dead body is being buried in the ground. This seventh richa also appears in the Atharvaveda at (XVIII.3.57) and (XII.2.31).

उदीर्ष्व नार्यभि जीवलोकंगतासुमेतमुप शेष एहि।
हस्तग्राभस्य दिधिषोस्तवेदं पत्युर्जनित्वमभि सं बभूथ ॥8॥
(RV: X.18.8)

The eighth richa (X.18.8) specifically and expressly commands a Hindu widow to return alive to her home. HH Wilson translates: "Rise, woman, (and go) to the world of living beings; come, this man near whom you sleep is lifeless; you have enjoyed this state of being the wife of your husband, the suitor who took you by the hand." This verse is to be recited by the dead husband's brother (i.e., the new husband etc.) to the widow, and, he has to make the widow leave her (dead) husband's body as per RV (X.18.3) and Asvalayana Grih Sutra (IV.2.18).

Dr. Wendy D. O'Flaherty, translates: "Rise up, woman, into the world of living. Come here; you are lying beside a man whose life's breath has gone. You were wife of this man who took your hand and desired to have you."

Pt. Shri Ram Sharma Acharya translates this richa: "*Hey mritak ki patni! Tumhara yeh pati mrityu ko prapta ho chuka hai–ab tum iske pass vyartha baidhi ho. Apne putradi aur ghar ka vichar karti hui uutho. Tum ish pati ke sath garbh dharan aadi stree kartavya ko pura kar chuki ho aur tum uske pran ke chale jaane ki baat bhi jaanati ho attah ghar ko lauto.*"

Dr. Ganga Sahai Sharma, translates: "*Hey mritak ki patni! Tum apne putro ewam ghar ka dhyana karke yeha se uutho. Aap marey huey vyakti ke pass kyo soyee ho? Ish Purusah ke panigrahan wa garbhadhan ke anuroop aap vyavahaar kar chuki ho. Aap ishke sath marane ka vichar chhodo.*"

Shrimali and Upadhyaya also give similar translation.

Arthur A. MacDonell, in his book 'A History of Sanskrit Literature' (page106) too says that (X.18.8) is addressed to the widow, who is called upon to rise and take the hand of her new husband, doubtless a brother of the deceased, in accordance with an ancient marriage custom. MacDonell quotes the following translation of (X.18.8) as given by Ralph T.H. Griffith:

Rise up; come to the world of life, O woman;
Thou liest here by one whose soul has left him.
Come: thou hast now entered upon the wifehood
Of this, thy lord, who takes thy hand and woos thee.

Thus, eight different authors from different places and different periods confirm that (X.18.8) actually commands a Hindu widow to return to the world of living beings, return alive to her home and return alive to her children, and take a new husband. Also, this very richa confers upon her full right on the house (matrimonial) of her deceased husband (*apne putradi aur ghar*). In 1995, the Supreme Court interpreted Section 14(1) of the Hindu Succession Act to the effect that a Hindu widow has full ownership rights over properties she inherits from her deceased husband. The Supreme Court said that object of the Hindu Succession Act was to wipe out disabilities imposed by Hindu Shastras. The Supreme Court, thus, restored rights conferred on widows under richa (X.18.8). This richa appears in the Atharvaveda at (XVIII.3.2) also. The Right of a wife on matrimonial home and her right to live with grandsons are reconfirmed in the following marriage richa RV (X.85.42):

इहैव स्तं मा वि यौष्टं विश्वमायुर्व्यश्नुतम्।
क्रीलन्तौ पुत्रैर्नप्तृभिर्मोदमानौ स्वे गृहे ॥42 ॥ RV (X.85.42)

"Abide here together; may you never be separated; live together all your lives, sporting with sons and grandsons, **happy in your own home**." One may note that in the Sanskrit text of this marriage hymn, the word used is *swa–grihe* i.e., one's own home. Thus, the Hindu wife has the Rigvedic right over her matrimonial home and no law can dispossess her. *Swa* implies absolute ownership of her matrimonial home, nothing less.

According to Achraya Sayana, it is the first six richas of

16th Sukta of Xth chapter of Rigveda (X.16.1 to 6), which are to be recited at funeral pyres; none of these six richas either call for burning of widows or make any reference to widows. RV (X.14) (X.16) and (X.154) are funeral hymns but, again, there is no reference to widow burning in these.

Those who misinterpret the Rigveda to say that it sanctions sati do this mischief by changing the last word of richa (X.18.7) to '*yomiagne*' neglecting commands of other richas. What role fire can play if the corpse is going to be buried in the next richas of this sukta? The last word of this richa is actually '*yomiagre*' as shown in the Sanskrit text given above from the Rigveda by HH Wilson and Pt. Shri Ram Sharma Acharya.

In fact, the body of dead husband is not burnt at all on a funeral pyre in this 18th Sukta!! Dr. Wendy O'Flaherty calls it 'the Burial Sukta' in her book, 'The Rigveda.' The dead body is buried in the ground (in a grave) vide tenth, eleventh, twelfth, thirteenth and fourteenth richas of this 18th Sukta. So, whose funeral pyre pro–sati lobby is asking a Hindu widow to mount if the corpse of her husband is being buried in a grave under this very sukta (X.18) of Rigveda!!! Thus, there is no richa in the Rigveda calling for widow burning. In fact, as I said earlier, the Rigveda commands a widow to return alive to her home with her new husband.

Even the discredited Manusmriti confers the right to life upon Hindu widows. Its sloka (V.160) reads "a virtuous wife who after the death of her husband constantly remains chaste, reaches heaven, though she has no son, just like those chaste men" (George Buhler).

Dr AS Altekar of the Banaras Hindu University in his book "The Position of Women in Hindu Civilization" (page 117–119) reconfirms that there is no mention of sati in the Avesta. Nor it is referred to in the funeral hymns of the Rigveda, where it would have been certainly mentioned, Altekar argues, if it had been in existence in the Rigvedic era. "We find no traces of it (i.e., sati)", Dr Altekar adds, "whatsoever down to 400 BC. The Brahamana literature (1500 BC to 700 BC) is silent about it, and the Grihyasutras (600 BC to 300 BC) though describe numerous rituals and sanskars make no mention of sati". According to Dr Altekar, the Buddhist literature is also unaware of sati. Had it existed during the life time of Buddha, he certainly would have opposed it in his sermons as he was opposed to sacrifice of even animals. Chanakya does not mention anything about sati. Authors of Dharmasutras (400 BC to 300 AD) and writers of early smritis like Manu and Yajnavalkya (100 AD to 300AD) have laid down detailed rules about women and widows but none of them, as per Dr Altekar, has suggested sati. The Manusmriti does not mention sati at all.

The custom of sati, Dr Altekar opines, appears to have begun in India from about 400AD. Some writers began referring to sati in their writings from 600AD onwards. Even these writers did not hold it to be mandatory for widows but only as a second alternative while regarding ascetic life preferable to committing sati. Such is the case, Dr. Altekar says, with Brihaspati, Parasara (IV.26–28) and the Agnipurana. From 700 A.D. fiery advocates of sati began to come forward to extol it in increasing numbers. During the period 700–1100 A.D., sati became more frequent in northern India During the period 1815–28, the Calcutta Division recorded 5099 incidents of sati and the orthodox Benares Division recorded much less 1165 incidents of sati showing that even in those days all Hindu widows were not burnt alive. Nor all Hindu widows used to opt for sati.

In short, sati is neither sanctioned by the Rigveda nor sanctioned by any Vedic literature.

7.3 Practices In Other Civilizations

Ancient records show that the custom of widow burning at

the funeral of her husband was prevailing among the Gauls, the Slavs, the Goths, the Norwegians, the Celts and the Thracians. It was common in the Scythians too.

During the medieval period, thousands of women were burnt alive on stakes in Europe after the Church had declared them to be witches. Jawaharlal Nehru in his 'Glimpses of World History' has written (page 230): "The Church started the reign of violence in religion, formally and officially, in 1233, by starting what is called the Inquisition. This was a kind of court which inquired into the orthodoxy of people's beliefs,and if they did not come upto the standard,their usual punishment was death by burning. There was a regular hunt for 'heretics' and hundreds of them were burnt alive at the stakes. Many poor and unfortunate women were accused of being witches and were burnt. They honestly believed that by burning a person at the stake, they were saving his soul or the souls of other persons." At page 290, Nehru adds, "All over Spain the Inquisition flourished and the most horrible tortures were inflicted on so–called heretics.From time to time great public festivals were arranged when batches of these 'heretics', men and women, were burnt alive on huge pyres in the presence of the king and royal family and ambassadors and thousands of people. *Autos–da–fe*, acts of faith, these public burnings were called". In the USA, African slaves were brutalized, lynched and sometimes burnt alive on stakes.

In his book 'In Search of Loving God,' Mark Mason (Chapter IX) has written that towards the end of the Dark Ages in Europe, Emperor Charlemagne had forbidden burning of the supposed witches. In the ninth century, the Church also repudiated the belief that witches had supernatural powers. Inquisition began in 1231 under Pope Gregory IX as a legal procedure to root out heretics, but in later decades and centuries, the Roman Catholic authorities allegedly began employing torture and execution to enforce orthodoxy. Papal Bull (ad extirpanda) issued by Pope Innocent III in 1252 authorised seizure of possessions of persons accused of not following the faith as laid down by the Church, their imprisonment and executions. Pope Innocent VIII issued the bull (1484) against witchcraft and appointed Inquisitors. It is alleged that a few million people were tortured and executed in Europe for witchcraft over three centuries and 85 percent of them were women who were burnt alive on fire stakes. Others claim that the figure of those burnt alive during 1450 to 1700 should be much less: only about two lakhs! No one knows the correct number of women who were burnt alive on stakes in medieval Europe. In June, 2004, the Vatican said that fewer witches were burnt at the stake and fewer heretics tortured into conversion during the dark centuries of the Inquisition than is generally believed, and also sought renewed forgiveness for sins committed by Roman Catholics in the name of Church doctrine (IHT, June 16, 2004).

In the Holy Qur'an, it is said at many places that Kafirs are inmates of fire such as surah (II.39), (III.10) (III.116) etc. Even in these days, it is reported from time to time that in rural India some women, accused of being witches, were killed or harassed. So, burning of women was not exclusive to Hinduism.

In modern era, without recalling the past bitter memories, we should look forward; follow the policy of 'live and let live', policy of peaceful co–existence with the Vedic norm of gender equality.

7.4 Nine Vedic Richas Sanctioning Widow Remarriages

In RV (X.18.9), the new husband takes bow (or any symbol or any item) from the hand of dead husband, and while taking the widow as his wife says to her: "let us launch a new life of valour and strength begetting male children overcoming all enemies who may assail us." HH Wilson translates: "Taking his bow from hand of dead man, (new husband says) for the sake of our vigour, energy and strength, I say you (dead) are there (in grave); may we (who are) here (on ground), blessed with male offspring, overcome all enemies who assail us".

युवं ह कृशं युवमश्विना शयुं युवं विधन्तं विधवामरूष्यथः ।
युवं सनिभ्यः स्तनयन्तमश्विनाप व्रजमूर्णुथः सप्तास्यम् ॥8 ॥
(RV: X.40.8)

The above richa (X.40.8) of the Rigveda praises Ashwin gods for protecting a widow. It shows gods were praised by the Vedic people for protecting widows. How could gods go to protect widows if Rigveda had actually commanded burning of widows?

कुह स्विद्दोषा कुह वस्तोरश्विना कुहाभिपित्वं करतः कुहोषतुः ।
को वां शयुत्रा विधवेव देवंर मर्य न योषा कृणुते सधस्थ आ ॥2 ॥
(RV: X.40.2)

Another richa (X.40.2) may come as a complete surprise to many Hindus who wrongly presume that widow remarriages are not allowed in Hinduism. HH Wilson translates it: "Where are you, Asvins, by night? Where are you by day? Where do you sojourn? Where do you dwell? Who brings you into his presence in the same place (of sacrifice) as on her couch a widow (brings) her husband's brother, as a woman (brings) her husband (to her)".

Dr. Wendy D. O'Flaherty translates: "Where are the Asvins in the evening, where in the morning, where do they stop and where have they spent the night? Who invites you as a widow takes her husband's brother to her bed, as a young woman takes a young man to a room."

Ralph T.H. Griffith translates (X.40.2): "Where are ye, Asvins, in the evening, where at morn? Where is your halting place, where rest ye for the night? Who brings you homeward, as the widow bedward draws her husbands's brother, as the bride attracts groom?"

Dr. Ganga Sahay Sharma translates in Hindi: "*Hey Ashwin kumaroo! Tum raat aur din mey kaha rahate ho? Tumhara samaya kaha bitataa hai? tum kaha nivas karate ho? Jisprakar vidhawa apne devar ko aur sadhawa apne pati ko charpayee par bulaati hai ushiprakar merey atirikta kaun yajaman tumhe yajnavedi par apne anukul banaataa hai?*" Thus, Rigveda not only sanctions survival of a widow but also sanctions her marriage and her living with her *devar* as his wife with full dignity and honour in the family. It expressly sanctions widow re–marriage.

In the Atharvaveda, there are many richas which sanction or instruct remarriage of widows, such as, AV (IX.5.27–28) and AV (XVIII.3.1–4). WD Whitney translates AV (IX.5.27): "Whoever (a female) having gained a former husband, then gains another later one, if they (both) shall give a goat with five rice dishes, they shall not be separated". AV (IX.5.28) reads: "Her later husband comes to have the same world with his remarried spouse who gives a goat with five rice dishes with light of sacrificial gifts".

AV (XVIII.3.1) blesses a widow with progeny (children) and property in this lifetime. AV (XVIII.3.2) is a repeat of RV (X.18.8). WD Whitney & Joshi translate: "Go up, O woman, to the world of living; you stand by this one who is deceased. Come to him who grasps your hand, your second spouse (didhisu), you have now entered into the relation of wife to husband."

AV (XVIII.3.3) is interpreted as the command to turn back a maiden (young calf or young woman) away from dead to home. WD Whitney translates: "I saw the maiden being led, being led about, alive, for the dead; as she was enclosed with blind darkness (agyanataa), then, I led her off–ward from in front." Thus, AV specifically prohibits sacrificing women or cows for dead.

AV (XVIII.3.4) is translated by another author as: "O ye inviolable one! (The widow) tread the path of wise in front of thee, and choose this man (another suitor) as thy husband. Joyfully receive him and may the two of you mount the world of happiness." In this richa word 'aghnya' has been used for widow, which means a widow cannot be killed. As a cow cannot be killed so a widow cannot be killed.

R.C. Majumdar and others too in their book "An Advanced History of India' have attested (page 30) that remarriage of widows was permitted in the Vedic age.

Contradicting translation of RV (X.18.7) attributed to him (PV Kane) by a website (www.dalistan.com) as given in the fifth paragraph above, Kane's own 'History of Dharmashastra' has been quoted by other authors containing verses to the effect that: another man is ordained for a woman in five calamities viz., (i) when husband is missing and is unheard of, (ii) husband dies, (iii) is impotent, (iv) becomes ascetic; (v) husband is declared depraved. Agnipurana (154.5–5), Parasar Smriti (IV.30) and Narad Smriti (V.97) are also quoted in support.

The Widow Remarriage Act was enacted by the British in 1856.

7.5 Sati Not Mandatory In Ramayana and Mahabharata Too

Veda, Ramayana (Valmiki) and Gita are the three and the only three supreme scriptures of the Hindus. All others (like *Brahamanas*, *Upanishads*, *Purana*, *Dharma Shastras*, *Sutras*, etc.) are just commentaries, explanatory notes written by individuals. As commentaries written on the Constitution of India cannot over–ride the Articles of the Constitution of India; and, as laws passed by the Parliament or State Assemblies cannot supersede the Articles of the Constitution of India, similarly, commentaries/explanations on the Vedas cannot supersede richas of Vedas or Ramayana or Bhagwadgita. Maharishi Vedvyas has himself instructed in the Mahabharata that in cases of conflicting views, Vedas shall supersede all other writings:

श्रुतिस्मशतिपुराणानां विरोधो यत्र दश्श्यते।
तत्र श्रौतं प्रमाणन्तु तयोर्द्वैधे स्मशतिर्त्वरा॥

"Whenever there is a conflict between what is declared in the Vedas and provisions in any of the Smritis, Puranas, etc. what is declared in the Vedas shall prevail." (See paras 2.2 and 2.3 also)

In the Ramayana, everyone knows that after the death of King Dasharath, his wives were never asked to step into his funeral pyre. Rather, they lived in the family with full honour and Bhagwan Shri Ram always bowed his head before his widowed mothers with full respect. In the Mahabharata, Kunti, mother of Pandavas did not commit sati and she was active in all family matters and was accorded full respect by all including Lord Krishna. Dharmaraj Yudhishthir, being the *gyata* of Dharma, would certainly have asked his widowed mother Kunti to commit sati if it was a requirement of Dharma. Yudhishthir never did so means committing sati was not a requirement of Dharma. Thus, there is no command either in the Ramayana or in the Gita to commit *suttee/sati*.

7.6 Vedic Rights Of Hindu Women

The third chapter of the Rigveda is considered to be its oldest part. Richa (III.31.1) commands that a son–less father accepts the son of his daughter as his own son i.e., all properties of a son–less father shall be inherited by the son of his daughter.

Richa (III.31.2) commands that if parents have both a son and a daughter, the son performs holy acts of *pindadaan* (after death of father) and the daughter has to be enriched with gifts (*rinadhan* i.e., to be made wealthy). Richa (II.17.7) also attests share of a daughter in property of her father. A Division Bench of the Supreme Court of India comprising JJ R.C. Lahoti and Ashok Bhan decided, "a father can make a gift of ancestral immovable property within reasonable limits, keeping in view the total extent of the property held by the family in favour of his daughter at the time of marriage or even long after." (Indian Express, December 15, 2003) A father has unfettered right to gift his self–acquired properties to his son(s) or daughter(s) as he may choose.

The custom of daughter being given freedom to select her husband is attested in RV (X.27.12).

Richas (X.18.8) and (X.85.42) confirm wife's rights over the matrimonial home.

Dr. Altekar informs at page 92 of his book that since the Indo–Iranian times, the husband and wife were regarded as the joint owners of the household. The Vedic word for the couple, *dampati* etymologically means the joint owners of the house. The Avesta (Yashta 15, 4) describes the husband and wife as nmano–paiti and nmano–pathni, showing thereby that they were equal partners and joint owners of the common household. RV (III.53.4) says: "A man's wife is his dwelling; verily she is his place of birth". It means the Rigveda identifies a household with the housewife. She is the owner of the household; she is the proprietor of the household. RV (X.85) and Atharvaveda (XIV.1 & 2) declare wife to be the 'empress' of the house. AV (XIV.1.44) reads: "Be you (bride) supreme among fathers–in–law, supreme also among brothers–in–law, be you supreme over sisters–in–law, supreme over mother–in–law" basically because it is the bride who carries forward the family line of her in–laws household. In AV (XIV.1.43) the bride has been specifically declared to be *samrajani* (i.e., empress) of her matrimonial (in–laws') household.

The Rigveda also specifically defines the status of a bride in the household of her in–laws: "Be a queen to your father–in–law, be a queen to your mother–in–law, be a queen to your husband's sister, be a queen to your husband's brothers." (HH Wilson & Joshi)

सम्राज्ञी श्वशुरे भव सम्राज्ञी श्वश्र्वां भव।
ननान्दरि सम्राज्ञी भव सम्राज्ञी अधि देवृषु॥46॥
RV (X.85.46)

It is sad that rights conferred upon Hindu women by the Vedas were slowly whittled down mostly under literature composed during the Christian era. Let us restore the supremacy of canonical Vedas.

7.7 Conclusions

Over centuries relatives have been murdering relatives or getting them assassinated for property, and it will continue in the coming centuries also. Greed is human nature. If greedy people incite a widow at the time when she is emotionally the most shattered, to commit suicide on the funeral pyre of her husband so as to deprive her of her gold, silver and land, let us not say or believe that widow burning is sanctified by the Rigveda or by Hinduism. Richa (X.18.3) commands a Hindu widow to separate from dead, and richa (X.10.8) commands her to return alive to her children, to her home. RV (X.18.9), RV (X.40.2), AV (IX.5.27–28) & AV (XVIII.3.1–4) command her to be remarried immediately to another person (the second husband, later husband, *didhisu*).

Thus, for their own empowerment, Hindu women will be well advised to remember the seven richas of the Rigveda viz., (II.17.7) (III.31.1) (III.31.2) (X.18.3) (X.18.8) (X.18.9) and (X.40.2) to assert gender equality and to claim their status and Vedic rights both in the Hindu Samaj and in the Courts of Law.

Eight

VEDAS, BEEF AND MEDICAL SCIENCES

Option is truly yours to invite, or not to invite non-curable diseases by taking beef

8.1 Constitutional Position

Article 48 of the Constitution of India states that the State shall take steps for preserving and improving the breeds and prohibiting the slaughter of cows and calves and other milch and draught cattle. About eighteen State Govts in India, mostly led by Congress Party, have passed legislations banning cow slaughter in their respective provinces.

In this book, only the question of permissibility of cow slaughter in the Vedas, and ill effects of taking beef on human health as per contemporary medical sciences have been examined. Related administrative, economic, legal, legislative, political and social issues have not been touched upon.

8.2 Diplomatic Dinners And Beef

When I was selected for the Indian Foreign Service in 1971, my father firmly told me that I should never take beef as it was against the Hindu Dharma and prohibited by the Vedas, though I could take other non–vegetarian dishes. Modern medical sciences do not rule out role of beef in causing diseases (CJD, vCJD, etc.), which are fatal, noncurable like AIDS, infectious (from one person to another) and genetic (from one generation to another generation). Beef may terminate family tree line of some beef eaters. Almost all ambassadors who invite/invited us for diplomatic dinners make/made it a point not to serve any beef item to us, as they are aware that Hindus generally do not take beef. At diplomatic sitdown dinners, it oftenly used to crop up as to why we did not take beef when other guests were served with beef but we were served with chicken or fish or vegetables. This also encouraged me to study in depth as to why we did not take beef. Generally, Muslims do not take pork. Jews take only 'kosher' meat and Muslims take only 'halal' meat. For this reason, some Muslim and Jewish guests to our India House parties do not take nonvegetarian items except fish. In this background, it came as a shock and surprise to see articles appearing in Indian media quoting richas after richas of the Vedas to claim that cow slaughter and beef eating were acceptable norms in India. Articles by learned Dr. D.N. Jha of the Delhi University (Hindustan Times –17th & 18th Dec, 2001) and an article on (www.allaahuakbar.net/jain/religious.htm) are worth looking at, without any acrimony or personal bitterness, for these being at least specific in quoting richa numbers of Vedas make it easier to knock out their claims simply by going into details, by looking at original Sanskrit texts of the Vedic richas. They translate the word *ghrit* (clarified butter) into "fat implying tallow of cattle", *mahisa* (buffalo) into cow, and invoke 'funeral fire'and 'forest fire' richas into their kitchens.

8.3 Vedas Ban Cow Slaugther

Two basic things never to be forgotten on this subject are firstly, that Vedas being the revealed texts, being canonical, are the Supreme among all Hindu religious books; secondly, that in the Vedas, the word aghnya (अघन्य) refers to cows.

In Vedic literature, aghnya has been universally accepted to mean cows. Aghnya means "one which cannot and should not be killed or slaughtered." Nirukta (VI.43) explains aghnya to mean "one that does not deserve to be killed." There are at least sixteen Vedic richas in which the word aghnya has been used. Rigvedic richas in which the word aghnya appears are (I.164.27), (I.164.40), (IV.1.6), (V.83.8), (VII.68.9), (VIII.69.2), (IX.1.9), (IX.93.3) and (X.87.16). In the Atharvaveda, there are many richas containing the word aghnya such as (III.30.1), (VIII.3.15), (IX.4.2), (IX.4.4) (IX.4.17), (IX.5.19) and (XVIII.3.4), etc. In the very first richa of the Yajurveda, cow has been declared aghnya.

Eight richas of RV (VI.28) are devoted to cows as devata (deity). Twenty–six richas of Atharvaveda (IX.7) are devoted to the worship of cows. Twenty–four richas of the Atharvaveda (IX.4) are devoted to the worship of bull (*risabh*) as a deity.

RV (VIII.101.15) more specifically commands not to kill a cow. HH Wilson, Arya and Joshi translate RV (VIII.101.15): "(She who is) the mother of the Rudras, the daughter of the Vasus, the sister of the Adityas, the home of ambrosia (*amrita*),–I have spoken to men of understanding,– **kill not her, the sinless inviolate cow."** The other four richas, which command not to kill, not to harm cows, are given below:

(i) RV (VI.28.3): "Let not the Cows be lost: let no thief carry them away: **let no hostile weapon fall upon them**: may the master of the cattle be long possessed of those with (i.e., milk, butter, curds, etc.) which he sacrifices, and which he presents to the gods." (HH Wilson)

(ii) RV (VI.28.4): "Let not the dust–spurning (war) horse reach them nor let them fall in the way of sacrificial consecration, let the cattle of the man who offers sacrifice wander about at large and without fear." (HH Wilson). Pandit Satyakam Vidyalankar translates this richa:

"The charger, whirling up the dust, does not reach them, They never make their way to the slaughtering stool, The cows of the worshipping man roam about Over the Widespread pastures, free from all danger."

(iii) RV (VI.28.7): "May you, Cows, have many calves grazing upon good pasture, and drinking pure water at accessible ponds: may no thief be your master; no beast of prey (assail you), and may the (fatal) weapon of Rudra avoid you." (HH Wilson)
Pandit Satyakam Vidyalankar in his book 'The Holy Vedas' translates this richa:

"May you have many calves, graze on pastures
And drink pure water at drinking places;
May not the thief master you, nor the wicked,
And, may the darts of the fierce Lord leave you aside."

(iv) RV (VIII.101.16): "The divine cow, who herself utters, speech and gives speech to others, who comes attended by every kind of utterance, who helps me for my worship of the gods, – **it is only the fool who abandons her."** (HH Wilson)
The following seven richas pray Agni to kill and burn flesh–eating raksasas: (HH Wilson's translation)

(i) RV (X.87.2): "Jatavedas (Agni), who have teeth of iron, consume the Yatudhanas flame when kindled, destroy the destructive (spirits) with your tongue, cut up the eaters of flesh, and put them in your mouth."

(ii) RV (X.87.3): "Agni, the destroyer (of the Raksasas), who have two (rows of teeth), sharpening them both, apply them to (the Raksasas, and preserve) both the upper and the lower (world); and march, radiant (Agni, against the Raksasas) in the firmament, seize the Yatudhanas with your jaws."

(iii) RV (X.87.4): "Agni, do you, bending your arrows by means on our sacrifices and praise, and sharpening the javelins with your splendours, pierce with them the Yatudhanas to the heart, break their arms when raised against you."

(iv) RV (X.87.5): "Agni Jatavedas, cut through the skin of the Yatudhanas, let your destructive thunderbolt destroy him with its fire; sever his joints, may the flesh–desiring flesh–eater devour his mutilated body."

(v) RV (X.87.16): "The Yatudhana, who fills himself with the flesh of man, and he who fills himself with the flesh of horses or of other animals, and he who steals the milk of the cow cut off their heads with your flame."

(vi) RV (X.87.18): "Let the Yatudhana drink poison from the cattle i.e., let their milk turn into poison; let the (Raksasas) hard to overcome be cut to pieces for the sake of Aditi; may the divine Savita give them over (to destruction), may they be deprived of the food of herbs."

(vii) RV (X.87.19): "You, Agni, have from old time opposed the Yatudhanas; the Raksasas have never overcome you in battles; burn the murderous flesh–eating (Raksasas) one by one; let them not escape your divine weapon."

The Atharvaveda reiterates the above penalties. AV (I.16.4) instructs, "If you kill our cow or horse or men, we shall kill you with lead balls." WD Whitney translates AV (VIII.3.15): "The sorcerer that smears himself with the flesh of men, who with that of horses, with cattle, who bears (off) the milk of the inviolable (cow), O Agni! Their heads cut you into with flame."

Therefore, the Vedas not only prohibit slaughter of cows but also sanction slaughter and burning of killers of cows. Beef eating was, thus, banned and was not a socially accepted custom and was not a general practice. AV (VIII.6.2) commands that a mother should reject as her daughter's husband, a meat–eater, companions of meat–eaters, a man violent in nature etc.

In any society, some persons always go against the norms of the society but exceptions by a few do not constitute the general norm of that society. For example, rape is banned in India by law, but rapes do take place and Indian courts keep punishing the rapists. We all know that rape is not an acceptable social norm of our society. Therefore, relying upon court records of today, whether future historians, say, after a thousand years, will be justified to assert that rape was frequent so must have been an accepted social practice in India of today. Future historians may present court documents of today as historical documentary proof but we know how off the mark they would be. Exceptions (by a few) do not constitute the rule i.e., the general norm of the society.

8.4 Similies And Metaphors In The Vedas

Similies, metaphors, etc. are always used in poems. In Hindi/ Sanskrit, one comes across phrases like Chandramukhi (चन्द्रमुखी), mriganayani (मृगनयनी), etc. Chandramukhi means one with a beautiful face; it never means a face physically created from the rocks of moon. Mriganayani means one who has beautiful eyes; it never means eyes physically plucked out from a deer and implanted into the face of a woman. When we say he is like a bull, it only means he is physically strong like a bull; it never means he has eaten a bull to become bull–

like. Thus, the Rigveda being in poetry form is full of similies, metaphors etc.

Explaining the difficulties in understanding and translating Rigvedic richas, use of mutually illuminating metaphors, Dr. Wendy Doniger O'Flaherty in her book 'The Rigveda' (Penguin Books) (page 17) says the problem arises when one tries to determine which of these are in the foreground and which in the background of a particular hymn: are the cows symbolic of the sun, or is the sun a metaphor for cows?

AA MacDonell (1854–1930), Professor of Sanskrit at Oxford University, in his 'A History of Sanskrit Literature' (1896 AD),p.81, has written that "the ninth chapter of Rigveda mainly consists of incantations sung over the soma while it is pressed by the stones and flows through the woollen strainer into the wooden vats, in which it is finally offered as a beverage to the gods on a litter of grass. The poets are chiefly concerned with these processes, overlaying them with chaotic imagery and mystical fancies of almost infinite variety. When Soma is described as being purified by the ten maidens who are sisters, or by the daughters of Vivasvat (the rising sun), the ten fingers are meant. The stones used in pounding the shoots on a skin are implied by verse–"chew him on the hide of a cow". The flowing of the juice into jars or vats after passing through the filter of sheep's wool is described in various ways. The streams of soma rush to the forest of the vats like buffaloes. The god flies like a bird to settle in the vats. The Tawny One settles in the bowls like a bird sitting on a tree. The juice being mixed with water in the vat, Soma is said to rush into the lap of the waters like a roaring bull on the herd. Clothing himself in waters, he rushes around the vat, impelled by the singers. Playing in the wood, he is cleansed by the ten maidens (ten fingers). He is the embryo or child of waters, which are called his mothers. When the priests add milk to soma, "they clothe him in cow–garments." The sound made by the Soma juice flowing into the vats or bowls is often referred to in hyperbolical language. Thus, a poet says "the sweet drop flows over the filter like the din of combatants." RV (IX.96.6). This sound is constantly described as roaring, bellowing, or occasionally even thundering. In such passages, Soma is commonly compared with or called a bull, and the waters, with or without milk, are termed cows."

In RV (IX.III.9), Soma is compared to a bull. In (IX.III.10), it has might of a hundred radiant (bulls). In (IX.86.26), Soma rushes through filters sporting like a horse. In (IX.89.3), Soma is compared to a lion. In (IX.97.28), Soma is said to nigh like a horse and terrible like a lion. RV (IX.63.29): "Destroying Raksasas, pour forth, Soma, with a noise, brilliant and excellent vigour." In RV (IX.47.1), Soma is moving like a bull. In (IX.33.1), the intelligent Soma juices rush along like waves of water, like buffaloes to the forest. So, where Soma is poured into fire, it does not mean that lions, bulls, buffaloes are to be thrown into fire.

MacDonell further writes (page 91), "The cow, however, is the animal which figures most largely in the Rigveda. This is undoubtedly due to the important position, resulting from its pre–eminent utility, occupied by this animal even in the remotest period of Indian life. The beams of dawn and the clouds are cows. The rain–cloud, personified under the name of Prisni, 'the speckled one,' is a cow, the mother of the Storm–gods. The bountiful clouds on which all wealth in India depended, were doubtless the prototypes of the many–coloured cows which yield all desires in the heaven described by the Atharvaveda, and which are the forerunners of the 'Cow of Plenty' (Kamaduh) (Kamdhenu) so familiar to post–Vedic poetry. The earth itself is often spoken of by the poets of the Rigveda as a cow. That, this animal already possessed a sacred character is shown by the fact that one Rishi addresses a cow as Aditi and a goddess, impressing upon his hearers that she should not be slain. Aghnya (not to be killed) which is a frequent designation of the cow in the Rigveda points in the same direction. Indeed the evidence of the Avesta proves that the sanctity of this animal goes back even to the Indo–Iranian period. In the Atharvaveda the worship of the cow is fully recognised, while the **Satapatha Brahamana emphasises the evil consequences of eating beef.** The sanctity of the cow has not only survived in India down to the present day, but has even gathered strength with the lapse of time. The part played by the greased cartridges in the Indian Mutiny (1857) is sufficient to prove this statement." In Yaj (III.6): Prisni stands for the sun (spotted bull): "The earth with all its waters revolves around the sun (prisni)."

One may note that in 1899 MacDonell advised that Satapatha Brahamana emphasises evil consequences of eating beef.

While being on the subject matter of metaphors and similies, richa AV (IX.7.18) (**अभ्रं पीवो मज्जा निधनम्॥**) is translated by WD Whitney: "clouds are fat of cow and conclusions (i.e., nidhans) are its marrow". In richa AV (IX.4.4), it is expressly said that calf, fresh milk, curds, ghrit are seeds of bull. In AV (IX.4.1) bull is said to be rich in milk as without bull there will be no milk. In AV (IX.4.7), ghrit is again said to be the seed of a bull. The idea is that it is the seed (semen) of a bull, which makes a cow to deliver a calf and yield milk, which, in turn, yields curd, ghrit, and butter. The Atharvaveda clarifies that in Vedic Sanhitas names of material used in yajna (fire ceremony) are sometimes named after names of animals. AV (XVIII.4.32, 33, 34). For example, in AV (XVIII.4.32) rice is named as cow and sesame is named a calf. Richas (33rd and 34th) again say, "With sesame as calf." In the 34th Richa grains (yellow, white, black, red) are equated "as your cow."

धाना धेनुरभवद् वत्सो अस्यास्तिलोऽभवत्।
तां वै यमस्य राज्ये अक्षितामुप जीवति॥32॥
AV(XVIII.4.32)

WD Whitney translates AV (XVIII.4.32): "The grains became a milch–cow; the sesame became her calf; upon her, unexhausted, one lives in Yama's realm." So, when grain and sesame are to be offered into fire, one is expected to have common sense not to push cows and calves into fire.

8.5 Scholarly Manipulations And Genuine Translation Difficulties

Readers may recall that allegations of fat (i.e., tallow, animal fat) of cows and pigs being used in cartridges sparked the 1857 Rebellion against the British Govt. by Indian soldiers in the British Army. From 1857 onwards, the British imperialist interests, therefore, became active to find ways and means, on one hand to lower reverence and sacredness that Hindus have for the Vedas & cows and on the other hand, to prove that Hindus too were as much foreigners in India as the British were. By overpaying, British started renting European and Indian 'scholars' to 'invent' evidence of beef eating in the Vedas as well as to promote the Aryan Invasion Theory. One Rajendra Lal Mitra published the first article entitled 'Beef in Ancient India' in 1872 in the Journal of the Asiatic Society of Bengal. Later, when Mahatma Gandhi took up protection of cows in his Go–Raksha movement, one Swami Bhoomanand published the same essay in the form of a booklet.

In his voluminous book 'Vachaspatyam,' Pandit Taranath, a Professor of Vyakarna at Calcutta Sanskrit College, has translated **"गोध्न । गां हन्ति हन् । गोहन्तरि।"** *Goghn ga hanti han: gohantari* to mean "killer of a cow." Vachaspatyam is a huge Sanskrit–to–Sanskrit dictionary in six volumes used by Sanskrit scholars. H.H. Swami Prakashanand Saraswati in his book, 'The True History and Religion of India' (page–274) explains, "**गोघ्न** (*goghn)* means the donee guest who receives a cow as gift. Maharishi Panini formed a special sutra "**दाशगोघ्नौ सम्प्रदाने।**" (3/4/73) (*Dashgoghno Sampradane*) for this purpose which means that the words **दाश** (*Dash)* and **गोघ्न** (*goghn*) represent the receiver of the charity **(सम्प्रदान)**. In this way, Maharishi Panini clarified and established the correct meaning of the Vedic word **गोघ्न** (*goghn)* by especially making a rule that the word "*goghn*" shall only mean the receiver of a cow. But Pandit Taranath over–ruled even the supreme authority of Panini in a grammatical matter! Great! Why did Taranath do so? Obviously, for monetary considerations! Swami Saraswati informs that in 1866 Pt. Taranath was given an advance commitment in writing by the then British Govt. of Bengal (Letter No. 507 dt. 26th January, 1866, Fort William) to purchase 200 copies of his books @ Rs. 50/– per copy aggregating Rs. 10,000/– after the Sanskrit Dictionary was complete. Pt. Taranath and his publisher were thus assured to receive Rs. 10,000/– from the British Govt., which at present market value will be more than Rs. 20 lakhs. Sir William Gray, the then Lt.Governor of Bengal (letter No.3480 dated 12th Dec 1870) also granted extension of time for completing Vachaspatyam to Taranath.

In 1847, the East India Company agreed to pay £ 200 per annum to Max Müller, a German national, for translation of Vedas etc. upto 50 sheet per annum £ 4 per sheet. In 1853, the annual salary of a male teacher in Britain was £ 90 and that of a lady teacher was only £ 60. (See paras 1.7 and 9.4). Swami Sarasvati has given quotations from letters written by Max Müller showing Max Müller's "bias and contempt against the Vedas & Hindus". Nevertheless, on the positive side, it must always be kept in mind that if British wanted they could also have systematically destroyed all Hindu manuscripts but they carefully collected and preserved these; systematic works on these started in Europe. Hindu Samaj should always appreciate this great service of the British and other Europeans to preserve Hindu sacred books.

European professors translated these into their languages as best as they could. However, in translations, as we all know, there are always two major difficulties: (i) some words in one language have no exact corresponding words in another language, and (ii) a translator is constrained by depth of his own knowledge of the cultural ethos of language being translated, his own cultural ethos and his own religious values. For example, the Hindi word Achchha (अच्छा) has many meanings depending upon how it is pronounced, such as (i) Good, I agree (ii) Oh, I see, I have heard (without any commitment) (iii) Is it so (with surprise)? (iv) It is ok with me, (v) it is better (than the other), etc. Similarly, it is difficult to pinpoint a word for मन (Manas) or चित्त (Chitta) in English. A European scholar who has not lived long enough in India is not expected to understand all these finer details. A European who has studied in India will generally translate better than those Europeans who have not studied in India. It is always open to younger generations to improve upon works done by glorious predecessors, without any acrimony, without any bad blood. This is how generations make progress. It is the prerogative, privilege and duty of the younger generation, to improve upon works done by older generations. In the academic world, let hundred flowers bloom.

8.6 Vedic Richas Mis–Quoted To Support Cow Slaughter

Let us focus, just for sake of academic discussions, on Prof. D.N. Jha's article 'Paradox of the Indian Cow'. Prof. Jha has written, "A guest, therefore, came to be described by Panini as a *goghna* (one for whom the cow is slain)." This meaning of *goghna* as seen above is not by Panini but by Pandit Taranath indirectly hired by British for Rs. 10,000 in 1866 AD.

Prof. Jha adds, "The sacred thread ceremony was not all that sacred; for it was necessary for a snatak to wear an upper garment made from cowhide." Nevertheless, everyone knows that there is no ban in the Vedas to skin a dead cow, so, it is common sense that one can always have cowhides without slaughtering a cow.

Prof. Jha writes, "The thick fat of the cow was used to cover the dead body RV (X.14–18) and a bull was burnt along with the corpse to enable the departed to ride with in the nether world. The funerary rights included, feeding of the Brahamans after the prescribed period and quite often the flesh of cow/ox was offered to the dead (AV XII.2.48)." Let us closely examine these contentions of Prof. Jha. From RV (X.14) to RV (X.18) there are 72 richas in HH Wilson's book but Prof. Jha has not specified which richa he has in mind in asserting that dead body was covered by thick fat of cow. However, if he had RV (X.18.12) in mind, this richa in its Sanskrit text has used word Ghrit (**घृत**) which is certainly not "thick fat of the cow" (i.e., tallow). Readers may themselves see the Sanskrit text of this richa, which is given below:

उच्छञ्चमाना पशथिवी सु तिष्ठतु सहस्त्रं मित उप हि श्रयन्ताम।
ते गश्हासो घश्तश्चुतो भवन्तु विश्वहास्मै शरणाः सन्त्वत्र ॥12॥
RV (X.18.12)

HH Wilson translates: "May the earth heaped over him lie light: may thousands of particles (of dust) envelope him; may these mansions distil *ghi* (for him); may they every day be an asylum to him in this world."

Dr. Wendy D. O'Flaherty in her 'The Rigveda' translates this very richa: ......"let there be houses dripping with butter for him." Even a schoolchild knows that butter/ghrit and tallow (thick fat of cow) are two different things though chemically both are animal fat, obtained differently. Butter is obtained from milk of live cows but tallow is obtained only after death/ slaughter of cattle. Ghrit is obtained by heating butter. So, what foreigners like Wilson and Dr. Wendy call ghee/butter, Prof. Jha, being an Indian, calls 'thick fat of cow' (implying tallow, slaughtering of cow)! Further, as we have seen in para (7.2), in RV (X.18), dead body is being buried in a grave in the ground; where is the question of burning a bull along with the corpse under RV (X.18)?

In RV (X.14) to RV (X.18) there is no stipulation of burning of a bull along with corpse. Jha's AV (XII.2.48) quotation is nowhere near to support him. WD Whitney & KL Joshi translate this richa: "Let you hold after the draft – ox (as) float; he shall carry you out of difficulty (and) reproach; mount this boat of Savita; may we cross over misery by six wide [directions]". There is, thus, no burning of bull or offering flesh of cow/ox to dead in this AV richa. Richas 45, 46, 47, 48 of AV (XII.2) are addressed to living people. Even in AV (XII.2.48), it is said, "may we cross over misery" implying it is addressed to living beings (we).

In the Vedas, a clear distinction has been made time and again between Holy Fire (Jataveda Agni), which is auspicious, welcome and carries oblations to Gods; and unholy/ unwelcome fire (Kravyad Agni). Kravyad Agni is the 'funeral fire' (**श्मशान अग्नि, चिता की अग्नि**). RV (X.16.9) says: "I send flesh devouring (Kravyad) Agni, to a distance, let him bearing away sin repair to King Yama, but let this other Jataveda Agni who is known by all convey oblation to the Gods." RV (X.16.10) says, "The flesh–devouring (Kravyad) deity Agni, who has entered your dwellings I turn him out, for the worship of the Pitrs, upon beholding this other (Agni) Jatavedas; let him celebrate the sacrifice (to Pitrs) in the most excellent assembly." Yaj (35.19) says "I drive corpse eating Agni to a distance: sin laden let him go to Yama's kingdom. Here let this other Jatavedas, carry oblation to Deities." AV (XII.2.7, 8, 10) push out Kravyad–Agni and AV (XII.2.34–39) instruct to keep away from Kravyad (flesh devouring) Agni as it brings misfortune. AV (XII.2.42) says "O non–flesh eating Agni, push out the flesh eating one; bring out the god–sacrificing one." Thus, flesh–devouring Agni was not to be allowed into residences and had to be extinguished as soon as cremation was over. But, out of ignorance or mischief, some authors bring the kravyad agni in residence and quote Kravyad Agni richas to claim that Vedic people were roasting cattle in fire–ceremonies in their homes. One does not invoke funeral fire (kravyad Agni) within his home, so how can kravyad Agni richas be invoked to justify roasting of meat in the kitchen? Kravyad richas are misquoted to say that Agni is eater of flesh/meat; therefore, to say that Vedic Hindus were offering flesh/meat to Agni devata in yajna or havan is another cold–blooded mischief.Only in Jataveda role, Agni can be invoked for worshipping purposes.

Prof. Jha adds, "Indra had a special liking for bulls RV (V.29.7), (VI.17.11), (VIII.12.8) (X.27.2), (X.28.3), (X.86.14). Agni was not a tippler like Indra but was fond of animal food including flesh of horses, bulls and cows RV (VIII.43.11), (X.91.14)." Here in the Sanskrit texts of (V.29.7) (VI.17.11) and (VIII.12.8) word (*mahisha*) (**महिषाँ**) has been used which means buffaloes or demons. *Mahisha* does not mean bull of cow family. Even the illiterates understand the difference between buffaloes and bulls of cow family. Further, there is no ban on slaughter of mahisha (buffaloes) in Hindu culture.

In RV (V.29.7) quoted by Prof. Jha, Agni is declared a friend of Indra and Indra is going to war against demon Vritra. Naturally as a friend, either Agni offers three hundred he–

buffaloes to help Indra fight Vritra or Agni has burnt three hundred demon supporters of Vritra. Readers may recall killing of Mahishasur **(महिषाँसुर)** a demon by Godess Durga is celebrated every year during Ashtami celebrations. Wilson translates this richa: "To aid (the undertaking of) his friend, Agni, the friend (of Indra) has quickly consumed three hundred buffaloes; and Indra, for the destruction of Vritra, has at once quaffed vessels of soma, offered by Manu." Ralph T.H. Griffith: "As friend to aid a friend, Agni dressed quickly three hundred buffaloes, even as he willed it, And Indra, from man's gift, for Vritra's slaughter, drank of at once three lakes of pressed out soma." As Agni is not in flesh–devouring (Kravyad) role here, the interpretation as given by Ralph TH Griffith that Agni offered three hundred buffaloes to Indra to fight demon is the correct one. HH Wilson's translation is also correct so far as one remembers that fire consuming anything only means that it has been burnt to ashes/destroyed by fire. So, there is no eating of buffalo meat in this rich a (richa) by Indra. Fire consuming anything simply means it has been burnt/destroyed by fire.

HH Wilson translates RV (VI.17.11): "For you Indra, whom all the Maruts, alike pleased, exalt, may Pusan and Vishnu dress for you a hundred buffaloes, and to him may the three streams flow with the inebriating, foe–destroying Soma." Ralph T.H. Griffith also translates: "He dressed a hundred buffaloes." Neither Wilson nor Griffith says hundred buffaloes being eaten by Indra in this richa. In the previous richa (VI.17.10), Indra has killed Ahi and in the next richa (VI.17.12) Indra has set free blocked water channels. In this Sukta RV (VI.17), a war scene is going on in which Indra has been offered help of hundred buffaloes (fighters as strong as buffaloes: metaphor) to fight demons. There is no feasting in RV (VI.17).

HH Wilson translates RV (VIII.12.8) quoted by Prof. Jha:

"Great Indra, protector of the good, when you have slain thousands of mighty (foes: सहस्त्र महिषाँ), then your vast and special energy has been augmented." Here, foes have been killed. Again, there is no eating of buffaloes by Indra.

RV (X.27.2) translation by Wilson: "(Indra asks) If I encounter in combat the undevout, resplendent in their bodies, and then will I cook a vigorous bull for them?" Ralph TH Griffith translates: "Then will I, when I lead my friends to battle against radiant persons of godless, prepare for thee at home a vigorous bullock?" Ignoring the question form, this richa has been misquoted to say that bull (rishabh) is being cooked by Indra for feasting. The correct position is that in RV (X.27.2) Indra is asking a simple question: when at war agaist the undevout (apostate, *adharmi*), whether he should focus on defeating enemy or should he prepare a bull for his enemies (i.e., surrender to enemies)? It is common sense that one is forced to work for his enemies only after being defeated. In the Vedas, as we know, the enemies are *raksasas* who eat flesh. In RV (X.27.7) there is the reply to this question: "Indra, verily destroys (his foe), the other does not destroy (Indra)." In richa (X.27.8) Indra says he looks after the cowherd and in (X.27.10) says that he creates bipeds and quadrupeds. All these prove that in (X.27.2) Indra is asking a simple question whether (after being defeated) he should cook a bull for *raksasas* or he should focus to defeat *raksasas*. Therefore, to say that in (X.27.2) Indra is cooking a bull for himself is incorrect.

In Sukta (X.28), there is a dialogue between Indra and his son. In (X.28.1), (HH Wilson) daughter–in–law of Indra says, "May Indra eat the parched grain; and drink Soma; when he is well satisfied, may he return home." Here, readers may note, Indra is eating grains. In (X.28.2) Indra is standing as a roaring bull. HH Wilson translates (X.28.3): "(Vasukra speaks) your worshippers express with stone fast flowing exhilarating soma–juice for you, you drink them, they roast bulls for you, you eat them." Ralph T.H. Griffith does not use the word 'roast' but translates "Bulls they dress for thee, and of these thou eatest." No fire has been invoked anywhere in (X.28), so where are bulls being roasted? There is no Kravyad Agni in (X.28). One is reminded of AA MacDonell that in such Soma passages, Soma is commonly compared with or called a bull. (See para 8.4) So, in (X.28.3) use of the word bull is a metaphor for soma. There is no roasting of an actual bull in this sukta but only 'hot/warm' Soma and parched grains are being served to Indra.

Dr. Wendy (page 258) says that Renou has called RV (X.86) the strangest poem in the Rigveda dealing with conflict and resolution on at least four levels in one Sukta. At the time before the conversation in this hymn takes place, Indra has ceased to be offered soma. Substitute offerings are being made to transfer monkey's (vrisakapi) potency to Indra. In richa (X.86.13) (not quoted by Dr. Jha), vrisakapi says, "Let Indra eat your bulls (uksno) (give him) the beloved and most delightful ghrit." In Richa (X.86.14) (Wilson): "(Indra speaks) the worshippers dress for me fifteen (and) twenty bulls (uksno), I eat them and (become) fat, they fill both sides of my belly." Ralph TH Griffith translates: "Fifteen in number, then, for me a score of bullocks they prepare, And I devour the fat thereof, they fill my belly full with food." And, fat of bulls as explained above in para 8.4, is nothing but ghrit; butter collected from 15 to 20 cows impregnated by bulls of Vrisakapi. There cannot be any roasting of bulls in these hymns as, there is again no Kravyad Agni in (X.86).

Richa (X.16.7) not quoted by Dr. Jha but quoted in (www.allaahuakbar.net) is recited at funeral pyre. Dr. Wendy O'Flaherty in her 'The Rigveda' explains (page 51) that in this richa skin of a **dead** cow is mentioned to cover corpse as armour/shield against fire, while the corpse would be anointed with fat and suet (ghrit). Ralph TH Griffith translates: (X.16.7) "Shield thee with flesh against the flames of Agni, encompass thee about with fat and marrow, so will the Bold One, eager to attack thee with fierce glow fail to girdle and consume thee." In Griffith's translation, also there is no mention of hide and flesh of cow at all. Soul of dead man is being told a very simple fact in this richa that flesh and fat of his own corpse is initially, temporarily, a shield against kravyad Agni, but not for a long time.

Prof. Jha has quoted the following richa RV (VIII.43.11) to assert that Agni was fond of animal food including flesh of horses, bulls and cows:

> **उक्षान्नाय वशान्नाय सोमपृष्ठाय वेधसे। स्तोमैर्विधेमोग्नये ॥11॥**
> **RV (VIII.43.11)**

The above richa says that *uksannaya* (**उक्षान्नाय**) i.e., grains as strong/healthy as bulls, and, *washannaya* (**वशान्नाय**) i.e., grains soaked in fat (*ghrit*) be offered in *havan* (fire–sacrifice). As per common sense, even today, whenever we conduct havan, we use better quality grains (*baail jaisa mota achcha daanaa*) soaked in ghee. Dr. Ganga Sahai Sharma, and Shri Ram Sharma agree with this. When two nouns are joined, the first one generally functions as adjective to the other one. Here uksa (bull) is adjective to annaya (grains). Similarly, washa (fat) is adjective to annaya (grains). But Wilson and Griffith both have wrongly translated this richa. Wilson translates: "Let us adore with hymns, Agni, the granter (of desires), the eater of ox, the eater of marrows, on whose back the libation is poured." Griffith translates RV (VIII.43.11): "Let us serve Agni with our hymns, Disposer, fed on ox and cow, Who bears the Soma on his back." In this very sukta, richas (VIII.43.3–7–8–9) declare that Agni's food is forest/ vegetations. In (VIII.43.10) and in (VIII.43.22) butter/ghrita is being offered as food to Agni. Over and above, in RV (VIII.43), Agni is not in Kravyad Agni role. So, not oxen and cows but only healthy grains soaked with ghee are being offered to Agni in (VIII.43.11) which we do even now while performing havans.

Yajurveda, which focuses on Yajna (*havan*) ceremonies, prohibits animal sacrifice by saying at (XIX.20) that one gets "*pashutva*" (i.e., 'animal–hood' or 'animal–like') by offering 'animals' as sacrifice. No sane person wants to become an animal. In (XIX.21–23), Yajurveda describes milk, a mixture of boiled and coagulated milk, curd, roasted grain, barley– meal, grains of roasted rice, parched wheat etc. as offerings/sacrificial food, which we follow even now.

RV (X.91.14) Sukta RV (X.91) is devoted to deity Agni (fire) which in many religions is poetically taken to represent God and Agni is believed to be in direct communication with God. High reverence paid by the Parsis to fire is well known. In Yasna (36.1) it is written: "To the fire as symbol of Ahura Mazda who appears in blazing flame." In Exodus (3.2), God appears in the form of fire or encompassed by fire. In Exodus (19.18) one reads, "And Mount Sinai was altogether on a smoke because Lord descended upon it in fire." Again, "And sight of glory of Lord was like devouring fire on the top of mount in eyes of children of Israel." In the movie 'Ten Commandments', actor Charles Heston as Moses sees presence of God in form of flames of Agni and God makes ten commands inscribed on stone by flames of fire. Flames are acting as hands of God in this movie. In (X.91) Agni is not Kravyad Agni; so it is not flesh devouring one. In (X.91.3) Agni is dispenser of wealth, lord of treasures of heaven and earth. In (X.91.5–6) plants and forests are foods of Agni. One may note that in the Sanskrit text of (X.91.14) word used is vasha (**वशा**) (fat, butter), which is wrongly inferred by Wilson and Griffith to imply barren cows.

यस्मिन्नश्राय ऋषभास उक्षणो वशा मेषा अवसृष्टास आहुताः
कीलालपे सोमपृष्ठाय वेधसे हृदा मतिं जनये चारुमग्ये ॥14॥
RV (X.91.14)

HH Wilson translates (X.91.14): "I offer graceful praise with all my heart to Agni, the drinker of Soma, the ordainer (of the rite), to whom vigorous horses, and bulls and barren cows and sheep are consigned as burnt offerings." Does it mean these animals are being pushed into fire one by one? No, certainly not because fire in (X.91) is not Kravyad Agni. In richa (X.91.14) vigorous horses, bulls, cows, sheep are being gifted to the ordainer of the rites (i.e., to the Pujari who is conducting yajna). In fact, in RV (V.8.10) the sage accepts the cattle, which are to be gifted to Agni. In (X.91.12) Agni is specifically addressed as **Jataveda** Agni so it cannot consume animals. Griffith translates (X.91.15) "Into thy mouth is poured the offerings, Agni, as Soma into cup, oil into ladle. So, actual offerings to Agni are Soma and oil, not animals. In the Purusa Sukta (X.90.10), HH Wilson says: "From him were born horses and whatsoever animals have two rows of teeth; yea, cows were born from him; from him were born goats and sheep." Does it mean these cattle were physically born one after another from Purusha/Yajna? No, certainly not. What these richas are conveying is that God creates everything and everything belongs to Him.

RV (X.79.6) This richa (not quoted by Dr. Jha) (not quoted by allaahuakbar) is also used by the beef–lobbyists to justify cow slaughter. It describes forest–fire. H.H. Wilson translates: "Ignorant I ask you Agni, sporting (here) not sporting (there), golden–hued, eating what is to be eaten, you cut (your food) into pieces as the knife (cuts up) the cow." But in Ralph T.H. Griffith's translation no cow is knifed. Ralph's translation "Agni, hast thou committed sin or treason among the Gods? In ignorance, I ask thee. Playing, not playing, he gold–hued and toothless hath cut his food up as the knife a victim." What the rishi is conveying in (X.79.6) is that fire, being toothless cuts into woods as smoothly as knife cuts into butter. It is a well–known proverb still in use. Therefore, here both Wilson and Griffith have again erred in their translations.

A website (www.allaahuakbar.net) claims that Rigveda Sukta (X.85) mentions that during marriage ceremony guests are fed with meat. It asserts, "In magha days are oxen slain, in Arjuni they wed the bride" This site quotes a book 'The Vedic Age' by Dr. V.M. Apte (page 387) that on the occasion of marriage guests were served with beef of cows, slaughtered for the purpose (RV: X.85.13). This site asserts that Vedic Index (Vol.II page 145) also says that on occasion of marriage cows were slaughtered for feast and that it is also accepted in the Vedic Dictionary (page 374) of the Banaras Hindu University. Let us go into details, as usual. HH Wilson translates RV (X.85.13): "Surya's bridal procession which Savita despatched has advanced; the oxen are whipped along in the Magha (constellations); she is borne (to her husband's house) in the Arjuni (constellation)." HH Wilson says that (X.85.13) refers to some astronomical fact, theory or myth, which is difficult to trace. Therefore, there is no cow/ox slaughter in (X.85.13), only whipping of oxen, which is a normal thing.

Allaahuakbar.net says that Atharvaveda (IX.4.37–38–39) gives expression that cows' meat is most tasty of all other foods. But in WD Whitney's Atharvaveda (IX.4) has only 24 richas. Atharvaveda (XI.4) has 26 richas. AV (X.4) also has only 26 richas.

Allaahuakbar.net translates Yaj 35/20: "O **Jataveda,** take this particular hide of cow. You know the ancestors may the rivers of fat of that particular hide flow towards the ancestors and the desires of those, who donate for their ancestors, be fulfilled." Ralph T.H. Griffith & Arya give different translation where there is no reference to any hide of cow. Griffith translates, "Carry fat (ghee) to Fathers (pitr), **Jatavedas**, where, faraway, you know then established. Let rivulets of marrow (ghee) flow to meet them, and let their truthful wishes be accomplished." Please note that in this richa Agni is **Jatavedas** (i.e., sacred role) so by definition no hide/skin can be put into it.

8.7 Charak Samhita

Some people mention that in the therapeutic section, Charak Samhita (Sushruta and Vagbhatta) prescribes flesh of cow as medicine for various diseases, implying that cow slaughter and beef eating were sanctioned. Use of flesh of a cow in Charak Samhita does not necessarily mean open general licence (OGL) for cow–slaughter as flesh of a freshly dead cow is always available for preparing medicine or a small portion of flesh may be taken out without killing a cow. There is no ban on collecting fat from dead cows. Snake venom is used to prepare medicine against snakebite: does it mean we eat snake venom and offer venom to our guests? Snake is not killed for collecting its venom. Cow urine is also used as a medicine: does it mean all healthy Hindus drink it and offer it to their guests? Medicine is for sick people, it cannot be branded as staple diet for healthy people.

8.8 Mughal Emperors On Cow–Slaughter

Abul–Fazl Allami in his Ain–i–Akbari (as translated by H. Blockmann) has written in Ain 66 (Book: First) that throughout the happy regions of Hindustan, the cow is considered auspicious and held in great veneration. In Ain

26, he writes that Akbar cared very little for meat, and often expressed himself to that effect. Abul–Fazl adds "It is indeed from ignorance and cruelty that, although various kinds of food are obtainable, men are bent upon injuring living creatures, and lending a ready hand in killing and eating them". Babur in his letter of 935 hijri advised Humayun to stop cow–slaughter. Akbar in his firman of 1586 forbade cow slaughter. According to a Finnish collector of Mughal coins, who has the reputation of having the only five rupees silver coin of Aurangzeb's mint available today in the world, Aurngzeb did not eat meat. According to some writers, Akbar and Aurngzeb both always used Ganga water for drinking and in their kitchen both had long life and long reigns. Prof. Mazheruddin Siddiqi, Reader and Head of the Department of Muslim History, University of Sindh, Hyderabad, Pakistan has also recorded that Akbar required people to prostrate themselves before him and forbade circumcision, prohibited the use of beef, and discouraged the growing of beards.

8.9 Views Of The Supreme Court Of India And Others

The then Muslim League at its Amritsar session of 1919 had passed a resolution recommending the sacrifice of animals other than cows on Bakrid. After all, cow is not a native animal of Saudi Arabia. In November 1994, the Supreme Court of India, dismissing an appeal of the West Bengal Govt. ruled that it is not a part of religious requirements of Muslims to slaughter a cow. The three–judge bench comprising JJ Kuldip Singh, BL Hansaria and SB Majumdar also referred to an earlier decision of the Constitution Bench wherein it was held that "total ban on cow slaughter did not offend Article 25(i) of the Constitution."

Dr. Tahir Mahmood, Professor of Law, Delhi University in his article captioned 'Don't be cowed by Stereotypes' in the Hindustan Times (22nd August 2003) has written that it is reprehensible to overlook the large heartedness of the minorities in extending unconditional support to the cow–protection provision of the Constitution. Prof. Mahmood reminds the nation that "Muslim members of the Constituent Assembly were unanimous in their support for the proposed ban on the ground that they respected religious sentiments of their Hindu brethren" But the political cowboys, he laments, have been projecting the minorities as the culprit for failure to abolish cow slaughter. He clarifies that the general Muslim would, in fact, care the least for the ban on cow slaughter, as sacrificial killing of the cow and eating their meat has no special place in their religion .The Prophet (PBUH) had never directed, Prof. Mahmood asserts, that cows be (necessarily) sacrificed as part of the ritual, or that beef be essentially eaten on any religious occasion. "On the contrary, the Prophet (PBUH) is believed to have warned that cow's milk cures but its flesh causes disease," says Prof. Mahmood, a former Chairman of National Minorities Commission.

No wonder that many Muslim rulers had prohibited cow slaughter in India. Maulana Syed Athar Hussain Dehlavi, Chairman of Anjuman Minhaj–Rasool, told a journalist Swati Chopra (Voice of Sanity, Times of India, 30th April, 2002) that: "For instance, Hindus are troubled by the consumption of beef by Muslims and we have brought to their notice that in one holy book, the Prophet exhorted people to drink cow's milk. So, if the cow is sacred for Hindus, it is in a way so for us too."

Surah (V.5) of the Holy Qur'an says, "food of those who have been given the Book (i.e., Jews and Christians) is lawful for you". Holy Qur'an does not similarly authorise Muslims to eat food of people who are not people of the Book. As such, the meat of animals slaughtered by Hindus, Sikhs, and Buddhists etc. is, strictly speaking, not lawful for Muslims to eat. We are, therefore, not surprised when some Muslim guests take only vegetarian dishes at our 'India House'. Surah (II.173), (V.3) etc. prohibit carrion, blood and meat of pork, what dies of itself, carnivorous animals, birds of prey (eagles, falcon') etc. Surah (II.173), (V.3) etc. prohibit Muslims to eat meat of animals not slaughtered as per Islamic process (zabah) and on which name of Allah was not invoked at the time of slaughter or name of other gods was invoked. Surah (VI.118) instructs, "Therefore, eat of that on which Allah's name has been invoked." Surah (V.1) says, "The beast of cattle is made lawful unto you (for food) except that which is announced unto you (herein)". Thus, the Holy Qur'an does not make it an obligatory/mandatory requirement to slaughter a cow as correctly concluded by the Supreme Court, and by Prof. Mahmood. Further, cattle are not to be slaughtered when in "al jalalah". In fact, title of surah II is "THE COW".

The Indian Express of 3rd Feb, 2004 has quoted Maulana Ansar Shah Kashmiri of Darul Uloom Waqf saying: "We have been issuing posters and urging members of Muslim community to leave the cow for qurbani on Bakrid every year since 1947."

The Hindustan Times, in its report "Deoband School asks Muslims to avoid sacrificing cows on Baqr'id", dated 2nd Feb, 2004 quotes Mufti Habibur Rahman of Darul Uloom saying: "as Hindus respected and worshipped cow, the Muslim community should sacrifice instead of cows, other four–legged animals." This advice/Fatwa was issued by a bench of three Muftis of Darul Uloom. Jamait Ulema–e–Hind President Maulana Mehmood Madani has also been quoted as saying that Muslims should voluntarily stop killing cows and that Jamiat had passed a resolution more than a year ago to this effect. Dr. M.S. Usmani, Vice President of National Minorities Commission, has been quoted by Dainik Jagran (5th Feb., 2004) saying that this recommendation/Fatwa of Darul Uloom should be applied all over India.

8.10 Vedas Supersede All Secondary Sources

Everyone knows that the Vedas are the Supreme religious canonical scriptures of the Hindus and supersede anything and everything to the contrary. This is not a new principle that I am enunciating. This is what Maharishi Vedvyas, who composed the Mahabharata, Gita and Puranas has himself written in the Mahabharata:

श्रुतिस्मशतिपुराणानां विरोधो यत्र दश्श्यते।
तत्र श्रौतं प्रमाणन्तु तयोर्द्वैधे स्मशतिर्त्वरा॥

"Whenever there is conflict between what is declared in the Vedas and provisions in any of the Smritis, Puranas etc. what is declared in the Vedas shall prevail." (See paras 2.2 and 2.3 also)

Satpath Brahamana is a commentary on the Yajurveda by Yajnavalkya. AA MacDonell (page 364) informs that the Manusmriti assumed its present form not much later than 200 AD. Yajnavalkya Dharma Sutra was composed around 1300 AD. Bharat Ratna PV Kane has written that beyond the name Vasistha there is hardly anything special about Vasistha Dharma Sutra (VDS) to connect it with the Rigveda. Kane also adds, "Grave doubts have been entertained about authenticity of the whole text of VDS as the manuscripts contain varying numbers of chapters from 6 to 30, and as the text is hopelessly corrupt in several places. Many sutras bear the imprints of comparatively late age."

Prof. Jha in his article has cited many **secondary sources** like Taittiriya Brahaman, Satapath Brahaman, Grihyasutras, Dharmasustras, Manusmriti, Yajnavalkya etc. to supersede ban on cow slaughter (aghnya) imposed by the Vedas, the **primary source**. Prof. Romila Thapar (Hindustan Times, 9th Dec., 2001) also says that Satpath Brahamana (3.4.1.2) and Vasistha Dharmasutra (4.8) etc. mention honouring guests with serving beef. So, Romila's quotations are in conflict with the views of MacDonell. As we have seen in para 8.4 above, AA MacDonell wrote in 1899 that Satapath Brahaman emphasised evil consequences of beef eating, so how can the same Satpath Brahaman be quoted to honour guests with beef. PV Kane has doubted the very authenticity of Vishnu Dharma Sutra. Jha's and Thapar's quotations from secondary sources to supersede the primary source (i.e., Vedas) are like attempts to supersede the Constitution of India by commentaries on the Constitution, or, to supersede decisions of the Supreme Court of India by the opinions of munsifs. These historians commit another basic blunder of placing Vedas and commentaries on Vedas on the same footings. A simple common sense fact is that secondary sources cannot supersede the primary source. Secondary sources always yield to primary source. It is a simple principle of jurisprudence. Canonical scriptures can neither be equated with nor superseded by non–canonical compositions. Sources which themselves concede primacy & supremacy to Vedas are, by definition, secondary sources.

Prof. Jha and others have cited a number of shlokas of the Manusmriti to justify beef eating such as (V.18) (V.31, 32) (V.39), etc. However, in (XI.116) the same Manusmriti prescribes penance for killing a cow. In (XI.96) Manusmriti says that flesh is food of *Pisachas & Raksasas* (demons). In (V.45 to 54), killing of animals and eating of flesh have been prohibited in the Manusmriti. (V.54) says that totally avoiding eating flesh is a great reward (*punya*). These internal self–contradictions within the Manusmriti prove beyond doubt that its text currently available is corrupted and interpolated one, justifying calls to discard Manusmriti lock, stock and barrel.

8.11 Animal Fat And Rheumatism

People who often consume beef /red meat, suffer from

rheumatism, more so, if they happen to live in a cold and damp climate. One way in which things we eat can cause arthritis, medical experts say, is by contributing to the formation of persistent immune complexes. Animal proteins, especially those from dairy sources, enter the blood stream and combine there with specific antibodies produced against them to form these 'immune complexes.' In most people these complexes would be 'eaten up' by scavenger cells found in liver, the spleen, and along the lining of blood vessels, and would quickly be removed from the blood stream. However, in the unfortunate victims of arthritis these complexes persist, and are not removed by scavenger cells. Eventually, they are filtered out of the blood stream by the capillaries traversing the tissues of the joints. There, embedded in the tiny blood vessels of the joint tissues, these complexes act much like slivers of wood stuck under the skin, causing severe inflammation of the joints. High animal fat, high cholesterol diet may inhibit activities of our immune system/scavenger cells leading to arthritis. Beef has some special proteins very high in carbon chains which liver of some persons is not able to break with the result that these get deposited into fluids between joints causing non–curable arthritis. Animal fats increase production of prostaglandin hormones that cause blood vessels to constrict which may slow the flow of blood and increase chance of blood clotting and heart attack/stroke/paralysis (www.drmcdougall.com).

8.12 Bovine Spongiform Encephalopathy (BSE): Mad Cow Disease.

The **mad cow disease** is known to spread from infected cows. Foot and mouth disease (FMD) is another disease among cattle. Bovine spongiform encephalopathies (BSE), Creutzfeldt–Jacob disease (CJD), vCJD, are deadly fatal, one–way traffic diseases caused by taking beef and marrow of diseased cows. Slaughter houses in India and world over do not know in advance whether the cattle being slaughtered is BSE infected or not; nor there is any testing machine available yet for this purpose. It is interesting to watch beef–ban trade war between Japan and the US, between Canada and the U.S.A etc.

CJD is now admitted to be transmitted genetically from one generation to another generation in the family. Dr. Frederick A. Murphy, Dean of the School of Veterinary Medicine, University of California Davis replied in the affirmative when asked if there was any evidence that CJD can appear as a genetic disease. He said Kuru and CJD should be thought of as two different spongiform encephalopathies. Kuru studies were instructive since they showed for the first time that a slowly progressive neurological disease of humans can be infectious, that is, transmitted from one person to another. For this discovery, Carleton Gajdusek was awarded the Nobel Prize. (www.accessexcellence.org). When asked whether there is any evidence that CJD can appear as a genetic disease, Dr. Murphy replied in the positive and said "Yes, there is familial form of CJD." The prion protein in familial cases is the same in each family member that has it and different in all other families. The pedigree of prion can always be determined. Thus, beef eating has the potential to terminate the family line of some beef–eaters who develop vCJD (human form of BSE).

Bovine spongiform encephalopathy (BSE) is a fatal brain disease of the cattle, which enters into human beings basically through bone marrow/spinal cord of affected cattle via food chain. BSE is an example of a Transmissible Spongiform Encephalopathy (TSE). Other TSE are Bovine Scrapie and kuru and Creutzfeldt–Jakob diseases (both in humans). Other examples of TSE are Gerstmann–Straussler–Scheinker syndrome (GSSS) and fatal familial insomnia (both in humans), chronic wasting disease of deer (CWD) and elk wasting disease (EWD). Scrapie is a fatal brain disease of sheep and goats endemic in many countries.

During 1974–1997 about 178,000 confirmed cases of BSE were reported in the UK alone and over 5 million infected cows were slaughtered and burnt there. More than 120 people died in the UK through infected meat. Mad cow disease was reported in Canada in May 2003. In the USA, mad cow infection was reported in Dec 2003. The infective agent of BSE is distorted prion. Infected prion has no nucleic acid and keeps replicating fast making the brain porus like sponge. It is not curable. The European Union Scientific Steering Committee in its Dec. 1997 Report did not rule out a inkage between beef and BSE saying, "current risk from beef is considered to be extremely small however the risk estimate has a wide range of uncertainty." Why did this Committee not totally rule out any linkage between beef and BSE, vCJD? Because such experts in Europe and in North America will be forced to pay millions of dollars in damages if, as defending experts, they failed to prove in a class suite that such a linkage was totally deniable. And death of 120 persons in UK alone does not rule out possibility of such a linkage.

There is no treatment or cure for BSE or vCJD. It is a one–way traffic like AIDS. The exact mechanisms of transmissions of infectivity to central nervous system are at present insufficiently understood and there is no rapid ante–mortem diagnostic test for BSE or vCJD. It is not known at what stage of incubation a BSE–incubating would give a positive result in an ante–mortem test if one existed (Institute of Food Science & Technology, UK, Oct., 2001).

The International Herald Tribune (17th Feb., 2004) reports that a new form of mad cow disease has been found in Italy and scientists believe that it may be the cause of some cases of human brain–wasting disease. Unusual forms of the mad cow disease have also been reported recently in France and Japan. Leading experts in prions, the mis–folded proteins believed to cause the disease, said the discoveries suggest that many cases of 'sporadic' human disease' by far the most common kind ' are not spontaneous at all, but come from eating brains or meat. The disease found in two aged dairy cows in Italy is so different from Bovine Spongiform encephalopathy (BSE) in cows and 'variant' Creutzfeldt–Jakob disease in humans that its discoverers gave it a new name, Bovine Amyloidotic Spongiform Encephalopathy, or BASE, because it forms amyloid plaques in the brain 'round, dark clumps of sticky protein debris'. Also, the new prions collect in different parts of the brain the olfactory bulb and thalamus, rather than the brain stem. And the two cows had relatively fewer of the 'holes' that turn the brains spongy. These characteristics resemble those found in about 30 percent of humans who have 'sporadic' Creutzfeldt–Jakob disease.

In the U.S.A, about 300 cases of sporadic CJD are reported every year. Only one person in the U.S.A is known to have died of variant CJD, the human form of mad cow disease, which was first described in the 1990s and has killed about 150 Europeans.

Food Standards Agency of the UK (www.foodstandards.gov.uk) informs that recent evidence has shown that the protein that accumulates in the brains of individuals with this new form of CJD is similar to the protein found in the cattle infected with BSE. Because of this newly discovered evidence, the new illness in humans is known as vCJD. Occurrence of vCJD in the UK, where there is a high incidence of BSE, suggests that there may be direct links between two diseases. Some individuals who have developed vCJD are known to have eaten BSE infected meat. vCJD is always fatal in humans.

As of March 2001, 95 cases of vCJD were discovered in the UK. The cattle also suffer from bovine tuberculosis.

Scientists have found evidence suggesting the human form of mad cow disease might be hitting a wider section of people than believed so far. All the people who died of vCJD in the UK had a genetic signature seen in about 35 per cent of Caucasians. In August, 2004, the Lancet medical journal reported spread of vCJD through blood transfusion from a mad cow disease infected person; and the genetic profile of new victim was more common that occurs in half of all Caucasians. It is less common among others ethnicities. (for further details see IHT, August 7–8, 2004, page 3)

8.13 Cancer, Cholesterol

Beef contains significant quantities of toxic organic chemical DIOXIN which causes cancer, endometriosis, Attention Deficit Order, chronic fatigue syndrome, rare nerve and blood disorders, immune system deficiency, etc. For more details see (www.cqs.com/beef.htm)

Beef harbours a deadly germ COLI 0157:H7 causing food poisoning. Because of 0157:H7 contamination, 25 million pound of beef was recalled in August 1997 in the USA. The International Herald Tribune (11th June, 2003) has carried a detailed article under the caption "From farm to fork, risk persists, How safe is your food?"

The Business Line of the Hindu Group (4th Sept., 2001) quoted Shri A.M. Dinshaw of Al Kabeer Exports saying that the world market does not require Indian beef and what they export is buffalo meat. According to Shri Dinshaw, buffalo meat from India is in demand because it is relatively lean with fat content being below two percent as against ten percent in beef. Buffalo meat has lower cholesterol.

Red meat has methyl nitro–amines, which cause cancer. Charred tandoori food has polycyclic aromatic hydrocarbons, which cause cancer. (www.atsdr.cde.gov). When meat and chicken are grilled turning brownish, chemical composition of food proteins changes becoming high in HFAs, which cause cancer. Grilled chicken has 400 times more HFA than non–grilled chicken.

There is a popular misconception that beef has high protein content which cannot be supplemented otherwise. Beef has only 22% protein, much below soyabean (43%), groundnut (31%), pulses (24%) etc.. Cholesterol per one hundred gramme of various items are: chicken breast (39mg), fish(60mg), pork(79), chicken leg(95), beef(99), lamb(100), cheese(100), butter(240), beef liver(300), ox liver(376), chicken eggs(548), lamb liver(610), chicken liver(748), beef kidney(800), beef encephalon (2300), pork encephalon(2530) etc. That is why doctors advise that lean white meat is safer than red meat. Cheese, butter, ghee, and chicken eggs are equally harmful.

Flu among chickens, the H5N1 strain, was first noted to have jumped into humans in Hong Kong in 1997. It was then brought under control by quickly slaughtering millions of birds. In January 2004, this flu, also called **avian flu**, was reported in China, Japan, South Korea, Thailand, Indonesia, etc. jumping into humans causing death of many humans. This deadly disease has been found to be transmitted from birds to humans; also, from avian flu affected humans to other humans. So, chicken is also not very safe. In January/February, 2004, millions of chickens were again slaughtered in these countries after millions of birds died of this flu. Some other strains of birds' flu are (H9N9) and (H9N2). In July 2004, Scientists voiced growing alarm that avian influenza may have become impossible to eradicate and may spread easily among humans. According to the WHO, about 34 people were infected early this year (2004) with a high mortality rate (IHT: July 08, 2004).

8.14 Cardiologists' Advice

Cardiologists also advise that meals high in animal fat raise blood cholesterol levels which may cause arteries to constrict and blood to clot more rapidly due to release of thromboxane and Factor VIII hormone leading to sudden cardiac arrests. Saturated fat (which comes from animal meat and coconut) impairs the ability of the liver to remove LDL (bad cholesterol) from blood circulation. A higher level of LDL is a factor leading to heart attack.

In August 2002, Indian newspapers reported that Kerala generates and consumes the maximum quantity of beef in India, and beef constituted nearly 40 percent of total meat consumed in Kerala. No wonder due to the deadly combination of beef and coconut oil, incidence of Dyslipedemia and Coronary Artery disease (CAD) are on the higher side in those areas. The Indian Medical Association, Kerala branch (www.imakerala.org) paper by Dr. N.G. Kaimal of Alleppey (March, 2001) informs that in India there is a geographical variation for the prevalence of CAD, only seven to nine percent in the northern region; and twelve to fourteen percent in the South (http://www.imakerala.org/cme/dyslipedimia.htm). As it is well known, dominant majority of people in the Northern India do not take beef. Dr. Kaimal advises that CAD mortality is 30% less in a vegetarian. Average serum cholesterol is 5.9 mm01/l in meat eaters, 5.6 mm01/l in fish eaters and, 5 mm01/l in vegetarians.

Coconut oil has the highest level of saturated fat (about 92%), which raises LDL (bad) cholesterol. The LDL responses of coconut oil are the highest (+36) with high levels of Atherogenicity and Thrombogenicity.

The world famous cardiologist, Dr. Dean Ornish of U.S.A, advises to do yoga and totally stop taking animal meat and animal fat and oils (triglycerides) to reopen closed coronary arteries without any medication and without bypass surgery. Dr. Ornish advises more or less to return to the the Vedic life style (i.e., morning walk, yoga, light vegetarian food without oils and without ghee) to regain a healthy heart. Dr. S.C. Manchanda, Head of Cardiology at the Metro Hospital, Delhi and Dr. K.K. Talwar, Head of Cardiology at the All India Institute of Medical Sciences (AIIMS), Delhi have also been quoted (Hindustan Times' 22nd May, 2003) advising that low–fat low–salt diet and yoga therapy reverse heart disease and hypertension.

Indians, both within and outside India, are more susceptible to get coronary artery diseases (CAD) when compared to other ethnic groups, perhaps, due to genetic predisposition, a non–resident Indian cardiologist, Dr K. Mohankishore, said while delivering his lecture at the International Institute of Medical Sciences at Vijaywada on 11th February, 2005.

Dr K. Mohankishore said a study conducted on patients revealed that despite the identical level of standard risk factors, including diabetes and metabolic syndrome, the absolute risk of CAD among Indians was double than that of other populations. It was paradoxical that the incidence was high among Indians despite low rates of obesity, smoking and hypertension, he said. Similarly, the high rates prevailed among the vegetarians as well as non–vegetarians and those living inside and outside the Indian subcontinent, he said. The prevalence of CAD in India, which was just four per cent during 1960, rose to 11 per cent during 2001, he said.

Philosophy narrated in the Holy Gita is considered by many cardiologists to be the best for stress management, neither be too attached nor be too detached: concentrate on doing efforts as doing so is in your control; do not be too attached to results (*phala*) as it is not in your own hand.

8.15 Option is Truly Yours

Thus, in terms of sixteen Vedic richas in which cow has been declared aghnya (अघन्य), there is not only total ban on cow slaughter in the Vedas, but they also call for slaughter of the killers of cows. Let those who enjoy beef and thus self–invite non–curable family line terminating genetic diseases like vCJD, do so openly without distorting the Vedas. There is no need or justification for them to distort Vedas and, thus, cause pain & anguish to millions of religious Hindus just to fulfil their own lust or taste for beef. The Vedas prescribe a life style for a disease free hundred year long (शतायु) life span for human beings (Yaj 36.24 & 40.2) but if a Hindu opts to terminate his life span earlier, let him do so, let him not blame the Vedas for not having cautioned him. RV (I.89.9) reads, "Since a hundred years were appointed (for the life of man), interpose not, Gods, in the midst of our passing existence, by inflicting infirmity in our bodies so that our sons become our sires i.e., let us not become so infirm requiring the paternal care of our own sons." RV (X.161) also confers hundred–year life span.

How many of us reach the age of hundred years without inviting infirmities? And, the reply is, how many of us follow the Vedas and the Vedic life style? It is internationally known that Indian men & women (irrespective of their religion) are genetically the most vulnerable group to cardiac problems, so, option is truly yours, whether or not, to further aggravate this genetic vulnerability by taking beef, and thereby self–invite non–curable and genetically terminating diseases.

"Genetically Indians are at higher risk of contracting diseases even when their weight is relatively lower than people in the West" says Dr. Catherine Le–Gales Camus, Assistant Director General, WHO, Geneva (Hindustan Times 31st March, 2004–page 9). Let's take better care of our own health. Should we, should we not is the real option.

Nine

MYTHS OF ARYAN–DRAVIDA DIVIDE

Experts agree that the words Aryans and Dravidians do not carry any racial connotation nor were intended to carry any such connotation. These words always implied only linguistic differences.

9.1 Meaning Of Arya And Dravida In Vedas

In the Vedas, 'arya' (आर्य) basically means 'sir', a noble person, an educated or cultured person, of course, following the Vedic religion, but with no racial connotation.

The word Dravida (द्रविण) occurs in many richas in the Vedas. It will be interesting to know the meaning assigned to word dravida in Vedas. The word 'Dravida' occurs in RV (III.58.6), (III.61.6), (IV.5.11–12), (V.28.2), (VI.69.1, 3, 5, 6), (VII.16.11), (IX.85.1), (X.31.2), (X.80.7), (X.81.1), (X.92.11) and (X.82.4) etc and implies wealth, opulence, treasure, prosperity. In Atharvaveda (XII.1.6), (XVIII.3.1), (XIX.31.6) and in Samaveda (55, 561, 1573) too, the word dravida occurs many times and always means property or wealth. Therefore, the Vedas do not attribute any derogatory meaning to word dravida. These are the East India Company historians who preached that dravida means black coloured people. No society expels the rich. Therefore, why did 'Aryans' act against common sense and why did they expel rich people is another fatal weakness of Aryan/ Dravida conflict hypothesis:

ऋतारी दिवो अर्कैरबोध्या रेवती रोदसी चित्रमस्थात्।
आयतीमग्न उषसं विभाती वाममेषि द्रविणं भिक्षमाणः ॥6॥
(RV:III.61.6)

"The possessor of truth is recognized in the sky by her rays: the possessor of wealth has taken a marvelous station in earth and heaven: Agni, soliciting alms of the radiant advancing Usas, you obtain your desired treasure (of oblations)."

* * * * *

ऋतं वोचे नमसा पृच्छ्यमानस्तवाशसा जातवेदो यदीदम।
त्वमस्य क्षयसि यद्ध विश्वं दिवि यदु द्रविणं यत्पृथिव्याम॥11॥
RV (IV.5.11)

"Interrogated with respect, I declare the truth, that this (wealth is acquired), Jatavedas, by the praise of you: you rule over it, (over) all that (it may be), the wealth that is in heaven or on earth."

* * * * *

किं नो अस्य द्रविणं कद्ध रत्नं वि नो वोचो जातवेदश्चिकित्वान।
गुहाध्वनः परमं यन्नो अस्य रेकु पदं न निदाना अगन्म॥21॥
RV (IV.5.12)

"What is the value of this (wealth) to us? what is its advantage? inform us, Jatavedas, for you know; (tell us) what is the best (course) for us on this secret path, so that we may follow unreproached the direct road." .

In Rigvedic sukta (II.37) and (I.96) deity (i.e., devata) is *Dravinoda–Agni*. So, the word dravida does not and cannot carry any derogatory connotation in the Vedas. RV (I.96.8) reads, "May *Dravinoda* grant us (a portion) of moveable wealth, may *Dravinoda* grant us (a portion) of that which is stationary, may *Dravinoda* give us food attended by progeny, may *Dravinoda* bestow upon us long life"

9.2 Confusion About Word 'Aryans'

There is a great confusion about the correct meaning and connotation of the word Aryans. Dr. Romila Thapar, a reputed Indian historian, has beautifully explained it in her Oct 99 JNU lecture on 'The Aryan Question Revisited' as under:

"The term Aryan as it is used in English with a capital 'A' was invented in the nineteenth century. It was invented by European scholars, who then proceeded to project Aryan both as a language and as a race. I will come to that in a moment. The term Aryan itself is derived from two sources. There is a very famous ancient text from Iran, the Avesta, which is linked to the religion of Zoroaster, what is known these days and practiced virtually only by the Parsis. The Avesta which was probably written at approximately the same time as the Rigveda uses the term 'airiya' for describing the authors of the text. The authors refer to themselves as 'airiya' from which of course later on you get Iran. And the Rigveda uses the term Arya. So, taking both these terms into consideration, it was decided that this new language and these new people were to be called Aryan. Now the nineteenth century scholars, this includes people like Max Müller, were fully aware that language and race are different things and yet frequently they confused languages with the race and equated them. And that is where in many ways the problem arises. They talked about an Aryan race on the basis of people speaking the same languages. Strictly speaking, they should be speaking about the Aryan (languages) speaking people. But, since this is an awkward phrase to use, it got cut down to the Aryans. It ceased to be just a language label and became a label for a racial entity as well. The difference between language and race is enormous. The two cannot be equated. Why? Because language is cultural."

"Race on the other hand is physical, biological descent. It has got nothing to do with social construction. So, language and race are in fact totally separate distinct features and the two cannot be equated. But, right through the nineteenth century with reference to the Aryans the two were equated and right through the twentieth century in the popular mind in India they continue to be equated. So please keep this in mind that you cannot talk about an Aryan race. Similarly, you cannot talk about a Dravidian race because once again the notion Dravidian race is based on language group, the Dravidian language group and it is incorrect to equate the two. Nor can you talk about a Munda race. These are all language labels and you have to be very careful to keep them as such." (http://members.tripod.com/ascjnu/aryan.html)

Jawaharlal Nehru has mentioned another (the third) source for word Aryan.We have seen in para 2.5 above that Jawaharlal Nehru was of the view that word Arya came from a root the word meaning to till, and Aryans as a whole were agriculturists.

9.3 Aryan–Dravida Divide : Myths And Realities

Some scholars assert that the Aryans were/are fair complexioned people and the Dravidians were/are dark skinned. They also claim that the four varnas were based on colours of skin. This is just not true as Lord Rama and Lord Krishna are always depicted in coloured pictures as dark complexioned (*shyama Varna*). Rishi Ved Vyas who compiled/ redacted the Vedas was himself of dark complexion (*Krishna dwaipayan*) born to a fisher woman. The Rigveda itself informs that Rishi Kanva who richly contributed to it was himself a dark skinned person vide RV (X.31.11):

उत कण्वं नृषदः पुत्रमाहुरुत श्यावो धनमादत्त।
प्र कृष्णाय रुशदपिन्वतोधर्ऋतमत्र नकिरस्मा अपीपेत्॥11॥
(RV:X.31.11)

On this subject of skin colour, I would again like to quote what Dr. Romila Thapar, a distinguished historian from India, said in her Oct. 99 address on 'The Aryan Question Revisited.' She said: "In fact, I cannot think of a single varna reference that actually refers to skin colour, except one, for example, the ninth book (Rigveda) which deals with the ritual of the soma karman where they talk about the hide turning black, the hide on which the ritual is carried out. Most of the references are used in a symbolic sense. You have the varna of the dawn, of the day, of the night, and of the clouds, and there is frequent reference to the dasas as the dark ones. They could be evil. They don't have to be necessarily always black skinned. In the same way as the Avesta refers to the daivas and says that they are the dark ones, the evil ones. These are the few, very few references to physical features. One which is frequently discussed *tvacamkrisnam*, which occurs only once in a very late section of the Rigveda. And the question of course is if the skin was black why it isn't mentioned more frequently and in the earlier hymns. Why do they wait till this one reference right in the late period.......Sayana was a very interesting person. He lived in the 14th century and did a commentary on the Vedic texts. I think it is very important for us as historians not just to stay with Max Müller's commentary on the Vedas but go back and look at what Sayana says. Sayana for example, when it comes to *tvacam krsna* says there was an asura called *Krsna* whose skin was torn apart by Indra. He does not read it a black skinned. There isn't single racial connotation in any of Sayana's commentaries. So anasa, he says was an–asa which means without a mouth i.e., people who didn't know the language and were, therefore, speechless. Alternatively, there is no reference to the Aryas being fair skinned or white skinned, the other contrast, which one would expect. Also, what is interesting and this is simply my reading, I may be incorrect on this, but I would nevertheless like to float it. There are one or two places where the word arya is used in a verbal sense–aryanti, they honour, and the root dasa is used again in a verbal sense–dasati–to treat with hostility. If these words, arya and dasa can be used not only as nouns and adjectives, but also as verbs, it is most unlikely that these can be interpreted as races."

There is no mention of forced southward migration of people either in Rigveda or in literatures now called Dravidian. Anthropological studies also do not attest hypothesis of any large scale migration of people right from the Harappa days into South India. However, starting from the East India Company historians, many scholars assert that fair skinned Aryans came from the West, invaded India during 1500 BC and defeated local Harappa culture people who were dark skinned and pushed them into South India. Bishop Robert Caldwell, a British Christian missionary, was the first in 1875 to have called the dark skinned people living in the South India collectively as Dravidians; and, Tamil, Telugu, Malayalam languages etc as Dravidian languages. Bishop Caldwell who initiated the Aryan–Dravida divide theory has himself admitted that his linguistic theories were of 'vast political and moral importance' implying that these served well British colonial interests. Another Indologist WW Hunter said, "Scholarship is warmed with the holy flame of Christian zeal". Such scholars end up with Dravidian Invasion Theory concluding that their 'Dravidians' too migrated into India (before their fair coloured Aryans) from the Mediterranean regions!

Sir John Marshall in 1924 suggested that the presence of

Brahui in Baluchistan would suggest that the Dravidian languages entered into India through this area. In recent decades, Marshall's view has been endorsed by leading Dravidologists including M.S. Andronov etc who see Brahui as the first group that broke off from the mainstream of Dravidian languages when they entered the Indian subcontinent around the fourth millennium BC (Parpola, Deciphering the Indus Script; Page 161).

In 1953, Christoph Von Furer–Haimendorf suggested that Dravidian languages came to India via Iran around 700 BC with Megalithic culture persons.

A scholar, Gopinathan (http://www.indiadefence.com/whoweare.htm) claims that languages like Latin and Greek have a number of loan words from Dravidian languages, so, he presumes that original Dravidians were of Mediterranean/Armenoid stock who in 4th millennium BC had settled in India and created the Indus Valley Civilization (IVC). Presence of Dravidian loan words in Greek/Latin does show contact between the two sets of languages implying movement either from the east to the west or from the west to the east, but Gopinathan presumes it to be only from the west to east.

Website (www.dalitchristians.com) claims that Dravidians were not the first inhabitants of India. It considers that Negritos, the first, followed by Australoids as the second inhabitants, the Mongoloids as the third; and, the Dravidians as the fourth immigrant inhabitants of India who came from the eastern Mediterranean in the third millennium BC and created IVC from Lothal to Mohen–jo–daro and had cultural links with Sumer.

Surprisingly, Shri SK Chatterji is of the opinion that: "No kind of man originated in India; all her human inhabitants having arrived from other lands." (Page 142, History & Culture of Indian People, Vol I) implying the British had as much claim over India as other Indians had.

Another website (www.zulunation.com) claims that Dravidians founded Hinduism in 3200BC who were Ethiopian invaders from Ethiopia in 3250–2750 BC and set up Indus Valley Civilization.The claim of this website is that Harappan people were Ethiopians.

Dr. Samar Abbas in his May 2003 paper 'India's Parthian Colony' (www.iranchamber.com) has claimed that the Pallava dynasty of South India was Iranian in origin.

In his interview of January1998, Ahmad Hassan Dani of Pakistan, who excavated at Mohen–jo–daro etc., told that (www.harappa.com) he did not agree with the presumption that Harappan people were Dravidians having links with the present day inhabitants of South India. If people of South India were really descendants of Harappan people, Dani argues, how is it that neither Harappan seals, nor Harappan language, nor Harappan urban/town planning structures or river dammings have been found in South India? Dani adds that we do not find any evidence of dam in Kaveri River, for example, the most important river in Tamil Nadu, earlier than first or second century AD. Ahmad Hassan Dani says that Prof. Asko Parpola of the University of Helsinki and others have been working on their *suo moto* presumptions that languages of the Indus/Harappan people were Dravidian, and, that people who built the Indus Civilization were Dravidian. But, he as well as Prof. BB Lal of India have not been able to agree with these subjective presumptions. To be fair, Prof. Parpola in his book "Deciphering the Indus Script" (page 174) says only in probabilistic terms that Harappan language is most likely to have belonged to the Dravidian family.

Dr. Subramanian Swamy, a former Minister in the Govt of India, wrote in the Frontline (June, 2003) that the British imperialists had wanted an instrument to 'divide and rule' over South India, and seized upon the fallacious Aryan–Dravidian

Divide theory propounded by the East India company historians. Dr. Swamy says that Justice Iyer in New India (July 3–16, 1916) had articulated his views debunking birth based caste system among Hindus, and that, Sanskrit and Tamil share about 40% of the vocabulary; the script of both have links with Brahmi. Therefore, people of North India and South India have common heritage.

Prof. Asko Parpola advises in his book 'Deciphering the Indus Script'(page 133) that for a period of thousand years, from the late second to the late first millennium BC, literary records available from South Asia are exclusively in Indo–Aryan languages. According to Prof Parpola, the first of the non–Aryan languages of South Asia to be recorded is Tamil, known from inscriptions and literature that go back to the last centuries preceding the Christian era. Therefore, it is logical to presume that before the advent of Tamil, our ancestors spoke a similar/common language. This is the objective reason why so many Sanskrit words are there in Tamil, Telugu, Malayalam, Kannada, etc.

Sri Aurovindo also advised that 'Aryan' and 'Dravidian' divide was artificial divide of one and the same people. Second series of dental letters ṭ, ḍ, ṇ, ḷ, ṣ, are taken as characterstic of 'Dravidian' languages but these are there in the Rigvedic Sanskrit though not in all other languages which are classified as 'Aryan' languages. This proves linkage/common heritage between Rigvedic Sanskrit and 'Dravidian' languages.

The sentence structures of Indo–Aryan languages and "Dravidian" languages are remarkably similar. A sentence in Tamil, Telugu etc. becomes good Bengali or Hindi by substituting Bengali/Hindi words for Tamil/Telugu words without modifying the word order. It is not only in cases of new Indo–Aryan languages but it began from the Middle Indo–Aryan syntax of Pali and Prakrit. Sanskrit words are there in

Malayalam, Tamil, Telugu, Kannada, Thai, Kumer, Indonesian bhasa etc. The Rigvedic Sanskrit has one cerebral consonant (ष) in excess of proto–Dravidian four (ṭ,ṇ,ḷ,ḷ). Burushaski has seven cerebrals spoken in the North–West Kashmir but it is admittedly not a Dravidian language. Korean and Japanese have sentence structures similar to that in Hindi. The following examples show similarity of sentence structure in the Indian languages:

Namaste, How do you do?
Namaskar, kemon achhen (Bangla)
Namaste! Kem Chho? (Gujrati)
नमस्ते आप कैसे हैं? (Hindi)
Konichi wa, anata wa ii desu ka (Japanese)
Namaskar! Channagiddira? (Kannada)
Namaskaram, Sukham tanne yalle? (Malyalam)
Namaskar! Kase bay (Marathi)
Vanakkam! Soukhyama? (Tamil)
Namaste! Baga unnara? (Telugu)

This language is not known to me:
Ami ei bhashati jani na (Bangla)
Mane a bhasha aavati nathi (Gujrati)
मैं यह भाषा नहीं जानता हूं। (Hindi)
Watukushi wa kono go o wakarimasan (Japanese)
Ee bhashe nanage tiliyuvudill (Kannada)
Ee bhash enikku ariyiall (Malayalam)
Mala hi bhasha yet nahie (Marathi)
Yenakk inda moli teriyadu (Tamil)
Naku ee bhasha teligadu (Telugu)

9.4 Aryan Invasion Theory: Now Discarded

In 1784, Sir William Jones, an employee of the East India Company, and President of the Asiatic Society in his paper

'On the Gods of Greece, Italy and India' claimed some resemblances among their gods and, later, pointing out some similarities in Sanskrit, other Indian languages, Greek, Latin, German etc suggested that these languages might be having a common source. Jones collectively called these as Indo–European languages. His knowledge about Hindu Gods could be gauged from this article in which he wrote that Kush was father of Lord Rama!

In 1816, Franz Bopp produced his first work; in 1852, his detailed work inventing proto–Indo–European language, the supposed mother of all Indo–European languages appeared. In this background, in 1853, Friedrich Max Müller introduced the word Arya into English and European usage with the connotation of race. Max Müller argued that the Aryan race originated in Central Asia, one branch came to Iran then continued to India; another branch went to Europe. In other words, Max Müller's hypothesis was that the same group of people having common roots laid the foundations of European, Iranian and Indian civilizations.

The Aryan Invasion Theory, one school claims, was developed by Max Müller, a highly paid German employee of the East India Company to deny political & moral grounds to Hindus (Aryans plus Dravidians) to claim independence from the British as they (Hindus), too, under this theory were as much foreigners in India (from Russian steppes or Mediterranean) as the British. (See para 8.5) This imperialist theory was designed to confer as much political legitimacy and political rights on British over India as Hindus (Aryans and Dravidians) claimed over India— all being foreigners, all being immigrants. Later, when the rule of the East India Co. had lapsed over India after 1857, and, Max Müller had become well established in the society, he too in 1888 conceded, "Aryan in scientific language is utterly inapplicable to race. It means language and nothing but language. Aryans are those who speak Aryan languages with Aryan grammar whatever their colour, whatever their blood." Therefore, Max Müller mercifully conceded that even black Indians could be his mythical 'Aryans'. However, Max Müller persisted with his concept of an 'Aryan language'. In the Rigveda, Arya means an educated one, neither race nor language. Sanskrit was the language of the Vedic people and continues to be the language of their descendants. Ideologues of Nazi Germany picked up this theory of Max Müller, a German and developed the Theory of Racial Supremacy of blonde Aryans with which Hinduism has nothing to do.

Some reputed linguists (Allen, Pissani, Salta and Trubetskoy etc.) question the very necessity to artificially invent the (so called mother) Indo–European language as they don't consider it necessary to postulate simply to justify similarities among many languages clubbed under this category of Indo–European languages. According to them, similarities in various languages could have arisen through borrowing and not necessarily due to a common ancestry. Further, there is no unanimity among scholars on the text/composition of the mythical 'mother' Indo–European language. Max Müller, Burrow Thieme and others have postulated different forms of the mother Indo–European language.

In 1875, General Alexander Cunningham published an article on Harappa with illustrations of the few antiques discovered there. Sir John Marshall, Director General of the Archaeological Survey of India asked Dr. Sahani to begin excavations at Harappa in January 1921. R.D. Banerjee discovered similar seals in 1923–3 at Mohen–jo–Daro in Sindh, some 650 km to the South–West of Harappa.

Prof. G.F. Dales of the Berkley University, USA, in his 1964 paper, has written that nine years of extensive excavations at

Mohen–jo–daro (1922–31) 'a city of three miles in circuit'yielded a total of some 37 skeletons, or parts thereof, which can be attributed with some certainty to the period of IVC. Some of these were found in contorted positions and groupings that suggested anything but orderly burials .He asks: "Where are the burnt fortresses, the arrowheads, weapons, pieces of armour, the smashed chariots and bodies of the invaders and defendants?" Prof. Dales adds, "Despite the extensive excavations at the largest Harappan sites, there is not a single bit of evidence that can be brought forth as unconditional proof of an armed conquest and destruction on the supposed scale of the Aryan invasion."

Prof Colin Renfrew (Cambridge) in his work "Archeology and Language: The Puzzle of Indo– European Origins" (1988) has written that as far as he could see there is nothing in the Hymns of Rigveda which demonstrates that Vedic speaking people were intrusive into India; the coming of the Indo–Europeans into India is just a presumption. Prof. Colin opines that we should seriously consider the possibility that the religion and culture of Rigveda was essentially a product of the soil of India, and that it was not imported ready–made on backs of the steeds of the Indo–Aryans.

Prof. Asko Parpola in his book "Deciphering the Indus Script" (1994) has written (page 22) that Harappan towns of transitional phase were burnt down and destroyed by Harappan people themselves while founding Mature Harappan settlements.

In fact, there is no mention of any foreign land in the Vedas. How could all the rishis of Rigveda (more than 414 in number spread over hundreds of years) forget to mention extra–territoriality in the Rigveda, if it was really true i.e., if they had really come from some foreign land into India, particularly when a number of richas such as RV (I.1.2), (I.131.4), (IV.1.13) and (VII.76.3,4), etc. frequently recall ancient (*purva*) and contemporary (*nutan*) risis, piters (our mortal human fore–fathers) etc.? How is it that all the sacred places of we Hindus are only within pre–partition Indian subcontinent, none in any area outside in the west beyond Afghanistan/Gandhar? On the contrary, Avesta does recall earlier/former areas of their habitation.

MS Elphinstone(1841), the first Governor of the Bombay Presidency, in his book, 'History of India',has concluded that there is no reason whatsoever for thinking that Hindus ever inhabited any country but their present one.

That wars mentioned in the Rigveda were always waged by the 'so called fair colour Aryans' against "dark skin dasa/dasyus" is sheer propaganda; it is just not true as in the richas RV(VI.19.8) and (VI.33.3) a fight takes place against kinsmen too. In RV (VIII.51.9), Indra is declared to belong to both Aryas and to Dasas "Good Lord of Wealth to whom all Aryas, Dasas here belong." In RV (IV.30.18), Indra slays Arna and Citraratha who are declared in this very richa to be Aryas (followers of Veda). Name of one of Rigvedic risi is trdasyu vasista who was revealed RV (IV.42), (V.27) and (IX.110) etc.

Again, very revealing is Wheeler's general observation: "Indeed, the anthropologists who have recently described the skeltons from Harappa remark that there, as at Lothal, the population would appear, on the available evidence, to have remained more or less stable from Harappan times to the present day." It means from Harappan times there was neither large–scale invasions by other races nor large–scale internal displacements of people.

The Aryan Invasion Theory has been totally discarded but now some scholars believe in the eastward migrations (no more large–scale armed invasions) in small small numbers of their

"Indo–Aryans" from Europe/ Ural Mountains into India. These are called "acculturation" models. Prof. Romila Thapar has written in the Frontline (13th Oct, 2000) that AIT has come to be discarded in favour of alternative theories of a series of migrations by Indo–Aryans into India. She says that in 1968 she had argued at a Session of the Indian History Council that the Aryan Invasion Theory was untenable. Prof. Michael Witzel of the Harvard University also wrote in the Outlook (20th Nov 2000) that the theory that Aryans were responsible for disintegration of the Indus civilization is no longer maintainable.

Prof. J. Mark Kenoyer of the Wisconsin University and many others have suggested that the Indus Civilization did not die but people there had to relocate elsewhere after one of their most important rivers (Gagra Kakhra) dried up. The Saraswati river dried up by 2200 BC. (See para 1.6) Another suspected cause of weathering away of Harappa civilization is presumed to be a shift in the course of the Indus River. Another is that Harappa people indiscriminately dammed the water along lower portions of the Indus without realizing the consequences: temporary but fatal flooding up river, flooding that would explain the thick layers of silt thirty feet above the level of the river at the site of Mohen–jo–daro. Some suggest that there was a long spell of draught spread over about three hundred years in which IVC slowly declined in the second millennium by continuous shift of residents into greener areas.

R.C. Majumdar, Raychaudhuri & Datta in their book 'An Advanced History of India' (page 15) have briefly covered the Harappan culture. "Archaeological excavations were carried out at Mohenjo–Daro in the Larkana district, Sindh and at Harappa, in the Montgomery district of the Punjab (Pakistan). Mohenjo–Daro — 'Mound of the Dead' — is the local name of a high mound situated in the plains of Larkana in a narrow strip of land between the main bed of the Indus River and the western Nara canal. Here a city was built some five thousand years ago. This city was successively destroyed and rebuilt no less than seven times, the inundation by the Indus being perhaps the chief agency of destruction. The rebuilding did not always immediately follow the destruction, but sometimes the city remained in ruins for a considerable period before a new city rose upon them."

"The Mohen–jo–Daro city is fairly big. The dwelling houses are many in number and vary in size from a small building with two rooms to a palatial structure having a frontage of 26 metres and a depth of 29.5 metres, with outer walls 1.25 to 1.5 metres thick. They are made of bricks, which are usually well burnt and of good quality. Sometimes very large bricks, measuring 51.5 centimetres long, 26.5 centimetres broad and 9 centimetres thick, are used. The big houses have two or more storeys, furnished with paved floors and courtyards, doors, windows and narrow stairways. It is especially noteworthy that almost every house has wells, drains and bathrooms. The streets of the city are wide and straight and are furnished with an elaborate drainage system together with soak–pits for sediment. On the whole, the ruins leave no doubt that there was on this site a large, populous and flourishing town whose inhabitants freely enjoyed, to a degree unknown elsewhere in the ancient world, not only the sanitary conveniences but also the luxuries and comforts of a highly–developed municipal life". "We must also conclude", Majumdar & others suggest, "That the art of building had reached a high degree of perfection in the Indus Valley Civilization. Kiln baked bricks of uniform size (1:2:4) and civil constructions including multi–storey houses using such bricks were especialities or characteristic marks of the Indus Valley Civilization".

In 1923, Earnest Mackay (who later excavated at Mohen–

jo–daro also) discovered a Harappan type seal at Tell Uhaimir under a pavement built by King Samsu–iluna (1749–12 BC). By 1932, about 30 Harappan seals were found in the Middle East. Nine seals found in Mesopotamia (Iraq) have been attributed to Akkadian period (2334–2154 BC). Some locally made Harappan seals were found in Ur, Susa, Tell Asmar and Tell as–Sulema etc. These prove that there was connection/ exchange among various cultures, and these were not unknown to each other.

Kot Diji, Amri, Gomal, Kalibangan (Rajasthan) are agreed to be pre–Harappan sites as pottery and other cultural items predating 2500 BC, and; Rana Ghundai III pottery culture items of 3500 BC were found at these sites. These items were found under debris of Harappa and low levels (–32 feet) of Mohen–jo–Daro. Excavations at Ghumla show a long cultural sequence in which Harappan culture comes fourth from the bottom. Asko Parpola also believes (page 15) that recent works clearly show that the Indus Valley civilization grew out of earlier local cultures and that these represent an essentially indigenous development. It means Harappan culture was not imported into India from the Mediterrarean region.Most important have been the French excavations carried out since 1974 at Mehrgarh and Nausharo creating unbroken cultural sequence from the end of eighth to the beginning of the second millennium BC. In his book 'Deciphering the Indus Script,' Dr. Asko Parpola has presented these various pre–Harappan cultures in detail (Page 18–19). Thus, there were admittedly pre–Harappa cultures in India. If so, what were these?

There is a very strange situation: one culture (the Indus Valley Civilization) has only archaeology and no literature (except seals); and another culture (the Vedic culture) has no archaeology but only heavy corpus of literature though both are accepted by all to have flourished more or less in the same geographical area, one following the other. The hypothesis of Vedic people invading the Indus Valley having failed, experts are now addressing the question whether the Indus Valley Civilization was actually the Vedic civilization, whether Harappan people were the descendants of the Vedic people. Mr. Egbert Richter–Ushanas, a German writer, in his 1997 book "The Indus Script and the Rigveda" has actually linked many Indus Valley seals to Rigvedic richas. About 200 inscriptions, among them the longest and those with the most interesting motifs, have been decoded in this book by setting them syllable for syllable in relation to the Rigvedic richas. However, universally acceptable decipherment of Harappan seals/language is still awaited.

It raises a very relevant question, whether Rigveda precedes the Harappan civilization. So far, the dominant view has been that Harappan or Indus Valley Civilization preceded the Rigveda. The mature IVC is accepted by all to have withered away by 1750 BC, if not before, whereas RV is believed by this school (Max Müller etc.) to have been composed only after 1500 BC. This view (Harappa pre–dating Vedic period) does not answer some simple questions. Such as, if RV is really post–Harappan, why there is no mention of remains of the characteristic Harappan urban structures (brick houses, roads, drainage etc) in RV? A simple answer appears to be: either there were no remains of Harappan civic structures when RV was being composed implying RV pre–dates Harappan civilization, or, these Harappan remains had got buried deep in the ground by the time the Rigvedic people are supposed to have arrived. However, to presume that all the 1400 Harappan sites spread over a million square kilometer area had got buried under ground by the time the Rigvedic people came is too much to presume. Someone who has visited Agra on horseback but has not mentioned the Taj Mahal in his memoir would only mean that he visited Agra before the Taj was constructed. India was visited by the Chinese Buddhist pilgrims Fa Hian (399 AD), Hiouen Thsano (630–645 AD) and I. Tsing (671–695 AD) and records of their travels are well–preserved but there will be no mention of Taj Mahal of Agra or Red Fort of Delhi in their records because they came to India before the Taj Mahal/Red Fort were built.

Experts opine that Harappan civilization was urban with features of town planning etc. And the Rigvedic Society was pre–urban having no urban centres and the Rigvedic people are believed to have been agro–pastoralists with small scale village societies. The claim that Rigveda is post–Harappa leads to another very awkward scenario; urban centres being taken over or replaced by rural small–scale societies without large scale armed invasion or without violent annihilation of Harappan people by the Rigvedic people. Why did 'victorious' Aryans not occupy brick made houses of 'defeated' Harappans? Why did the Rigvedic people not use Harappan bricks of uniform/standardized size in their constructions? Did the Harappans forget brick making and building civil town structures by the time Rigvedic people came? Why did the Rigvedic people not improve upon techniques of town planning of Harappans or force 'defeated' Harappans to make Harappa type houses for them (Rigvedic people)?

In September 2004, when I put these questions to Prof. Parpola,he suggested that, "The earliest Aryan speakers led a semi–nomadic life, trekking around,living in their waggons and houses built of wood, such as the temporary sheds built for the Vedics 'rauta rituals' please note that in the Vedic worship, there were no permanent temples. Unburnt earthen 'bricks'were used to build funeral mounds for distinguished dead, and burnt bricks of various sizes (not standardized single size as in the Indus civilization) were used to build Vedic fire altars." Prof. Parpola does not attest to use of homes made of fire burnt uniform size bricks by the Aryan speakers. Specific question posed by me to Prof. Parpola was, "Whether there is any mention of fire baked brick made homes (other than forts/ puram) for common citizens (Harappa type) or Harappan civil constructions (road, bathroom, drainage etc.) in Rigveda or other Vedas?"

The Yajurveda is aware of bricks in preparing fireplaces (Yajna vedi) such as Yaj (XVII.2) but still, Rigvedic people did not make brick houses for their own living or, force Harppan people to build brick houses for them (Aryans)! Victorious people living in temporary sheds or in wooden homes and defeated people living in multi–storey homes does not appeal to common sense. The simple answer seems to be that there were no Harappan bricks or Harappan urban structures during the Rigvedic period; so these find no mention in the Vedas. In other words, the Rigvedic people, one could argue, preceded the Harappan people, not the other way about. Villages grow into urban centres, not the other way.

The famous (M–304) seal found in Mohen–jo–Daro has the figure of a person sitting in yoga–mudra (either Padmasana or Siddhasana) wearing two horns of an animal, may be a water buffalo. A water buffalo is depicted in the seal along with a tiger, an elephant and a rhinoceros. All these four are noted for their ferocity and are prominent symbols of war, death and fertility. The other seal is (M305). Experts who hold the view that Indo–Aryans succeeded Harappans quote this figure in M(304 & 305) as Harappan form of Lord Shiva and call it 'Proto–Siva' as these seals depict characterizations of Rudra described in the Rigveda; they postulate that therefore, being successors to Harappan civilization, the Rigveda adopted the Harappan Proto–Siva as the Vedic Lord Shiva. Lord Shiva in Hinduism is also called 'Pasupati' i.e., overlord of animals and in (M304 & 305) 'deity' is surrounded by ferocious wild animals, it is assumed to represent Lord Shiva. The question is whether any statue of Pasupati had been excavated in IVC, if so, how many and where? If the Rigvedic people were not aware of brick–made double storey homes of rich Harappans, it will be reasonable to presume that they (Rigvedic people) would not have come across much smaller seals (M304 & 305) as well. So the question of Rigvedic risis basing their praise of Rudra on depictions in small objects like (M304 & 305), not seen by them, does not arise. The explanation that appears more reasonable is that Harappans succeeded Rigvedic people; they gave physical presentations or picturisations (in form of M304 & 305) to qualities attributed to Rudra in the Rigveda such as in RV (II.33) etc. One may see Sanskrit texts of three richas of RV (II.33) in para (5.7). Indra has himself been addressed as *shiva* in many Rigvedic richas such as (II.20.3), (VI.45.17) and (VIII.93.3) etc. so *shiva* is very much a Rigvedic deity. In these richas, the word *shiva* occurs in Devnagari script.

Mohen–jo–Daro seals (M296A) and (M296A bis), when rotated 90 degrees anti–clockwise from position generally printed in textbooks appear similar to omkar symbol as written in the Rigveda.

Swastika is mentioned many times in the Rigveda. Swastika appears in RV (I.90.5) meaning prosperity and in RV (IV.55.3) as goddess Svasti and as the abode of happiness. Well being is the usual meaning of Swastika. In RV (I.89.5), it means our welfare. Eighteen swastika (solitaire) seals in Mohen–jo–Daro (M332A to M348A and M435A) and fifteen swastika (solitaire) seals in Harappa (H104A to H118A) have been found. Swastika seals at Lothal have also been found (L–69, L–70). So, what is mentioned in the Rigveda has been found in physical form of seals in Mohen–jo–Daro and Harappa such as Pasupati (Proto–Siva), Swastika, Omkar but what was physically available in Harappan civilization (such as uniform size fire baked bricks, brick made mutli–storey houses, roads, bathrooms etc.) do not find any mention in the Rigveda. The Rigvedic people certainly did not have uniform– sized–brick made homes for themselves. Now, it is accepted that 'fire–pits' or fire–altars were there in Harappan civilization too. A row of seven fire altars (yajna–vedi) has been found in Kalibangan. At Lothal also, ritual fire places have been discovered in Mautre Harappan layers, from the earliest (II A) to the latest (IV) period. So, should Rigveda not precede Harappan civilization? The Times of UK carried a full–page report explaining that "one of the oldest known swastikas was painted on a palaeolithic cave 10,000 years ago and swastikas have been found on pottery and coins from ancient India, China and Greece". (HT January 20, 2005). Swastika in deep blue colour was the insignia of the Finnish Air Force, and in black colour that of the Finnish Army. In the Finnish language, it is called hakaristi (good luck, lucky).

There is a general misconception that Rigvedic people were more pastoralists than agriculturists. It is not true. Whereas some were in animal husbandry, others were in regular agriculture. Rigvedic people prayed for monsoon and ploughed their fields as farmers do even these days. This is evident from RV (IV.57.2, 4, 7, 8). RV (IV.57.2) reads, "Lord of the field, bestow upon us sweet abundant, (water), as the milch cow (yields her) milk, dropping like honey, blend as butter: may the lords of the water make us happy." RV (IV.57.4) reads, "May the oxen (draw) happily, the men (labour); the plough furrow happily; may the traces bind happily: wield the goad happily." RV (IV.57.7) reads, "May Indra take hold of Sita; may Pusan guide her; may she, well stored with water, yield it as milk, year after year." RV (IV.57.8) reads: "May the plough shares break up our land happily; may the ploughman go happily with the oxen; may Parjanya (water the earth) with sweet showers happily: grant, Suna and Sira, prosperity to us".

शुनं नः फला वि कृषन्तु भूमिं शूनं कीनाशा अभि यन्तु वाहैः।
शुनं पर्जन्यो मधुना पयोभिः शुनासीरा शुनमस्मासु धत्तम्॥8॥
RV (IV.57.8)

Those who plough the fields are not nomads by definition but are settled in regular agriculture. Farmers generally remain at one place for generations.

People assert that names of rivers also migrate. The Harahvati is claimed to become Saraswati, quite a distance away from Afghanistan to Punjab. But if RV was composed during 1500 BC to 800 BC, why should Rigvedic people have carried the name of Harahvati from Afghanistan to Punjab and give this name to an already dried up channel as Rigvedic Saraswati in the Punjab region. (Saraswati had dried up by 2200 BC. See paras 1.6 and 1.7)

The horse is central to Rigveda but it is said to be totally absent on seals of the Harappan culture. Absence of horse on Harappan seals is interpreted to mean total unfamiliarity of Harappan people with horses. Therefore, the argument is that as invading Aryans brought the horse into South Asia, Harappan culture must pre–date Rigvedic people. This school argues that as domestic horse, archaeologically speaking, does not appear in the Indian subcontinent before 2000 BC, Rigvedic richas cannot be older than 2000 BC. Experts are divided on this horse point. Some assert that horse bones of period 6000–5000 BC (pre–Harappa) have been found at Kila Gul Mohammad in Baluchistan. Dr. A.R. Alur, a veterinary doctor researched on excavations at Hallur, Dharwad, Karnataka (excavated in 1965) and claimed to have found horse bones of 1800 BC to 1500 BC on carbon dating. In 1980, the University of Allahabad reported finding bones of cattle, horse, sheep, etc in Vindhya/Ganga region of period 17,765±340 BC to 5540±240 BC showing human settlements in this region. Dr SR Rao also reports that horse bones have been found (after 1930–40) both from the 'Mature Harappan' and 'Late Harappan' levels.

In Septemer 2004 ,when I asked Prof. Parpola whether any seal in the Harappan civilization has been found depicting 'cow', he replied, 'The animals depicted on the seals'cattles and other species'appear to be all males,with the genitals clearly represented". In other words, no seal depicting 'cow' has been found in the Harappan civilization. Does it mean Harappans were not aware of 'cows'? Absence of cow seal does not and cannot mean absence of cows in the Harappan civilization as bulls have been known to Harappans. Similarly, absence of horse seals in the Harappan civilization may not necessarily imply absence of horses in the Harappan civilization. Absence of cow seals in the Harappan culture was explained by Prof. Parpola saying that, perhaps, worship of female cattle was not in vogue in the Harappan culture. May be horse worship too was not in vogue in the Harappan culture which explains absence of horses on the Harappan seals. If Harappa had followed Rigvedic period, absence of horse seals in Harappan culture would imply that Harappan people had given up the Rigvedic practice of worshipping horses. Prof Parpola disagreed with this analysis of mine. He pointed out that many different animals were represented in the Indus seals, but not the horse, which one would expect to be represented as a stallion and not as a mare. Prof. Parpola said it was impossible to place Rigveda before the Indus civilization (2500 to 1900 BC) because Rigveda many times refers to chariots pulled by horses, and the earliest known horse–chariots, so far, anywhere in the world are dated tp 2000BC (graves in sintashta–Arkaina culture of the Southern Urals.)

Harappan Seals

M-304 A ter

M-296 a

M-332 A

Another argument marshalled to suggest that Rigvedic people were outsiders to the Indian sub–continent is that in the Rigveda there is no reference to tiger, there are references only to *simha* as lions; and, as tiger is a basic animal in the lower Indus area, Rigvedic people would have known about tiger if they were indigenous people of Indus Valley. Firstly, RV is not a dictionary of animals; the absence of reference to any animal in RV does not necessarily mean unfamiliarity of Rigvedic people with that animal. Secondly, the name of one of Rigvedic rishi is Vyaghrapad Vasista (व्याघ्रपाद वासिष्ठ). Vyaghrapad means one who has feet like a tiger or who walks like a tiger. This risi composed RV (IX.97.16–18). Words tiger (व्याघ्र) and lion (सिंह) simultaneously appear in Atharvaveda (IV.8.7). The word tiger (व्याघ्र) occurs twice in AV (IV.8.4). Therefore, the Vedic people were aware of the tiger as well as the lion.

9.5 Ambedkar On Dasas, Dasyus, AIT And His Single Race Theory

Dr. BR Ambedkar had also emphatically rejected the Aryan Invasion Theory (AIT). The April 2001 Document (www.sabrang.com) quotes Ambedkar writing, "there is no evidence to show that the distinction between Aryans, Dasas and Dasyus was a racial distinction". Sri Aurovindo, a great expert on the Vedas, also concluded that the Vedas do not suggest any racial division between 'Aryans' and 'Dasas/Dasyus.' AA MacDonell and A.B. Keith too say, "The great difference between the Dasyus and the Aryans was their religion". It is significant that (in the Vedas) a constant reference is made to difference in religion between Aryans and Dasas & Dasyus."(The Vedic Index of Names and Subjects, pages 347, 356–7).

Ambedkar said that the 'Theory of Aryan Invasion' was an invention and just an assumption. The assertion that Aryans came from outside, Dr Ambedkar wrote, and invaded India, was not proved and the premise that Dasas and Dasyus were aboriginal tribes of India was demonstrably false. Ambedkar also quoted three richas of the Rigveda (I.117.5, 8) and (II.3.9) to assert that Vedic people had no preference for colour, and; that the Vedas do not support the contention that Vedic people were different in colour from Dasas and Dasyus. Ambedkar also mentioned the Rigvedic richa RV (X.31.11) to say that one of the composers of RV'rishi Kanva– was himself of black colour.

Ambedkar always rejected the hypothesis that fair colour upper caste Hindus were descendants of invading fair colour Aryans, and that the untouchables were from local black colour Dravidians. He always held the view that all castes of Hindus came from the same race. 'If the Brahamans are Aryans', Ambedkar said, "the untouchables are also Aryans, if the

Brahamans are Dravidians, the untouchables are also Dravidians". (BR Ambedkar, Writings and Speeches, Govt of Maharastra, 1986–90 volVII, page 85 and 302–303). At page 162 of 'Dalits and the Democratic Revolution' by Gail Omvedt, Dr. Ambedkar is quoted as having rejected the "non–Aryan theory" of origin of 'untouchables.'

Here, it is pertinent to recall what Jawaharlal Nehru, the first Prime Minister, had to say, "India for ages past is a country of pilgrimage. All over the country, you find ancient places from Badrinath, Kedarnath, and Amar Nath in the North to Kanyakumari in the South. **It is the feeling of one country and one culture that binds us together.**" (1961 Madurai Session, AICC).

9.6 Dasas, Dasyus; Aryans From The Same Racial Stock

The word Arya appears 36 times in 34 Rigvedic richas. The word Dasa appears in 54 hymns (63 richas) and word Dasyu is found in 65 hymns (85 richas) of the Rigveda. In Rigvedic phraseology, Dasas/Dasyus never meant black or Dravidians but only those who did not follow the Rigveda, and were called asraddha (faithless), ayajna (offering no yajna), avrata (without rituals) etc. People referred to as Dasas/Dasyus in the Vedas were most probably Indo–Iranian tribes and Zoroastrians.

Nineteenth century historians and the East India Company historians spread the myth that the fair–skinned Aryans defeated the black skinned Dravidians who are referred to as Dasas/Dasyus in the Rigveda; and that Aryans and Dasas/ Dasyus belonged to different races. Now, it is accepted that 'Dasas', 'Dasyus', and 'Aryans' belonged to the same racial stock but different language groups. In September 2004, Prof. Parpola replied to me, "Race and language are not bound together. Individuals and people can and do change language. But yes, in my opinion the Daasa language belonged to the same Indo–Iranian branch of the Indo–European language family as the (Vedic) Sanskrit, only it was a very early representative of 'Iranian' while the (Vedic) Sanskrit is 'Indo–Aryan'. The question asked by me was, 'Arya, Dasas, dasyus, I understand, are now accepted to belong to the same race, same stock, sharing same homeland but different language groups of Indo–European family– is it correct?" Later, Prof Parpola informed me that some scholars still think that Dasas and Dasyus spoke non–Aryan languages.

Dr Romila Thapar also suggests that there was no racial difference between the Aryas and the Dasas. In her talk of Oct'99 on "The Aryan Question Revisited," Dr. Romila Thapar clarified, "Let me turn now to the tricky question of the definition of the Arya and the Dasa. Was there in fact a racial distinction? Remember I told you that the argument was that the Arya race came and conquered the local race of the dasa. What is very interesting is that the physical differences that are mentioned all occur in the last books of the Rigveda, not in the first books. If there was a strong physical difference, marked physical difference, you would expect that from the very first compositions the composers would say that these dasa who are black skinned, thick lipped, bull jawed etc all the descriptions, but no, the descriptions come in the tail end in the second half of the first book and the tenth book of the Rigveda. What you have then if one looks for the definition of the arya varna and the dasa varna from the Rigveda, these are groups of people that have distinctive languages, because the dasas are spoken of as being mrdhravac, speaking a hostile language or not speaking the language correctly. They are also described frequently as avrata "they do not perform the rites, the religious rites, which the aryas (Vedic people) perform. They are also *akarman* they do not observe the customs that the aryas observe."

SG Talageri's view is that Dasas refer to non–Puru tribes (of Aryan language groups) and Dasyus mean their priestly class.

R.C. Majumdar, H.C. Raychaudhuri & Kalikinkar Datta at page–25 of their book 'An Advanced History of India' inform that, "The Indra–worshipping tribes seem to have been divided into two rival groups. One of these included the Srinjayas and their allies the Bharatas, both lauded by the priestly family of the Bharadvajas. To the other group belonged the Yadus, Turvasas, Druhyus, Anus and Purus who are found frequently in alliance with indigenous tribes. The first two tribes of the second group are branded as Dasas in one passage of the Rigveda, and of the remaining three, the Purus are styled mridhravachah, 'of hostile speech', an epithet otherwise applied only to the Dasyus."

Avesta and other Zoroastrian scriptures not only call their Gods..... Ahuras and their demons as Daevas but also call their own followers as Dahas and Dahyus and that they migrated to places where Avesta was composed from sixteen places including 'Airiyan Vajeo.' Indra, the dominant god in the Rigveda is a demon in Zoroastrian texts and the name of the supreme demon in Z–texts is Angara Manyu. In the Rigveda, Angiras are a risi family and rishi Manyu is composer of RV (X.83 and 84). These show hostility between them i.e., between Zoroastrians and Rigvedic tribes. So, the wars between 'dasas/dasyus' and 'Aryans' described in the Rigveda appear to be fights between Indo–Aryans and Indo–Iranians (Zoroastrians) i.e., between two language groups of the same stock/race. Rigveda is saga of conflict between two branches of Aryan languages speakers: one who remained in India; and those who migrated to Iran from "Airiyan Vajeo."

Prof. Parpola argues, in a paper published in Iranica Antiqua, (vol. 37, 2002) that the Dasas were the elite of BMAC (Bactria and Margiana Archaeological Complex) who had come from the Eurasiatic steppe and taken over the rule in the originally non–Indo–European languages speaking culture; that the Dasas were the Aryan (language) speakers, but represented a branch that had come to these parts earlier than the Rigvedic Aryans; and it was, Prof. Parpola further argues, through this BMAC culture that the Aryan speech first spread from Central Asia to Iran and to India. In other words, Dasas and Rigvedic Aryans were two branches from same stock, sharing same 'homeland' but different languages.

Prof. Parpola's hypothesis is that about 2100 BC the first wave of BMAC Aryans, a group of pre–Proto–Iranian speakers, ancestors of Dasas, came to Southern Central Asia from lower Volga–Ural steppes and took over the rule of BMAC in Southern Bactria (in northern Afghanistan and Southern Taj Kistan) and Sapalli in northern Bactria and that they infiltrated the elite of the Indus Civilization as well, some proceeding as far east as the Ganges–Yamuna region. Parpola presumes that linguistic differences between the Indo–Aryan and the Iranian branches appeared only after 1900 BC. He postulates that a second Proto–Indo–Aryan wave of Aryan language speakers replaced pre–proto–Iranians as rulers of the BMAC around 1900 BC. The third also Proto–Indo–Aryan speaking wave is supposed to have come to the BMAG from the north around 1700 BC.

This third wave of Aryan language speakers is believed by Parpola to have been fused with their predecessors (Dasas) and the resulting mixture is supposed to have extended westward taking over the rule in the Mittani Kingdom of Syria. The same stock is supposed to have come to South Asia via Swat. Prof. Parpola believes that this third wave of BMAC Aryan language group constituted the first wave of the Rigvedic Aryans (including the tribes of Yadus and Turvasas) represented by the Kanva poets of the 8th and 1st books of the

Rigveda. The fourth wave of Aryan speakers to come to Southern Central Asia were the Proto–Iranians of the classical Timber Grave culture of eastern Europe around 1300 BC. Their coming Parpola postulates, made a part of Proto–Indo–Aryans of the Central Asia and 'Greater Iran' to move into South Asia resulting in a second wave of Rigvedic Aryans, the Purus and Bharata tribes. They came via eastern Afghanistan fighting there with earlier arrived Dasas.

To be fair, Prof. Parpola has put a disclaimer in his paper saying that above is his present understandings of how Aryan speakers came into South Asia. Nevertheless, he makes it clear that the war described in the Rigveda is not between people of different races (Aryans and Dravidians) but among different language groups of people of the same stock.

9.7 Some Points

A place slowly starts developing into an urban centre (in pre–industrial era) as the need for trading the surplus produce (agriculture, handicraft, dairy, etc.) of surrounding or nearby villages grows. That is, emergence of urban centre follows growth of economy of nearby villages beyond a point. Majority of residents of non–industrial urban centres are in service/trade whereas majority of residents of villages are in production (agriculture, animal husbandry, dairy, handicrafts etc.). Academics suggest that the Rigvedic society was basically rural, based primarily on agriculture and animal husbandry; and the Indus Civilization was basically urban with characteristic town planning, outer boundary wall of town, grainary store, water–tanks, straight roads, community halls, houses with stair–cases, all made of fire–baked bricks of regular size (30x20x10 or 1:2:4). Following the normal course of growth of human settlements, i.e., the expanding rural economy giving birth to urban centres, Rigvedic society should precede the urban Harappan society, particularly when the view of violent destruction of Harappan society by non–Harappan people has now been discarded.

Another puzzle is that if Rigvedic society was that simple rural and nothing more, why and how should the concepts of Emperor and Empress, king & queen and nation appear in Rigveda? In RV (X.85.46) daughter–in–law is being blessed to attain status of Empress (samragyi) (सम्राज्ञी). RV (X.125.3) has word (mahisi) the mighty queen. Again, in RV (X.159.3) it is said, 'My daughter is an empress' (duhita viraat) (HH Wilson's translation). The word 'samrat' (सम्राट) occurs in AV (IV.1.5), RV (I.100.1) also. The words king (raja), queen (rani) also occur in the Vedas. The word raja in Devnagari script appears in RV (IX.97.56), (VII.27.3), (I.156.4), etc. meaning the sovereign. The word nation (राष्ट्र) appears in RV (X.124).

9.8 Migrations : Eastward or Westward

इमं मे गङ्गे यमुने सरस्वति शुतुद्रि स्तोमं सचता परुष्ण्या।
असिक्न्या मरुद्वृते वितस्तयार्जीकीये शृणुह्या सुषोमया।
(RV:X.75.5)

तृष्टामया प्रथमं यातवे सजूः सुसर्त्वा रसया श्वेत्या त्या।
त्वं सिन्धो कुभया गोमती कुमुं मेहत्न्वा सरथं याभिरीयसे ॥6॥
(RV:X.75.6)

Now, the theory of westward migration of Vedic people/ Indians from UP/Bihar region to Central Asia/ Europe is taking a sharper shape. One may see: Shrikant Talageri's The Rigveda: A Historical Analysis.

On this question of westward or eastward migration, readers may decide themselves by looking at shloka RV (X.75.5): "Accept this my praise, Ganga, Yamuna, Saraswati, Suturdi, Parushni, Marudvrdha, with Askini and Vitasta; listen, Arjikiya with Sumosa." Parusni is another name for Iravati, or Ravi; Arijkiya is the same as the Vipasa (Beas) and the Susoma is the Sindhu. The Suturdi is Sutlej; the Vitasa (Jhelum); the Askini (Chenab). In this shloka, readers may note that the direction of description of rivers is from the east to the west. Direction of description of rivers is not from the west (i.e.,from Sindhu) towards the east (i.e., Ganga) but from Ganga towards Sindhu. Thereafter, in the next richa, rivers beyond Sindhu are further mentioned in the westwardly direction. If the Vedic people had come into India from the west, order of rivers in (X.75.5) ought to have been just the opposite i.e., from west to east. After all, it is common sense that while enumerating/recalling names of popular rivers, cities, personalities etc, the most important or the most popular one is cited the first, followed by less and less important ones. This means the Ganga River was the most familiar one and the most important or most popular one among Rigvedic people implying that main place of habitation of Vedic people was in the Gangetic region. In the subsequent sloka (X.75.6) rivers of Afghanistan are mentioned which lends support to the hypothesis of westward migration of people from Central India region. Wilson translates (X.75.6) 'You, Sindhu, in order to reach the swift–moving Gomati, have united, yourself first with the Trstama: (now be united) with the Susartu, the Rasa, the Sveti, the Kubha, and the Mehatnu, in conjunction with which streams you do advance.' Gomati (Gomal), Kubha (Kabul), Krumu (Kurram) and Suvastu (Swat) are rivers in Afghanistan.

Some people claim that the river Saraswati mentioned in RV was actually somewhere in Western Afghanistan. This claim is knocked out by RV (X.75.5) as in this richa, Saraswati is mentioned (geographically speaking) between Yamuna and Suturdi (Sutlej); both are live and flowing rivers of today. (See Para 1.6)

The Rishi who composed RV (IX.96) and RV (X.179.2) says that he belonged to the family of King of Kashi (Varanasi, my hometown). Prof. Micheal Witzel disputes it and asserts that Kashi and other Gangetic lands mentioned in Talageri's book do not show up in the RV at all. Witzel says that Talageri has relied upon such an anukramani, which is not so old, and has 'Eastern' bias. Arya & Joshi also in their Rigveda mention the name of composer of RV (X.179.2) as Pratardana Kashiraj i.e., Pratardana from the royal family of Kashi.

In RV (III.53.14), Kikatas and their king Pramaganda are described; and kikatas were inhabitants of areas in Bihar. Prof. Witzel says that this richa speaks of kuruksetra, some 750 miles west of South Bihar. Arya and Joshi point out in their RV that kikata is usually identified with South Bihar in agreement with Talageri. Majumdar, Raychaudhury & Datta also asscociate Kikatas with South Bihar (An Advanced History of India, page 27). Sayana, following Yaska, Nirukta (VI.32), says kikatas to be countries inhabited by Anaryas, people who do not perform worship implying that Vedic Hinduism had not reached these provinces when richa (III.53.14) was composed. In any case, this richa confirms that the Rigvedic people knew about geography of Kikatas region.

In shloka RV (VIII.2.41), rishi Kanva Medhatithi praises king Vibhindu and in RV (VIII.3.21–24) praises another king Pakasthaman for their generous gifts; the Brihaddevata (VI.42) clearly informs that they were kings of Kashi and Bhoja (Madhya Pradesh) respectively. Rishika Lopamudra, wife of Agastya rishi was the daughter of the King of Vidarbha. She composed RV (I.179.1–2). Richas (VIII.5.37–39) expressly refer to Cedi Kings of Central India for their generous gifts and valour. AA MacDonell (page 131) informs that Cedis are found in epic age as settled in Magadha (South Bihar). MacDonell adds that Rigveda refers to a rich and powerful prince Iksvaku who ruled to the east of the Ganges at Ayodhya and was the founder of the Suryavanshi dynastry in which Lord Rama was born (MacDonell, page 133). These shlokas of the Rigveda seriously question the hypothesis that the Rigveda was composed exclusively or mostly in the Punjab/Afghanistan region.

The name of the river Ganga/Jahnavi appears in four richas RV (I.116.19), (III.58.6), (VI.45.31) and (X.75.5) Talageri argues that as the sixth mandala is the oldest chapter of the Rigveda, the original home of the Vedic Aryans was the Indo–Gangetic region. Talageri enforces his view that Jahnavi in RV (I.116.19) means the Ganges by stating that in richa (I.116.18) simsumara refers to Gangetic dolphin (suis). AP Arya & Joshi in their Rigveda Samhita (part I – page 291) also say that simsumara is a name of the Gangetic porpoise.

Following is the text of RV (VI.45.31):

अधि बृबुः पणीनां वर्षिष्ठे मूर्धन्नस्थात्। उरुः कक्षो न गाङ्ग्यः ॥32॥
(RV:VI.45.31)

"Brbu presided over the high places of the Panis, like the elevated bank of the Ganges."

River Yamuna is mentioned by name in RV (V.52.17) and RV (VII.18.19) reconfirming presence of Rigvedic people in the Gangetic plains:

सप्त मे सप्त शाकिन एकमेका शता ददुः।
यमुनायामधि श्रुतमुद्राधो गव्यं मृजे नि राधो अश्व्यं मृजे॥17॥
(RV:V.52.17)

"May the seven times seven all–potent (Maruts, aggregated as) as a single troop, bestow upon me hundreds (of cattle): may I possess wealth of cows, renowned upon the (banks of) the Yamuna: may I possess wealth of horses." Yamuna is mentioned in Atharvaveda (IV.9.10) also. In AV (XX.137.9)

River Yamuna is mentioned under the name Ansumati.

Prof. Michael Witzel of the Harvard University, a learned Indologist, has opined that in RV (I.116.19), Jahnavi is merely a female word meaning the wife or a female relation of Jahnu and that it does not imply the river Ganges. Witzel further states that the river dolphin is not just found in the Ganges but also in the Indus River. In fact, dolphins (suis) are found in many rivers of the Gangetic plains. Another argument of Witzel is that RV (I.116.18) and (I.116.19) are not closely connected, though, these are adjacent richas. So, (page 17, EJVS–7–2 htm) Witzel concludes that, "In short, jahnavi Ganges is not found in the Rigveda." However, readers may see in the above quoted Sanskrit texts of RV (VI.45.31) and (X.75.5), river Ganges is referred to in the Devanagari script under the name 'ganga' (गंगा) in the Rigveda. All Indians know that Jahnavi is a synonym of river Ganga, still in vogue; that it is a female name. Witzel argues that as per Oldenbereg's work (1888), RV (VI.45.31) is a late addition to the Sixth mandala at some uncertain time.

We see word Ganga in Devanagari script twice in RV and the word Yamuna in Devanagari script thrice. Therefore, it is not fair to say that RV was composed exclusively in Afghanistan/Punjab region.

The geographical area inhabited by the Rigvedic people is clearly indicated by the mention of certain rivers in the Vedas, which permit of easy identification. The most important among these are the Kubha (Kabul), the Suvastu (Swat), the Krumu (Kurram), the Gomati (Gumal), the Sindhu (Indus), the Sushoma (Sohan/Sindhu), the Vitasta (Jhelum), the Asikni (Chenab), the Marudvridha (Maruwardwan), the Parushni (Ravi), the Vipas (Bias), the Sutudri (Sutlej), the Saraswati, the Drishadvati (the Rakshi or Chitang), the Jumna, the Ganga and the Sarayu. The mention of these rivers in the Vedas implies the possession by the Rigvedic people of a considerable portion of the country stretching from eastern Afghanistan to the upper valley of the Ganges (RC Majumdar & others, page 27).

9.9 Westward Migration of Rroma people: From India to Europe

Now, it is accepted that Rroma or Roma people (also known as Gypsies in Europe) had their origin in India. They are descendants of Indians who left India thousands of years ago. Gypsy is the 16th century English translation of Spanish word Gitano. Moreover, Gitano is the 15th century Spanish word for people from Egypt. There is no unanimity as to when they first left India and in how many waves. Some believe that few artisans and black smiths left India along with returning armies of victorious Alexander the Great as camp attendants who were later left behind in Egypt. From Egypt, they moved into Spain so their name Gitano i.e., ones from Egypt.

Some believe that Roma people are descendants of such Indians, who were taken slaves by Mahmud of Ghazani during his Indian invasions and taken to Kabul, but being surplus, were later released in Afghanistan; rather than returning to India, they kept wandering westward into Europe via Egypt, Syria etc. In Arab chronicles there are numerous references to a wandering tribe called Zotts (Jats). Prof. Asko Parpola in his 'Decipherinig the Indus Script' (page 163) informs that Siraiki language of Pakistan is known in Baluchi language as Jatki i.e., the language of Jatt people. The ethnicon Jatt comes from Middle Indo–Aryan Jatta, from Old Indo–Aryan Jarta, known from the Mahabharata in the form Jartika as the name of people living in the northern Indus Valley. Five Brahui and several Baluch tribes claim Jatt origin.

Walid (705–715) and Yazid II (716 AD) expelled Zotts to north of Baghdad, to Khanikin and to Ainzarba. In 856, the

Byzantians captured Ainzarba from Arabs. It is this time when Gypsies first appeared in Byzantine territory. Another wave of westward migrants from India is believed to be survivors of the army of Prithvi Raj Chouhan after his disastrous defeat at the hands of Muhammad Ghori in 1192 at Tarain. Many Rroma people believe that their ancestors migrated from India in this wave in 1192 AD.

In Romani legends, India is commonly referred as the Baro Than (the Great Land). One of their legends claims their antiquity in India as far back as the invasion of Alexander. Romani language has many dialects but the root language is ancient Punjabi or Hindi. Of all the evidence linking Romanis with India, the linguistic one is considered the most important. The philological/linguistic similarity was steadily brought out by Stefan Valyi (a Hungarian) in 1763, J.C. Rudiger in 1782, by August Friedrich Pott in 1844, Paspati in 1870 and by an Austrian philologist Franz Miklosich in 1872–81. John Sampson published his work 'The Dialect of the Gypsies of Wales' in 1926.

Romani language is related to Sanskrit/Hindi as may be seen below:

Romani	Hindi	English
yek	ek	one
dui	do	two
trin	tin	three
star or chtar	char	four
pansh	panc	five
sho	chha	six
eft (half in Persian)	sat	seven
okht–octo	ath	eight
nu	nau	nine
dash	das	ten

The following are a few examples of Romani words with their Hindi and English equivalents:

Romani	Hindi	English
yakh	ankh	eye
yag	ag	fire
kalo	kala	black
ker	kar	to do, make
kan	kan	ear
devata	devata	deity
nak	nak	nose
bal	bal	hair
rat	rakt	blood
tud	dudh	milk
marva	marna	to die
amaro	hamara	ours
gra	ghora	horse
dant	dant	teeth
lon	lun, noon	salt
lameva	kam	love
than	sthan	land
mas	mans	meat
tu	tum, tu	you
chib	jibh	tongue
manush	manush	man
puro	burha	old
slao	sala	brother–in–law
phen	bahin, bhne	sister
phral	bhrata, bhai	brother
dzamutro	jamatar	son–in–law
sasro	sasur	father–in–law
sasuy	sas	mother–in–law
kak	kaka	uncle

The sentence is generally constructed in the same way in Romani and Hindi. For example:

Romani: Ja, kik kon chalavelo o vurdo.

Hindi: Ja, dekh kaun chalayya dvar ko.
English: Go and see who has come to the door.
Romani: Main hun kalo.
Hindi: Main hun kala.
English: I am dark.

Romani: Mero sero dukkers.
Hindi: Mero sir dukhe.
English: My head aches.

Conjugations of verbs etc., follow the Hindi pattern. The feminine ending i. is found in both. Romani has two genders: o represents the masculine and i the feminine. For instance, boro rye means a great man, and bori rani means a great lady. In Romani, the feminine of kalo is kali, as in Hindi the feminine of kala is kali, in both the adjective means 'black'.

As in Hindi, Gypsies use the same word (kaliko) for tomorrow and yesterday, which again is very close to Hindi kal (or kalko). Similiarrly, Gypsy shoshoi signifies both hare and rabbit as does Sanskrit sasa. The Gypsy habit of coining new words by compounding two or more words is also reminiscent of the Sanskrit Sandhi Samasa system. However, the Romani vocabulary is very limited and it has few verbs.

So westward migration, forced or otherwise, from India atleast in medieval times is an established fact. However, since when and in how many waves should be researched in details. Is it continuing from pre–history period? Whether Mitannies and Kassittes migrants into West Asia were from India? Is it from pre–history, pre–Vedic time or only from medieval time?

On the subject matter of westward migration of Asians into Europe, Jawaharlal Nehru in his book 'Glimpses of World History' (page 9) has written: "When you read history you will find that for long periods and stretches of time, Asia had been dominant. Her people went in wave after wave and conquered Euorpe. They ravaged Europe and civilized Europe. Aryans, Scythians, Huns, Arabs, Mongols, Turks they all came from somewhere in Asia and spread out over Asia and Europe." At page 14, Nehru adds: "Gradually the Aryans poured westwards from Asia, and invaded Greece and the neighbouring countries. These were the Aryan Greeks whom we now know and admire as the ancient Greeks."

Appendix I

VEDIC BROTHERHOOD

To annihilate the monster of casteism, the author made efforts to spread the principles of Vedic equality by getting his articles published gratis in newspapers (Indian Express, 4th Oct 02 & 17th Jan 03) and the Asian Age (23rd Oct., 2002). Sify.com portal carried all the artcles and even show–cased some articles on its www.samachar.com page. Many magazines and websites suo moto came forward to carry these, gratis, such as the Organiser, Jaiswal Jagriti (Dec., 2002), Jaiswal Gaurava (Jan., 2003), www.sify.com/news, www.jagran.com, www.atributetohinduism.com, www. caribbeanhindu.com, http://shastras.org/ambgupta.pdf, etc.

10.1 Steps Taken

In Sept. /Oct. 03, the author sent following letters to HH Swami Purna of London, UK and to HH Swami Dayanand Saraswati of Pennsylvania, USA:

"Dear Swamiji,

Jaishree Gopal, Chairman, Navyashastra, New York, USA, has been in touch with me on how to spread the cardinal message of Vedas and Gita i.e., equality of all Hindus by birth and gender equality. Recently, in my personal capacity, I penned some articles, which are displayed on Sify.com at the following page (http://sify.com/news/othernews/fullstory.php?id=13171234&vsv=579). Sanskrit texts of shlokas quoted in my articles do not appear in Sify.com due to some technical difficulty.

I am glad to learn from J. Gopal that you are going to organise a meeting of Acharyas to discuss concerns facing Sanatan Dharma. In my humble opinion, the biggest problem the Hindu Samaj has been facing over last one thousand years is the continuous decline in percentage of Hindu population; the root cause therefore in my personal view is our deviations from original teachings of Vedas & Gita.

Out of over 414 mantra–drasta rishis of Rigveda, about 30 are lady rishis (rishikas) implying gender equality that is Hindu women are neither to be discriminated nor to be prevented from gaining excellence. Therefore, Hindu women have equal access to and equal claim over Vedas & Gita. But, ignoring this very fact, some Acharyas discriminate against women quoting secondary sources. Can one supersede Vedas by subsidiary literature?

We have been either burning our widows and/or discouraging their remarriages. This is one of the major reasons for falling percentage of Hindus. Some Acharyas look down upon remarriage of Hindu widows whereas Vedas sanction widow remarriage vide RV (X.40.2), RV (X.18.8–9), AV (IX.5.27–28), and AV (XVIII.3.1–4).

Though many Acharyas lament and some actively oppose proselytization/conversion of Hindus into other religions but they ignore that it is they who, by misinterpretations of the Vedas & Gita, create fertile grounds for conversion activities of preachers of other religions. Many ignorant people quote RV (X.90.12) as Rigvedic authority to justify birth based casteism and consequent fragmentation of Hindu Samaj into four main castes at fratricidal war with each other, whereas, as explained in detail in my articles, RV (X.90) preaches total equality of all four professional classes. In a healthy person, mouth does not claim to be superior to legs, arms do not claim any superiority over legs, and arms do not function independently of head (Parkinson's disease) etc. as each part of body is functionally dependent on each other. No part of body is inferior or superior to any other part of the body; each dependent on the other; each complementary to the other, each supporting the other in a healthy person (Purusha). Thus, the Purusha Sukta commands that none of the four classes is inferior or superior to any other; and, each is dependent on the other for healthy survival. A Virat Purusha (i.e., a vibrant society) is created only when the four professions/classes work in as close harmony as four limbs of a healthy person.Thus, the Purusha Sukta, in my humble opinion, emphasises complementary role, supplementing each other. By throwing Sudras out of villages, followers of Manusmriti amputated Hinduism and made it crippled and invalid, ripe to be enslaved. In the Gita also, there is no birth–based caste as Lord Krishna says "Karmani pravibhaktani" (18.41). Lord Krishna does not say "Janmani pravibhaktani"

सं गच्छध्वं सं वदध्वं सं वो मनांसि जानताम्।
देवा भागं यथा पूर्वे सञ्जानाना उपासते ॥2॥
(RV:X.191.2)

समानो मन्त्रः समितिः समानी समान मनः सह चित्तमेषाम्।
समानं मन्त्रमभि मन्त्रये वः समानेन वो हविषा जुहोमि ॥3॥
(RV:X.191.3)

समानी व आकूतिः समाना हृदयानि वः।
समानमस्तु वो मनो यथा वः सुसहासति ॥4॥ (RV:X.191.4)

समानी प्रपा सह वोऽन्नभागः समाने योक्त्रे सह वो युनज्मि।
सम्यञ्चोऽग्निं सपर्यतारा नाभिमिवाभितः ॥6॥
(Atharveda: III.30.6)

Thus, the central command of the fifteen harmony seeking Vedic richas, and ten profession– not– hereditary Vedic richas (detailed in my articles) is that all Hindus are totally equal by birth, of one bunch, share the same water and food, worship together united in the same temple, common are the prayers, common be the purpose, common be thoughts, united like spokes of a wheel, common be oblation, friendly towards each others, etc. One becomes a warrior (Rajnya), Brahaman (educated ones) or rishi, not by birth but by his efforts/training (karma) vide RV (X.125.5).

अहमेव स्वयमिदं वदामि जुष्टं देवेभिरुत मानुषेभिः।
यं कामये तंतमुग्रं कृणोमि तं ब्रह्माणं तमृषिं तं सुमेधाम्॥5॥
(RV:X.125.5)

No one is superior by birth and no one is inferior by birth. In fact RV (V.60.5) reads, "No one is superior (ajyestasa) or inferior (akanishtasa). All are brothers (ete bhrataraha). All should strive for the interests of all and should progress collectively. (sowbhagaya sam va vridhuhu):

अज्येष्ठासो अकनिष्ठास एते सं भ्रातरो वावृधुः सौभागाय।
युवा पिता स्वपा रूद्र एषां सुदुधा पश्निः सुदिना मरूद्भयः॥5॥
(RV:V.60.5)

Transgressing and flouting the above, secondary literature has been used to divide and fragment the Hindu Samaj from within, into castes & sub castes. And, such a rotten social structure was created wherein only about 3% of Hindu population was expected to go to war whereas in Islam and in Christianity about 35% of population was eligible and made psychologically available/prepared to take on Kafirs and pagans. No wonder, therefore, Hindus were defeated by numerically small numbers of Turks, Mongols, Afghans, Mughals, and by even slave invaders. Millions of Hindus were butchered, their temples destroyed and their women raped and sold as slaves in Kabul, etc. Even in independent India, the percentage of Hindus is falling! History repeats itself if lessons of History are ignored in passive complacence. Should we not reappraise our socio–religious norms? Hinduism is the only religion which, by ill treatment of a section of its adherents, encourages them to walk over to other religions. As such, we may legitimately ask: is Hinduism not on the path of auto–destruction? We must act fast to put it back on right path of organic growth.

Let us restore the primacy and supremacy of Vedas. Let us stop incorrect practice of superseding Vedas by secondary sources or commentaries as the Rishi Veda Vyasa has himself instructed that Vedas are supreme and take precedence over everything:

> **श्रुतिस्मशतिपुराणानां विरोधो यत्र दशश्यते।**
> **तत्र श्रौतं प्रमाणन्तु तयोर्द्वैधे स्मशतिर्त्वरा॥**
> **(Mahabharata: 1–V–4)**

Acharya, above are my humble submissions in **my individual and personal capacity**. May I request you and your learned colleagues to help us restore original teachings of Vedas & Gita to all Hindus! In fact, Swamiji, RV (X.191) commands bringing all Hindus under one banner. I shall highly appreciate your views and guidance.

Yours sincerely,

(O. P. Gupta)
Ambassador of India
Helsinki, Finland"

****

10.2 HH Swami Purna informed that he had discussed the

above letter of mine with HH Shankaracharyaji of Jyotirmath Badrinath and other Swamis at their congregation at Haridwar and there was all–round support for reforming Hinduism and return to our Vedic roots of equality by birth and gender equality.Following is the text of reply received from HH Swami Purna:

"H.H. Prof. Dr. Sri Swami R.A.G. Purna Anand–apee–thadhiswar

Acharya Mahamandaleshwara Srimat Paramahamsa Brahmanista Yogiraj

17 Clarges Street, Mayfair, London W1J 8AE

Shri O.P. Gupta 2 February, 2004
Ambassador of India
Helsinki, Finland

Dear Sri Guptaji,

I have received your letter of September 29, 2003 and I have gone through all of your painstaking work and research thoroughly. Meanwhile we have been discussing the crucial issues raised in your documents intermittently over the last few months.

As you may recall, in the 1980's, I used to suggest to you that you should devote your private time to the study of the Vedas and related schools of philosophy in order to bring more light and wisdom to the divided Hindu community in India and overseas. You have rightly suggested that Manusmriti and other works have been distorted and corrupted by priests and scholars for their own selfish gain. Also mainly Western scholars outside India have tried to confuse the meaning by giving theories for their own vested interests, thus bringing more doubts, confusion and complexes in the minds of Hindus. It is time that Hindus awake after some 1,000 years of slumber and realise their treasure of knowledge, bring prosperity and revive the Golden Age, just as once India was described as the Golden Bird.

There is no doubt in my mind that the Vedas are the ultimate authority and basis for all the branches of Hindus including Buddh, Jain and Sikh that were inspired by Vedic knowledge. Buddha himself was brought up in the Vedic tradition, as were also Mahavira and Guru Nanak.

If anything is a contradiction or in violation of Vedic thought it should be dismissed as a deviation from the highest principles of the Golden Age. The Vedas in their entirety 'each shlok and sutra' represent the various aspects of life. If someone does not understand or does not grasp the richness of the Vedic philosophy, then that is his/her own shortcoming. All of the great propounders, philosophers and scholars have followed the path of the Vedas and created wonderful work successively 'even in the dark ages' until today.

In the Vedas, there is a clear cut direction and understanding of the structure of society. If one looks carefully at Hinduism one will find no better system has developed since Vedic times. The Vedas command: ***"You shall live one hundred or more...."shatamjivet***" and first developed Ayurveda, the science of life.

Accordingly, life is divided into four states:

- **Brahmacharya**: 25 years to build the body and mind and study;
- **Grihast**: 25 years as a householder with accompanying duties and responsibilities;
- **Vanaprasth**: 25 years of semi–retirement and dedi–cation to more scholarly and social work; and
- **Sanyas**: 25 years of total spiritual life and dedication to spirituality.

Of course, one can define each stage in great detail scientifically according to the system. That would take many pages and can be done on another occasion.

In conjunction with the four stages of life four objectives are set:

- **Arth**: Resources or wealth;
- **Dharma**: Duty, responsibility and obligation;
- **Kama**: Fulfilment of positive ambitions and desires; and
- **Moksha**: Liberation or enlightenment

These four objectives were blended and combined with the pursuit of the four stages of life, as well as with the four castes or classes '***varna***' to bring order and balance into society. The Vedas state the symbolical picture of where the ***varna*** originate in relation to the Cosmic God, Brahma:

- The Brahamins come from the mouth of the God;
- The Kshatriya come from the shoulder;
- The Vaishya come from the thigh; and
- The Shudra come from the feet.

The symbolism of the parts of the body can be likened to the parts of society. Without all four parts of the body it would not work; similarly society would not work without all of the ***varna***. Significantly, the ***varna*** were defined on the basis of quality, merit and work, not by birth. As you rightly point out in your article the engineer's son does not become an engineer by birth. Similarly, the scholar's son does not become a scholar by birth. He/she may claim the greatness of their ancestry, but only by achievement 'not birth' is he/she qualified. Effort, ***purushartha***, is a vital integral part of Hinduism. According to various mantras in the Vedas and the Manusmriti the Brahaman can become a Shudra if his work is Shudra in nature and the Shudra can become a Brahman if his work is Brahmin in nature. As Krishna stresses in the Gita: ***"Chatur Varnyam Maya Sristum Gunkarma Bibhagasha."*** Thus, the four varnas or categories are created according to ***guna*** and ***karma***, quality and work.

Of course, many ignorant people with vested interests interpret and practise Hindu teaching to suit their own desires and ambition. Wrong practice of any principle does not become right however long the practice continues, even after a few thousand years of practice by many. As we know, the Hindus have been divided by their own ignorance and wrong practices away from the true knowledge of the Vedas. When they became weak and divided outside forces have attached, as with the Law of Nature. This has led to confusion. They cannot be blamed as this is the nature of things, just as people like to fish in troubled waters. As Mahatma Gandhi has written: ***"The varnashrama of the shastras is today non–existent in practice. The present caste system is the very antithesis of varnashramadharma."***

Post Independent India has witnessed a greater rise in conversion to Christianity and Islam, based on political and demographic rationale. I have warned the successive Prime Ministers of India over these years. When Rajiv Gandhi was Prime Minister, I wrote a very detailed letter to which he replied in detail. I asked him to keep India free from the four forces of the World, the Christian Empire, the Muslim Empire, the Communist Empire and Multinationals, since these forces could destroy India and Hindus. I have advised different Prime Ministers, including Prime Minister Atal Bihari Vajpayee, that India should not become another U.S.A and that that would be the day of sorrow if India were to become a second America. Of course, I am not saying not to learn from the American experience– the Vedas say ***"....let knowledge and truth come***

from all sides...."–but India should not emulate the corruption, distortion and decadence of America.

In my letter of 13 February 1986 to the Pope John Paul II I pointed out that when he visited India:

"It would not be too much to suggest that you should declare publicly a reform in Catholic policy to announce non–conversion in favour of coexistence, humanitarianism, the promotion of population control, as well as a common platform for the meeting of spiritual and religious leaders to enable a constant dialogue on the basis of mutual recognition and acceptance."

Such a policy would be in the interests of peace worldwide and should be followed by the Muslim leaders. If we worship the same God, where is the place for conversion? Why break and destroy the culture of others? There are many paths to the same goal. But the objective here has not been peace and unity. Instead, the purpose is control and dominance through numbers and division. That is the real struggle and has been so throughout history. If Hinduism in India is to be sustained, all of India's policies and programme should be based on her great philosophy, spirituality and culture that is found in the Vedas and related works. India's policy cannot be based on borrowed external language and culture.

In accordance with the above, Sanskrit should be taught to every Indian as a compulsory subject. By learning Sanskrit, they can understand the true knowledge better. Knowledge is given freely to all. Those who proclaim that Shudras and women are not entitled to such knowledge and should live in darkness should recall that Shudras come from the feet of the Supreme and the feet are worshipped. How can they be untouchable or outcaste? Also, when the god of learning is the Goddess Saraswati, how can the female form be letter? As you say, there are thirty female rishies in the Rigveda alone.

One should note the famous stanza: ***"Where women are given due regard prosperity and gods dwell."*** Hinduism, above all, as a philosophy represents universality, something that exists and is open to all, like the sunshine, beauty and justice.

I have presented your research articles to Dharma Sansad in Rishikesh at the meeting in November 2003. They have greatly appreciated and welcomed your thoughts and are delighted that a person like you 'in the Foreign Service' understands the meaning and values of the Vedas. Their view is that ignorance abounds in government and bureaucratic circles. It is unusual to find someone in such a position with such understanding and knowledge. They hope that there will be more like you in government so that the policies and programmes of the Constitution are implemented properly.

I have been closely working with the Shankaracharya of Jyotirmath and he has given his unconditional support to your efforts. He is willing to carry on work with you and to see you when you are next in India in order to plan programmes and a comprehensive strategy. Indeed the leaders that I am in touch with are with you and bless this second social movement and yagna to eradicate the confusion and other ills in Indian society and to bring Hindus under their own Vedic banner.

It will be very important for India to have enlightened political leaders 'at home and in the Foreign Service' who can understand and carry out work for the overall betterment of the people of India in accordance with her Constitution. Today India is caught by casteism, communalism, religious conversion and religiosity, as well as negative politics and materialism. It is timely that Vedic knowledge, which deals with all aspects of life, be explained and implemented in people's day to day life through exemplary political leaders and capable bureaucrats in the true spirit of practical spirituality.

With my spiritual strength and blessings,

Svami Purna"

****

10.3 My letter to Swami Dayanandji was routed through the Navya Shastra of USA. In October, Swami Dayanand wrote to Navya Shastra as under:

"Dear Jaishree,

I have included Navya Shashtra's proposal for discussion in the Acharya Sabha Meet as you can see in the programme sent along with this letter. I have made arrangements for translating the main letter in Hindi, Tamil and Kannada which will be attached with the other papers and given to all the participants.

With best wishes and love
Yours truly,
Swami Dayananda"

****

The first historical Meeting of Acharya Sabha was held at Rani Meyyammai Hall, Engmore Chennai on Nov. 29 " Dec 1, 2003. This historic meeting of Acharyas was reported in the Indian Express of 22 Dec., 2003 under the caption *"Speak now and forever in single Hindu voice"* by Ms. Renuka Narayanan.

The following response was received from Jaishree Gopal, Chairman, Navya Shastra:

"Dear Ambassador Gupta,

We just wanted to thank you once again for helping us reach out to the Acharyas this year. At the very least, whether they reform right away or not, they all know that Hindus are beginning to question discriminatory practices that have no basis in the Vedas. They also know by now that the worldwide Hindu Samaj truly feels that we must make our dharma open, tolerant and available to all.

Your letter played a very big part in our campaign without it we would not nearly have had as much prestige, and we thank you sincerely for that. Your essays are gaining the recognition they deserve throughout India; hopefully Navya Shastra will continue to play a small role in propagating your vision.

After the holidays, we will call you to update you on our activities and to take your advice on some matters.

Sincerely,

Jaishree Gopal
Vikram Masson
Dec. 21, 2003"

****

Earlier, in June 2003, Navya Shastra Executive Committee had written as under:

"June 14, 2003

Yours Excellency,

We are writing to you on behalf of Navya Shastra, a global Hindu organisation of scholars, activists, priests and lay people committed to reforming the Hindu religion of caste and gender discrimination. We are especially concerned about the inequalities inherent in the shastras, particularly the smritis, and the continued use of these subordinate texts by religious leaders bent on perpetuating arbitrary differences that have the dangerous potential to destroy the foundations of our eternal Dharma. We are committed to engaging them in an ongoing dialogue about our future, given that they still carry immense prestige among the commonweal.

We are very impressed with your visionary readings of the Vedas, the Ramayana and the Bhagawadgita. In recent articles, you have incontrovertibly demonstrated that birth–based varna classifications were not known to our ancient Rishis, and that these injunctions are the machinations of later writers, like Manu and Gautama, who stratified the Hindu people into a mindless collection on tribes that were easily divided and conquered by medieval invaders.

We enjoyed your use of Bhagwadgita shloka 16:18 to excoriate the present–day upholders of Manu: "Given over to egotism, brute force, arrogance, etc., they hate Me dwelling in their own bodies as well as those of other." We cannot think of a more incisive rejoinder to the casteists among us, who are providing fodder for energetic missionaries in their proselytization efforts. It is most fitting that this rejoinder carries the weight of Bhavacan Himself.

Statesman, scholar and religious thinker, you represent the vanguard of fearless commentators on Hinduism today. Your incisive essays have enlivened and enlightened the Hindu mind, and given us all hope that the proportional decline in the Hindu population will eventually come to a halt. A tireless intellectual missionary, you have exhorted our religious leadership to spread our Dharma to whoever will listen. An uncompromising critic, you have chastised them for their continued approval of such vile practices as the prohibition of widow remarriage.

We take this opportunity to invite you to our organisation and our forum as an Advisor; we would like your sagacious counsel on all of our activities, and your guidance in negotiating the Hindu religious landscape. This will not entail attending any meetings or require any time commitments: we simply request your moral support.

We are not affiliated with any political party or organisation. Our membership reflects the astonishing diversity of the Hindu people. With your guidance, we will be able to persuade the religious leadership to cast off Manu and other divisive smritis forever, and to lead all Hindus in a movement for spiritual equality.

Our website is at www.shastras.org. We have included a short biography of our founding members and a copy of our press release centered around a recent communication to the Kanchi Shankaracharya, where we have asked Him to admit Harijans into the Veda Pathasala sponsored by the Kanchi mutt. We believe that spiritual equality cannot remain in the theoretical realm, and must be demonstrated by the most traditional of Acharyas. We believe so strongly in this that we have promised to fund the living and training expenses of these boys.

Most sincerely,

Vikram Masson
Jaishree Gopal (Chairman)
(On behalf of the Executive Committee)"

Appendix II

XIIth WORLD SANSKRIT CONFERENCE, HELSINKI

In July 2003, the XIIth World Sanskrit Conference was held at the University of Helsinki. It was organized by Prof. Asko Parpola of the University of Helsinki, and, Prof. Ram Karan Sharma, President, International Association of Sanskrit Studies, India. About four hundred international experts of Indology and Sanskrit attended it. Following is the text of address by the author:

"It is a great privilege and honour for me to speak before this august body of international Indologists. Many foreign diplomats showed in–depth knowledge of Indology. The first Finnish Ambassador to India Dr. Hugo Valvanne delivered a speech in India in Sanskrit.

I find there is rich tradition of Indology Departments in European Universities. Frankly speaking, my knowledge of Sanskrit is very elementary but over the last nine years that I have been Indian Ambassador, I was often asked how old are the Vedas, how old is Sanskrit, why widows were burnt in India, what is casteism, etc.

To find replies, I made my self–studies. Contrary to the views of many authors, the Purusha Sukta in my opinion commands total harmony and absolute equality among all. Vedic richas command that professions are not hereditary implying social mobility such as RV (X.125.5). Some authors quote RV (X.18.7) as Rigvedic sanction for sati but under this very Sukta dead body is being buried in a grave.

Antiquity of the Vedas and Sanskrit are other popular questions. Some experts opine that Vedas were composed around 1500 BC to 900 BC whereas others believe it to be older than 4500 BC. As per International Herald Tribune of 12th June, 2003 anatomically modern Homo sapiens were there on this globe nearly 160,000 years ago. How did they communicate amongst each other?

About 200,000 years ago genes creating language capability among human species developed and about 100,000 to 50,000 years ago, a gene called FOXP2 developed providing the last perfection of language capability making it totally modern. So,if Sanskrit is the oldest language; but is not older than 1500 BC, then, in which language did our forefathers communicate before Sanskrit?

Classical belief is that the three pyramids of Giza and sphinx were built around 2500 BC but on the Discovery Channel, it was claimed that these were built in 10,500 BC based on pattern of weathering of the upper parts of Sphinx—from top to downwards showing heavy torrential rains and lower parts showing horizontal weathering pattern by floods. There was rain and flooding in Giza in the last period of last ice age in 11000 BC. Astronomical argument was that in 10500 BC, sun was rising in the Constellation of Leo and three stars were located exactly above the three pyramids.

RV (IX.33.6) and RV (X.47.2) talk of four oceans, one each in four directions of India. Famous Sankalpa mantra (merodaksina bhage Jambudvipe bharatkhande ......) talks of Jambudvipe. It was millions of years ago that India was an Island. How did this information come into Rigveda?

RV (IV.58.2) is seen by astronomers suggesting that Sristi started 4.32 billion years ago. Modern Astrophysics says earth is about 4.6 billion years old. RV (I.164.11) informs that one year comprised 360 days and 360 nights. How many years ago earth was completing one circle around sun in 360 days? Prof. Carl Sagan, the Cornel University Astronomer told that Vedic tradition is the only tradition, which talks about the right time scale.

Sanskrit is an Indo-European language. To reply to the age old puzzle of how old are the Vedas, a multi-disciplinary research involving astronomy, astrophysics, archaeology, anthropology, meteorology in addition to linguist approach funded by UNESCO and other countries will, I am sure, help us in narrowing of social conflicts among different groups when it is realised more and more that linguistic roots of most of us, if not of all of us, is common, smoothening our march towards globalisation i.e., Vasudhaiva Kutumbakam."

* * * * * * *

[Note: Some details and photographs of above Conference are available at the following website: http://www.helsinki.fi/hum/aakkl/12wsc/]

Amb O.P. Gupta with the Delegates of World Sanskrit Conference
(Helsinki, July, 2003)

Amb O.P. Gupta with the Delegates of World Sanskrit Conference
(Helsinki, July, 2003)

Amb O.P. Gupta with the Delegates of World Sanskrit Conference
(Helsinki, July, 2003)

Appendix III

QUESTIONS AND ANSWERS

The portal Sify.com had posted my articles, showcased them on its main webpage www.samachar.com and later created an interactive webpage where readers posted many interesting questions at http://sify.com/news/othernews/fullstory.php?id=13171234. These are furnished below along with replies, a bit modified:

1. **Question posted By AMIT on 6/18/03**

   Is God personal human being who is supremely powerful or impersonal higher reality?

   Ambassador O P Gupta replies: Amit, in my humble view, God is impersonal higher reality. What could not be explained in terms of contemporary science falls within maayaa of God. Modern science cannot create a new life. It has so far succeeded in replicating a living cell, but not creating a new living cell. So, we say God creates life.

2. **Question posted By JAGDISH SARAN on 6/18/03**

   I have just phased out as a CEO of a technology company in U.S.A and currently researching on business leadership characterstics based on Indian culture, Vedas and scriptures. In this age, hi–tech is associated with entrepreneurship and India and Indians in U.S.A and other countries have played very important role in high tech development. So, what is your opinion about the relevance of our Vedas in this hi–tech age. Thanks

Ambassador O P Gupta replies: Jagdish Saran, One excels in his field only if he is at peace with himself during work, only if he has developed faculty of focused attention. The Vedas and Vedic life style no doubt help one attain these quickly and easily. Even before the IT age, our ancestors had much advanced knowledge of mathematics, decimal system, astronomy, concept of zero, Alefzero, etc.

3. **Question posted By SUSHEEL on 6/19/03**

I have read all the articles you have written on conversions, caste and sati, they should be an eye opening to all the ignorant Hindus. I have a question which is irrelevant to the question posted above, I would appreciate if you clarify this question. Is Hinduism a religion, is the word Hindu quoted in the Vedas or is it just man made like other religions of the world?

Ambassador O P Gupta replies: Yes, the Hinduism is a religion. Susheel, as far as I know, the word Hindu does not appear in the Vedas. It is a term given to inhabitants of areas east of Sindhu River by Arabs. In the Arabic language, all residents of this region (now India) are known as "al–Hindi" (whether a Hindu, a

Muslim or a Christian or Hindi speaking or Tamil or Malyali speaking etc.). Hinduism is the collective name of religion followed by the majority of inhabitants of this region. In Ki–swahili language, all Indians (whether Hindu, Muslim, Christian, Hindi Speaking or Malayalam speaking) are called 'mu–hindi' or 'wa–hindi.'

4. **Question posted By JEBEEN on 6/19/03**

Honorable Ambassador: I am an Indian Muslim from Assam, resident of New York City. I am so delighted to read your views on the following: *The Futility of Religious Conversions *Caste and Bhagwadgita *Caste and the Hindu Scripture *Rigveda and the Indian Woman. Please do continue in your effort to educate the masses to get rid of these problems that is killing Indian Society. My Best Regards, Syeda Jebeen S. Shah

Ambassador OP Gupta replies: Jabeen, thank you very much for your kind words of appreciation.

5. **Question posted By SURENDRA on 6/19/03**

I was very much delighted to read your views based on Vedas. I will appreciate your views about SATYARTH PRAKASH (Maharishi Dayanand) and interpretation of Vedic mantra, sloks, religion and criticism of religions like Jainism, Islam and Christanity. Is the English translation of Satyarth Prakash available? I would like to arrange your talk at Boston. Please reply if time permits. With great regards, Surendra P. Verma Ph.D.

Ambassador O P Gupta replies: Surendra, I have not yet gone through Satyarth Prakash. Thanks for your kind words of appreciation.

6. <u>Question posted By JAYA on 6/18/03</u>

It is important in these days that parents teach their children the value of principles/ knowledge/ culture as against the value for money. But if this does not happen AND the children somehow realize this fact and try to follow that, they enter a paradox of disobeying their parents and being unable to fulfill their fancy aspirations. How do we handle this situation?

Ambassador O P Gupta answers: Jaya, Children in all cultures initially copy their parents; and, for the first few years mother is their natural teacher.

7. <u>Question posted By NISHIT SAHAY on 6/18/03</u>

My regards to Shri Gupta. I am International Business Advisor in MASON ENTERPRISE CENTER, George Mason University, Virginia, USA. I have deep interest in Physics, Indian Philosophy and Bharaitya Culture. Shri Gupta your type & quality of people are very rare in Indian Administration and the present Bharat needs person like you, I am making this statement after reading your THOUGHTS on various burning topics. Regards Nishit

Ambassador O P Gupta replies: Thank you very much for your kind words of appreciation

8. <u>Posted By ARUN BAPAT on 6/19/03</u>

Dear Shri Gupta ji, I liked your interview. I am a seismologist and have been doing research in the fields of earthquake and allied subjects for last three decades. In addition, I have been helping people in curing diseases with Yogic techniques. I have prepared one audiocassette on meditation (Hindi: Dhyan Kaise Kare). I would like to know whether you would like to have it. If so I can send it.

Ambassador O P Gupta replies: Arun Bapat, Thank you very much for your kind words.

9. <u>Question posted By RAGHBENDRA JHA on 6/19/03</u>
I would like to thank you and congratulate you on your excellent writings on Hinduism. There can be no doubt that a properly interpreted Hinduism is perfectly consistent with the rapid technological advances of the hi–tech age. Keep up the good work and regards.

Ambassador O P Gupta replies: Raghbendra Jha, thank you very much for your kind words of appreciation.

10. <u>Posted By ARUNA on 6/20/03</u>
I have not gone through many of the Indian scriptures. But in whatever little I have gone through, there is no mention of casteism, sati or child marriage. I feel all these evil systems were seeded in to the Hindu society. These days one can see a lot of rift between the rich & poor. Scriptures say nothing about it.

Answer by Shri O P Gupta: There are a number of richas in the Vedas, some of which are given at page 5 of my article 'Caste and the Hindu Scripture', which call for harmony and social unity irrespective of one being rich or poor.

11. <u>Posted By PURUSH on 6/20/03</u>
Hon Shri Guptaji: Have you attempted to advise the

BJP leadership re: Broader outlook of Hinduism, especially in the context of other major religions, and how they can formulate their policies for India so it can be the greatest society in all nations?

Answer by Shri O P Gupta: No, Sir. I am sharing my personal views with public at large.

12. <u>Posted By ANANTA REDDY on 6/19/03</u>
I request you to go through the article published in June issue of National Geographic titled Untouchbles written by Tom On'il. Can you justify his views which are apparently based on mis–information?

Answer by Shri O P Gupta: Thanks for your advice.

13. <u>Posted By ANANTHARAMAN RANGAN on 6/19/03</u>
It is difficult to reconcile that a religion could sanction division of its adherents into compartments where some of the worst atrocities are practised by people in higher compartments on the people in lesser privileged compartments without any remorse or guilt. Even Bhagwadgita seems to sanction this "division according to work" when Lord Krishna says Chaturvarnam Mayaa srishtam.... None has clarified the anomaly as even the Shankaracharyas practice segregation with great devotion.

Answer from Shri O P Gupta: Anantharaman Rangan, no organisation will succeed if there was no 'division according to work'. Every corporation has to have a CEO, a CFO, middle level functionaries, engineers, accountants, workers, clerks and receptionists, etc.

Every hospital has division according to work, Cardiologists, Dermatologists, ENT experts, consultants, surgeons, nurses, accountants, etc. Any modern Army has to have a General, middle level officers and foot soldiers: division according to work. As I have shown in my articles with help of Vedic richas and shlokas of Gita, these two scriptures provide for social mobility from one profession to another; and prohibit birth–based social segregations into compartments. There are atleast eleven Vedic richas (see para 2.5 of the book) commanding that professions are not hereditary.

Richas after Richas of the Vedas attest that profession is not hereditary and that we are all from one stock. Birth based professions and social segregations into various airtight compartments are mischiefs created by secondary/subordinate literature which most of us out of our own ignorance, elevate to the status of 'scriptures.' Only the Vedas and Gita are our 'revealed' scriptures. Gita being the sermon directly from Lord Krishna is obiviously a revealed scripture. Chaturvarnam Mayaa Srishtam.... has to be read in the context of my interpretation of the PurusSukta RV (X.90) viz., that only when all the four professions act in as perfect harmony with each other as mouth, hands, thighs and feet of a healthy man act, that a powerful society is created. In Gita, Lord Krishna himself says that chaturvarnam division is based on 'guna, karma and swabhava' attained by an individual obviously in his present life, as this division takes place in the present life.This division of labour is ***'karmani*** pravibhaktani' ,not repeat not, "*janmani* pravi–bhaktani" (Gita 18.41)

If the four professions work in disharmony, society becomes paralytic with Parkinsons disease, and when disjointed (socially segregated), society dies i.e., becomes slave of others. Hindu Samaj suffered because we neglected our two revealed scriptures in favour of secondary/subordinate literature. Let us restore supremacy and primacy of the Vedas & Gita: our two and only two revealed scriptures.

14. <u>**Posted By SUBHASH BHAGWAT on 6/18/03**</u>

Shri Gupta quotes Gita: XVIII.68 as evidence that Hinduism is a missionary religion. (Gita: XVIII.68) He who, offering the highest love to Me, preaches the most profound gospel of the Gita among My devotees, shall come to Me alone; there is no doubt about it. I would like to point out that Krishna asks us to preach among my devotees i.e., among Hindus; not among others. It is wrong to claim missionary goals from this.

Answer from Shri O P Gupta: Shri Bhagwat presumes that Krishna's devotees can come only from among Hindus and uses his own presumption to conclude that Hinduism is, therefore, not a missionary religion. Shloka (XVIII.68) does not limit 'my devotees' only to Hindus as incorrectly presumed by Shri Bhagwat. Shloka (XVIII.71) is addressed to "the man who hears Gita with reverence": naturally, non–Hindus are not excluded from hearing sermons of the Holy Gita. There were/are many non–Hindus who were/are Krishna devotees (Raskhan, Malik Muham–mad Jaisee, ISKCON members etc.).

One may see many Jains, Sikhs, Muslims, Christians

attending discourses on the Gita. Shloka (18.69) makes the area of Gita preaching global. Shlokas (18.70) (18.71) are addressed to 'whosoever studies Gita' and 'one who hears Gita with reverence.' Therefore, Gita does not exclude non–Hindus. People become devotees or are made into devotees. Gita (18.42) casts duty on Brahamans (educated class) to teach (i.e., propagate) the Vedas. The fifteen harmony (assimilation) seeking Vedic richas such as RV (X.191), Yaj (26.02), etc. do attest missionary nature of Hinduism. Many Vedic richas cover strangers also such as Yaj (26.02).

15. **Posted By PPSINGH on 6/16/03**

Sati is like a glorification of barbaric murder. Marriage is meant for procreation, what a child would produce if married? God created a casteless society in the world, paradoxically, society got itself divided into castes. What is the caste of different Gods/Godesses? Some confusion is created in some old writings. The Holy Books have teachings for a universal society, with no inequality all over the human race.

Answer by Shri O P Gupta: I agree with Shri PP Singh. The Veda does confer right on a daughter to select her husband: RV (X.27.12). Naturally, a child has no mental capability to make informed choice, so it is obvious the Vedas do not sanction child marriage.

16. **Posted By PPS AHLUWALIA on 6/15/03**

Sir, there may be some controversial literature, but no Holly scriptures have allowed the inhuman and awfully degrading practices of child marriage/Sati/caste system.

Lack of knowledge/backwardness/ narrow–mindedness have made such shameful practices and the civilized world should condemn them. Look at marrying an innocent minor with a dog while media was making this horrible event as a big show; no one was shown to come to the rescue of the poor little girl. I saw this event on the ZeeTv recently.

Answer by Shri O P Gupta: I agree with Shri PPS Ahluwalia. It is only to remove ignorance/back–wardness that I have quoted exhaustively from primary scriptures (Veda & Gita), to convince people that these do prohibit Sati/child marriage/ gender discrimination/ casteism.

I have mentioned nine Vedic richas sanctioning widow remarriages. Mischief is created by secondary literature.

17. **Question by Amarjit Kandola:**
Hon' Mr Gupta nice to have a scholar on the Vedas. I'm basically a sceptic, and have read something not very complimentary to Vedas. I seek your guidance. The Vedas are considered great, Shri D'nand told us to go back to them. But I'm told the greatest among the is the Rigveda. No doubt their poets were great, their language full of vitality and very resonant. But they mostly contain: mantars for sacrifices, prayers for food, more wealth (cattle, mainly cows), smashing adversaries.

Answer by Mr. O P Gupta: The Vedas cover almost all walks of life, ethics, worship, yagya, war, medical sciences, astronomy, mathematics, astrology, agriculture, etc. (See opening paragraphs in Chapter–I).

18. **Question by Easwar Krishnan:**

Dear sir I am a young 15 year old boy who reads your article with deep interest and I am highly influenced by them. Hinduism is undoubtedly going through a tough time and something must be done inside and outside India. Sir, since you are in a comparitively powerful and influential position, you must use it and do something to protect the sanathan dharma (such as setting up Hindu schools). Thank you.

Answer by Mr. O P Gupta: I agree. Second generation socio religious reforms from within Hinduism are the need of the hour.

19. **Question by Karunakar Reddy:**

Dr. Gupta, I heard one BIG Brahaman who got trained for 6 years in one of six Asthanams in India. He says JESUS is there in Sama Vedam & Yajurvana Vedam. He says these SLOKHAS from SAMAVEDAM SARVA PAAPA PARIHARAM RAKTHA PROKSHANAMAVASYAKAM,TATH RAKTHAM PARAMATHMENAPUNYA DHA–ANA BHALIYAAGAM. What is SHIVA LINGAM? The shape has any meaning with Shiva? Please give me your mail ID to know further. I am in search of SATYAM & read your articles.

Answer by Mr O P Gupta: I have not seen any reference about Jesus Christ in the Vedas. Shiva Lingam is one of the manifestations of Lord Shiva.

20. **Question by Ram:**

Dear Guptaji, where in our Hindu scriptures does it

say that rebirth and present karma are interlinked? Does God really discriminate between a saint and a sinner? If 'Yes', how HE is considered to be all forgiving? Paramahamsa is reported to have pulled up Vivekananda for not being willing to help 'prostitutes'when they came to Dakshineswar temple. 'You are like a Dhobi. You must wash all clothes' Is this correct and valid as per your undestanding. Hoping to hear from you.

Answer by Mr O P Gupta: I have shown in great detail in my articles that neither the Vedas nor Gita stipulate any linkage between karma of past life and karma of present life. RV (X.125.5) itself says that by imparting training one can be turned into a warrior, a Brahaman, a rishi or a sage. The Vedas instruct that professions are not hereditary.

Whether God discriminates between a saint and a sinner or not, Nature does discriminate; saintly people live longer enjoying better health, sinners die early suffering bad health (blood pressure, tension, anxiety, etc.)

21. <u>Question by Ganesh Vaidhianathan:</u>
The Vedas are not written by ordinary human beings, the persons who wrote them are godly saints; they wrote the Vedas for the enlightment of human beings. While other countries are doing research about our Vedas the sad state is that we are moving to their way of life. Whatever they have told in the Vedas are not their views it is the reflection of Gods views.

Answer by Mr O P Gupta: I agree.

22. **<u>Question by Vishwanath:</u>**
Dear Mr. Gupta, I have a few queries on this topic. (a) When exactly were the Vedas written? (b) Who wrote them? What is your thought on the Aryan invasion theory? (c) Do you think that the Ramayana and Mahabharata really happened or they are just stories which became famous similar to the current Harry Potter series

Answer by O P Gupta: As I said in my article, no one knows how old the Vedas are. Some say about 1500 BC to 900 BC; others say more than 4500 BC old. Some scholars believe that the Rigveda was revealed much before 5000 BC as it does not mention cotton whereas the oldest cotton seeds found in Mehrgarh (Baluchistan) have been carbon dated to 5000 BC (Scientific American Journal, Aug, 1980). But, everyone agrees that these are the oldest books of all humankind, written in a language, which is still in vogue. The Aryan Invasion Theory, as mentioned in my article, was invented with a view to deny political basis to Indians for demanding that the British leave India; all being foreigners; all being immigrants under AIT. Motivation to invent A.I.T. was that older immigrants could not ask new immigrants to leave the country. I believe the Ramayana and Mahabharata to be true.

23. **<u>Question by Dinesh:</u>**
Dear Dr. Gupta It is so elevating to learn that an IFS is so deeply learned in the Vedas. I want to know 1.How 'Yagya' helps in spiritual practice? Is it not a waste of resources.2. What is the use of offerings to the gods like Varuna, Rudra, Agni who do not exist anymore

Answer by O P Gupta: These days we use air freshners. Yagya in a mechanical sense does the same without adverse side effects. Yagya is a social community effort aimed at stress–management and social harmony. These days, heart patients are advised to do community–singing (singing bhajans with family members) before going to bed to reduce stress. If one does yagna/puja everyday with focused concentration, his body starts secreting a hormone Dehydro–epiandrosterone (DHEA) which is anti–ageing. This hormone keeps him biologically younger than his actual age. And, in our normal religious language it was explained by rishis as he who does puja regularly with reverence is blessed by that deity. Regular moortipuja with meditation keeps one younger than his age by secretion of DHEA. Doing puja mech–anically may not help in secretion of DHEA. In our perceptions, Gods exist, though one may worship them under different names and by different modes in different ages.

24. **Question by Jagdish Saran:**

Ambassador Gupta, I thank you very much for answering my previous question. As I indicated before I am researching on Entrepreneurship and Business leadership and would like to get your opinion on which Veda or other Indian or Aryan Hindu/Buddhis scriptures I should read on these topics for getting maximum information for research.

Answer by O P Gupta: You may wish to go through (Penguins Classics') ARTHASHASTRA of Kautilya (Chanakya) by Ambassador L.N. Rangarajan; and, the

Rigveda & Atharvaveda in Hindi by Acharya Shri Ram Sharma of Bareilly, UP, India. These may be of great help to you in your research. You may also like to go through a book by Dr. V.R. Panchamukhi captioned "Indian Classical Thoughts on Economic Development and Management" (ISBN 81–85040–43–5).

25. **Question by Amarjit Kandola:**

Dear Mr Gupta, we are lucky to have a scholar of Vedic studies like you. I have some 'intelligent', some crazy, some difficult questions. Hope you won't mind (great minds never do). Q–1. Where does the word 'Hindu' first occur in our scriptures?

Q–2. Who were 'dasas and dasyus' who are described as "dark and ill–favoured, bull–lipped, snub–nosed worshippers of phallus, and of hostile speech?"

Q.3 Why are our gods 'Rama', 'Krishna' and others shown as 'dark/blue?

Answer by Mr. O P Gupta: Regarding the word Hindu, you may see my reply to Shri Susheel. The word BHARAT does occur at many places in the Vedas and in Gita. Dasyus still means thieves & robbers.

Dasa/Dasyus may also mean Indo–Iranian tribes, groups not following the Vedas. It all depends upon the context in which this word has been used in a richa. Now it is accepted that Aryans, dasas/dasyus belonged to one race. Some of our Gods are of dark/shyam complexions but not all, which, in turn, proves my central theme that we all are one irrespective of the colour of our skin. (See Chapter 9).

26. **Comment by Tarkeshwari Singh:**

Dear Sir, We are honoured to have you as our Ambassador who has such deep knowledge about the Vedas and Hinduism. I read your articles with interest and I must say they are very well written and give the true picture of what our Vedas say. These articles will definitely clear the wrong notions which Indian people have in their minds about Vedas. Do keep up this excellent work in future

Answer by Mr. O P Gupta: Thank you very much.

27. **Question by Man Mohan Bhanot:**

Dear Sir, I know that Vedas have supreme knowledge. A true Vedantist can solve the energy crishis on earth by extracting (seeking) it from father planet sun—not in small quantities but as much as needed. But then the one who gets to know the Vedas does not have any relevance for such talks

Answer by Mr. O P Gupta: Thank you very much. In my view, the Vedas & Gita make one a karma–yogi (doer, performer, optimist, achiever), not an escapist. Solar energy is a reality and is now being tapped more and more to generate electricity.Wind energy is also getting converted into energy.

28. **Question by Niraj Kumar Jaiswal:**

Sir, Please accept my congratulations on your excellent and thought provoking articles on Hindu caste system and other related topics. These articles present your

in–depth research and knowledge on these topics. With kind regards, Niraj Jaiswal, Ashgabat (Turkmenistan)
Answer by O P Gupta: Thank you very much.

29. **Question by Sangeeta Bhargava:**
How do you find similarity or adversity in connecting Vedas knowledge benefiting in today's life? Sangeeta Bhargava of Dar–es–Salaam Television.

Answer by Mr. O P Gupta: The Vedas, Gita and Yoga help one to be steady in achieving their objectives. So, these have eternal value. See my reply to question 23, these help by stimulating secretion of DHEA hormone.

30. **Question by Dilip Sanvordeker:**
Dear Shri Gupta, your research and details expressed in these writing are absolutely divine. As an intense on these Hindutva matters, I am deeply thankful to you on your efforts to educate us more in these matters. I am beginning to come to a belief that the Vedic age rishis or our Vedic seers have instilled their knowledge (antardhyana) in our genes and the world is benefiting from our Vedic heritage through high tech and maths foundations India has offered to the world. Please comment.

Answer by Mr. O P Gupta: Yes, I agree with you.

31. **Question by Krishna:**
One of the best I have read. We do not know what is in Hinduism and call ourselves Hindu. These articles should be circulated to many internet sites. Truly remarkable.

Answer by Mr O P Gupta: Thank you very much

32. **Question by Purush Reddy:**
Hon. Shri Gupta: I loved the article re: Futility of rel conv. I am amazed at your knowledge of various religions. India is held back because of religious strife and narrow views about what Hinduism is etc. Pl continue your writings so people like me can get enlightened.

Answer by Mr O P Gupta: Thank you very much.

33. **Question by Murali Vrindavanam:**
Dear Mr. Gupta, This question is very relevant to the present economy which we are facing. Do our Vedas tell us anything on World trade or how we should deal with open policies? How is it that we got a culture of individualism and not a team approach?

Answer by Mr O P Gupta: A number of richas listed in my article 'Caste and the Hindu Scripture' command team/community spirit/approach RV (X.191), AV (III.30), etc. We at one time had over thirty percent of world trade. The Vedas do tell us about these but in a different phraseology. The Mahabharata has chapters after chapters on politics.

34. **Question by Vasisht:**
I am greatly interested to read your articles on Hinduism. But I have a basic question. Who is a Hindu? What does the word Hindu mean? By adding ism, are we not unintentionally making it monolithic? I am a south Indian Brahaman having nothing in common

with a north Indian Brahaman. Even the way we pronounce the gayatri mantra is different. Nothern Indian temples have marble idols, in south it is stone made. Why? Why Hindu gods are from the north, three great acharyas (bhakti) are from south?

Answer by Mr O P Gupta: Kindly see my reply to Shri Susheel. I am a bit surprised when you say that being a South Indian Brahaman you have nothing in common with a North Indian Brahaman. You have common religion, common scriptures, common deities, etc. Gods are not regional. They are not even national but are global. Pronunciation in almost all languages differs from place to place, so, people may pronounce mantras a bit differently but the texts remain the same. The basic theme of Vedas & Geeta is that God is one; and that different deities are manifestations of one and the same God. RV (I.164.46)

35. **Question by Vivek Singh Sengar:**
Shri Guptaji. Sadar Pranam. I have not seen the Vedas, Sir, please describe how they look like, in which language they are written, where are the original books, and is their translation available in the market?

Answer from O P Gupta: At present, the Vedas are just like any other book. Thousands of years ago, these were passed on from one generation to another through oral recitations without letting in any mistake. These were later written down in the Sanskrit language on bark leaves. No one is certain about their antiquity; some say about 5000 BC old and others say not more than 1500 BC. Nevertheless, all agree that these are the oldest surviving books among all mankind, with the same text, same pronunciation, same meaning, and same way of writing.

Hindi and English translations are available. Rigveda mantras were revealed to about 414 rishies including about 30 women rishis (called rishika). You may visit http://www.sacred–texts.com for English translations, though English used therein is archaic. Rigveda (ISBN 81–7110–138–7), Yajurveda (ISBN 81–7110–136–0), Atharvaveda (ISBN 81–7110–172–0) and Samaveda (ISBN 81–7110–113–1) published by Parimal Publications, 27/28 Shakti Nagar, Delhi–110007, India have Sanskrit texts with English translations. Hindi translations of all the four Vedas by Acharya Shri Ram Sharma of Bareilly, UP, India are also available. You may visit http://www.gayatripariwar.org about books by Acharya Sharma.

36. **Question by Narayan Shetty:**
Guptaji, Why did Rama kill the shudra Shandaka who was performing tapas?

Answer from O P Gupta: Thanks, I am yet to go through the Valmiki Ramayan. Let us not forget that Rama killed Ravana, a Brahaman by birth & learned pandita in Vedas, and Rama ate at home of Sabri. But, as per the Vedic richas I have mentioned, there was no concept of birth based caste and birth based professions in Vedic time. Let us all be very clear and very firm about it. The Vedas are admitted by all Hindus to be the Supreme; and, let us not place other books at par with Vedas. Supreme must always remain Supreme.

37. **Question from Girish Shanbhag:**

Shri Guptaji, Your articles on Vedas and other scriptures are worth reading. Something to learn from and practicing it. I have one question. What do the Vedas or the Gita say about non–believers (atheists). Can an atheist get Moksha or Liberation

Answer from O P Gupta: The Vedas and Gita do not shut out non–believers. But Moksha is a religious concept, so, it is outside the self–imposed restricted domain of a non–believer.

38. **Question by Ramachandra Sakhdeo:**

My question is somewhat unrelated to the topic but concerns the Vedas. The stanza starting with "Krinvanto Vishwam Aryam" is said to be in the Vedas. One of my friends has asked to find out where exactly this stanza located? Could you please clarify?

Answer from O P Gupta: Thanks. With correct Sanskrit text, one may easily locate Vedic shlokas.

39. **Question from Sridhar Virakthi:**

Dear Sir, I congratulate you on your enormous knowledge by which I feel proud of being an Indian. I am currently in London and feel proud of the Vedas and our sciptures. I feel I should contribute more in spreading the words of truth. Can you suggest how I can go about on this mission of people getting to like the Vedas?

Answer from O P Gupta: Thanks for your comments. The best way to spread words of truth about the Vedas is now by e–mail interactions followed by meetings, seminars, etc.

40. <u>**Question from Govinda Buddiga**</u>:
Is there any good translation of Vedas? Can you please give me the info.

Answer from O P Gupta: Kindly see my reply to Shri Vivek Singh Sengar.

41. <u>**Question from Renjish:**</u>
How did the Vedic astronomers perceive the solar system? Was Earth considered to be in the centre of the universe? Please let me know where I could understand this more?

Answer from O P Gupta: By observation and calculations. In Vedic astronomy, earth was never considered stationary or the centre of the universe. RV (8.12.30) reads, "O Almighty God! When you stabilize this brilliant light, the sun in the heaven, the other planets of yours are put in motion."

RV (1.22.16): "Let all luminous objects and physical forces come to our safety because sun crosses the world by three steps – the dawn, noon and dusk. It sustains the earth with seven rays."

RV (X.85.2): "Adityas are strong by soma, gravitation, the grand earth is held by the soma, the gravitation. Soma, the gravitation is stationed in the vicinity of these Naksastras." Yaj (23.9): "Who does move on its own axis? Who does move around the other?"

Yaj (23.10) replies, "The sun moves on its own axis and the moon moves round the sun and the earth." RV (10.189.1): "This moon, being the satellite of the Earth, revolves round its mother planet i.e., the Earth and follows it in its revolution round the self–luminous the sun i.e., the father planet." Aitreya Brahaman (4.29) says that the sun neither sets nor rises. It is the earth, which by its rotation on its axis causes sunset, sunrise or nights and days.

RV (4.58.2) is seen by many suggesting that sristi (i.e., Creation) started 4.32 billion years ago. Modern Astrophysics says that earth is about 4.6 billion years old. Prof. Carl Sagan, the Cornel University (USA) astronomer told that Vedic tradition is the only tradition, which talks about the right time scale. Only our Vedic culture among all cultures of the world has been aware of precessional rotation of earth completing one circle in 25920 years. Therefore, Vedic astrology and Vedic zodiac always correspond to actual positions of stars and constellations in the sky.

RV (1.164.2) "The elliptical (trinabhichakra) path through which all celestial bodies move is imperishable and unslackened." Even Greek astronomer Ptolemy (178 AD) regarded earth as stationary; and, it was an accepted fact in Europe till Galileo's time. But Galileo (1564–1642 AD) escaped his death by agreeing to denounce this 'pagan' theory of revolving earth. Arya Bhatta (478 AD) calculated that sidereal period of one revolution of earth was 365.2586 days–that of Mercury 87.9698 days and that of Venus 224.699 days. Modern figures are 365.2563, 87.979 and 224.70008 respectively. See how accurate calculations of Arya Bhatta were.

For further details see (i) Science in Vedas by Acharya V.N. Shastri, published by Sarvadeshik Arya Pratinidhi Sabha, Ramlila Ground, New Delhi, India. (ii) A Digest of Sanskrit Science Exhibition by Rashtriya Sanskrit Vidyapeetha, Tirupati India. (iii) A History of Development of Mathematics in India by S. Grover (Mrs.) published by Atma Ram & Sons, Delhi, India and, (iv) Hinduism, Its Contributions to Science and Civilization: by Prabhakar Machwe.

42. **Question by Raghuvir Srinivasan:**
Sir, please elaborate on references in the Vedas, which describe the structure of the atom and matter. Some years ago I had met Prof. George Sudarshan, a distinguished physicist, who said that the ancient seers had already discerned the structure of the atom.

Answer by Ambassador O P Gupta: Dear Raghuvir, you are right. Vedic seers were aware of atomic nature of matter but with a different terminology. RV (X.81.3): "He whose eyes are everywhere" one Divine Being who has created the heaven and earth by the process of integration and disintegration of atoms."

RV (X.72.6) "In the end of Chaotic State the physical forces were endowed with the energy to assume the forms of creation. There did get rise multitude of atoms full of motion." Kanad developed Theory of Atoms further in his book Vaisesika sutra. "Though the structures built are perishable he wrote, atoms of which they are built are not perishable." "Only forms change. Individual atoms combine with others. Atoms do not exist in an uncombined state in creation."

Prof. Albert Einstein proved that mass is not destroyed and in our current terminology gave a quantitative formula that E is equal to mass into C square. In Gita (VIII.18 & 19), Lord Krishna says that this multitude of beings is dissolved at coming of the cosmic night; it rises again at the commencement of cosmic day, i.e., mass is not destroyed; it just transforms its forms. For further details, please see last para of my reply to Renjish.

43. **Question by GAURAV SHARMA:**

Dear Ambassador Gupta, did you see HH Kanchi Shankaracharya's replies to Nivedana (2003–07–08) that 'girls should not chant Gayatri Mantra' and to Mr. Por Sezhian (2003–07–09) that "all humans cannot chant Gayatri Mantra"? These directly contradict your basic theme that equality by birth and gender equality are the two cardinal vedic norms as per RV (V.60), RV (X.191), AV(III.30) etc. Thus, HH is contradicting the Vedas!!! Please comment.

Answer by Ambassador O P Gupta: The Rigveda contains divine revelations to over 414 rishis out of which about 30 are lady rishis (rishikas). This means Almighty God Himself considered women fit enough and eligible to receive divine revelations. Therefore, in my humble views, women have equal access and equal claim over the Vedas.

If God did not discriminate against women in matter of revealing Vedic richas to them, how could we? The Gayatri Mantra was revealed to rishi Vishwamitra Gathin who was a great warrior also. The Gayatri Mantra appears at RV (III.62.10), Yaj (III.35) (XXII.9) & (XXX.2) and Samaveda (1462). I have not yet seen any restriction imposed by mantra–drasta rishi VG on who should or should not recite it. Further, Vedic richas RV (X.191), AV(III.30), AV(VIII.54), Yaj (XXVI.02), Yaj (XXXVI.18) open gates of worship to all men as well as women without any gender discrimination. Vedas command common be prayers (samano mantrah, samano manah, samanam mantra–mbhi mantraye). You may also see 'Striyon ka Gayatri Adhikar' by Poojyawar Acharya Shri Ram Sharmaji at website (www.awgp.org) or (www.dsvv.org).

44. **Comment by YAKUB MULLA:**
Excellent articles, very objective and educative. I was generally aware that the Holy Quran does not accept basic tenets of Christianity but it was in these articles that sura numbers have been correctly quoted. Sify.com is doing good social service by hosting these.

Answer by Ambassador O P Gupta: Thank you very much. Sify.com is really doing a wonderful social service. Exposures to basics of others' religions without acrimony strengthen foundations of any secular society.

45. **Question by GSHEENH:**
Mr. Gupta you are a well intentioned person, but your knowledge of vedas is quite limited. Vedic Brahamans probably are quite upset that you are doing a Brahaman's duty. I have read that only a Brahaman

from pure Brahaman parents could learn vedas. People would pay more attention if you were a Brahaman. According to Lord Krishna you are tresspassing your prescribed duty and unfit for salvation.

Answer by Ambassador O P Gupta: Firstly, to propagate or justify birth based caste related disabilities is now a criminal offence in India.

The Hon'ble Supreme Court of India has also ruled that non–brahamans can be appointed as priests in Hindu temples, so, now it has full & final force of law.

Secondly, in my articles, I have quoted many Vedic richas RV (X.191), RV (X.125.5), RV (V.60.5), AV (III.30) etc. proving that the Vedas instruct unity, equality by birth and harmony. The Vedas themselves do not exclude any one, irrespective of his birth, from learning these.

In Gita, too, there is no birth based caste as Lord Krishna (XVIII.41) says 'Karmani pravibhaktani.' Lord Krishna does not say 'Janmani pravibhaktani'. So the term 'Vedic Brahamans' used by you in hereditary sense is definitely a fraudulent term, alien and contradictory to the Vedas & Gita. According to Vedas, Gita and Manusmriti all those who study and propagate Vedas are the real Brahamanas, see para 3.5 of this book. If your hereditary "Vedic Brahamans" could have led Hindus to salvation, Hindus would never have been defeated time and again by numerically small numbers of The Turks, Afghans, Mughals and Britishers etc.

Defeat after defeat of Hindus by small number of foreign

invaders was made possible because transgressing Veda and Gita, Hindu Samaj was fragmented from within. Despite being in numerical majority, Hindus for centuries were regularly sold as slaves in Multan, Kabul, etc. (Muslim Slave System in Medieval India by Prof. K.S. Lal). Why? Who are responsible for this misfortune of our forefathers?

It is the sacred duty of each one of us to study & analyse the causes of misfortunes which befell upon our forefathers and recently upon Kashmiri Hindus in 1989 so that our grandchildren do not suffer the same. It should no more be a matter of seeking individual salvation but the salvation of the whole Hindu Samaj.

One may notice that Hindu preachers (kathawachaks) who in line with the Vedas,Gita and Ramanaya open gates of their religious discourses to all Hindus are richer than those who practise casteism.

46. **Question by SWAPAN MUKHERJEE:**

I am very much interested in the Vedas. Please let me know how do I get all the four authentic (unabridged) Vedas (Books) in English or Hindi and if possible with narations. If it is in Sanskrit, naration is must.

Answer by Ambassador O P Gupta: Dear Swapan, please see my reply to Shri Vivek Singh Sengar. You may also wish to visit the following websites: (i) M/s Motilal Banarasidas at www.mlbdbooks.com, (ii) Interntaional Booksellers: www.dkagencies.com

47. **Comments By KARTY:**

Appreciate Shri Gupta's effort to spread the Vedic/

Gita knowledge, but I believe he needs to learn them in depth from revered Guru's. Some of the corrections to Shri Gupta's statements: First–Vedas alone are revealed scriptures (Shruti prasthana), while Gita is categorized under Smrithi Prasthana (Written from Memory). Two – Child marriages were in vogue and had the sanction of Shastras – pl refer The Hindu Dharma – a collection of teachings by The Sage of Kanchi – the true Living God.

Answer by Ambassador O P Gupta: My job is such that I keep meeting top religious leaders from all shades of Hinduism, Islam (Shiite, Sunni, Bohra, etc.), Jews, Christianity, Buddhism, Jainism, Sikhism, etc. and exchange views with them.

During my long public service, I have met many Hindu Gurus and Acharyas but found that most of them were unable to give me satisfactory replies to burning questions like: why Hindus were defeated time and again by much smaller numbers of foreign invaders, why the percentage of Hindus in total population has been declining even today, why Hindus recently (1989) got uprooted from Kashmir Valley, who are untouchables, why are they untouchables, who made them untouchables; are there untouchables in Islam, if not, why not; who are weakening Hinduism, etc.

Some said that being *sanyasis* (who have renounced the world) they were above such worldly (*saansaarik*) affairs. They tried to evade or escape from replying such questions. Many Hindu Gurus appeared somewhat unaware of the treatment prescribed for Kafirs in the Quran; many of them were also unaware that under strict Islamic laws, Hindus, not being ahle–kitab, are not even Kafirs but jimmis or dhimmis, a few steps below Kafirs.

In order to find answers to my questions, I had to self–educate myself and find time to study texts of the Holy Vedas (not commentaries or explanatory notes), Holy Qur'an and the Holy Bible, etc. and came to my conclusions that though in theory we all Hindus worship Veda & Gita; in practice, we have deviated from these in our day to day life which, in my humble view, is the root cause of our downfall.

You see Islam is expanding because Muslims do not allow other books & individuals to be placed on par with the Holy Qur'an. My articles attempt to restore Vedic norms of equality by birth and gender equality. Let us restore the Supremacy of Vedas.

Every Hindu knows that Gita is the sermon/revelation directly from Lord Krishna to Arjuna; simultaneously heard (shruti) by Sanjay with the help of *Divyadristi* provided by Vedvyas. What Sanjay could hear with the blessings of Vedvyas was obvisouly audible (shrawan/shruti) to Vedvyas.

As you know, Vedic richas also travelled from generation to generation by memory till reduced to a written form. Gita was written by Vedvyas who had himself heard (shruti) Lord Krishna revealing it to Arjuna.

What is in vogue need not always have sanction of

Vedas. As I mentioned in my article "Rigveda and the Indian Women;" and in my reply to Shri PP Singh (6/16/03), RV (X.27.12) commands: "She (bride) of herself chooses her husband amongst men." Naturally, a child has no mental capability to make informed choice of her husband amongst men, so, Rigveda does not sanction child marriage. You may advise, if you know of any Vedic richa to the contrary.

48. **Question by SRIHARI:**

I have few questions on your articles. You said that Kunti never committed Sati, but as far as I know the story, Pandu's second wife did commit Sati instead of Kunti. I did not remember her name but she is mother of Nakul and Sahadeva.

So using Kunti's example how could we justify Sati is wrong? Second question: the story of Ram who killed a Sudra for practising meditation which is against caste principles on the order of Vishwamitra. Isn't it true? If it is true how do you justify it?

Answer by Ambassador O P Gupta: Pandu's second wife Madri committed Sati and Kunti did not commit Sati. This only further proves my basic point that committing Sati was never a part of, nor, a mandatory requirement of Hindu Dharma. Kunti was not insulted or discarded for not committing Sati. She continued to receive full respect in the family. Some widows committing suicide does not make it sanctified or exemplary.

Rigvedic richa RV (X.18.7) is fraudulently quoted by pro–Sati lobby to claim Rigvedic sanction for Sati suppressing a very simple fact that in Sukta RV (X.18) the dead body is being buried in ground, so, there is no funeral pyre for a Hindu widow to mount under RV (X.18.7).

Further, the Rigveda sanctions life and remarriage of widows vide nine richas RV (X.40.2), RV (X.18.8–9), AV (IX.5.27–28) and AV (XVIII.3.1–4). For other part of your query, please see my reply to Shri Narayan Shetty.

49. **Comment By MAHESH MIKKILINENI:**
Dear Ambassador Gupta: Your writings on Veda are interesting– on age of Vedas etc. If you read the book written by Myle Dillon et. al Celtic History & Culture (I am sure, you know who these Celtics/Germanics are? All Europeans–from Greek/Roman/Austrian/French/Spanish/British & Irish and Germanic/Russian etc. M. Dillon is a Sr. Prof. at Dublin Institute for Celtic Studies, Prof. at Edinborogh, Wisconsin & Chicago etc.) Celtics are none other than Brahamans from Bharat.

Answer by Ambassador O P Gupta: Thank you very much for your kind words. In fact, now the theory of westward migration from present day India to Asia Minor and thence to Europe is taking a sharper shape. The Rigveda: A Historical Analysis by S.G. Talageri (ISBN 81–7742–010–0) is worth reading.

(APPENDIX IV)
FURTHER RESOURCES

Percentage Composition of Population of India

	1951	1961	1971	1981	1991	2000*
Hindus	84.98%	83.5%	82.7%	82.6%	82.41%	80.5%
Muslims	9.91%	10.7%	11.2%	11.4%	12.1%	13.4%
Christians	2.35%	2.4%	2.6%	2.4%	2.34%	2.33%
Sikhs	1.74%	1.8%	1.9%	2.0%	1.99%	1.84%
Buddists	0.05%	0.7%	0.7%	0.7%	0.77%	0.76%
Jains	0.45%	0.5%	0.5%	0.5%	0.41%	0.40%
Others	0.54%	0.4%	0.4%	0.4%	0.43%	0.64%

Composition of India's Population

(Number in Million)

	1951	1961	1971	1981	1991	2000*
Hindus	303.6	366.5	453.3	549.7	672.6	827
Muslims	35.4	46.9	61.4	75.6	95.2	138
Christians	8.4	10.7	14.2	16.2	18.9	24
Sikhs	6.2	7.8	10.4	13.1	16.3	19
Buddists	0.2	3.2	3.8	4.7	6.3	7.9
Jains	1.6	2.0	2.6	3.2	3.4	4.2
Others	1.8	1.6	2.2	2.8	3.5	6.6

Decadal Growth Rate

	1961-71	1971-81	1981-91	1991–2001*	Remark (2001)
Hindus	23.7%	24.1%	25.1%	20.3%	Decline
Muslims	30.85%	30.7%	34.5%	36.0%	Growth
Christians	32.6%	16.83%	21.5%	22.6%	Growth
Sikhs			24.3%	18.2%	Decline
Buddists			35.3%	24.5%	Decline
Jains			4.0%	26.0%	Growth

* Based on 6th September 2004 Data

India's Rank in the World

FIRST	Yoga & Meditation, inventor of zero, largest democracy in the world, largest cattle stock (cows and buffaloes), largest producer of milk (84.6 million tons, 2001–02); tractors, feature films, three–wheelers, sugar (15 million tons), tea (813 m. kg.), fruits (46.97 m. tons), pulses (16.1 m. tons), spices (2.7 m tons), cashew (0.44 m. tons), coconut, black pepper, mint oil, tomato, butter; largest exporter of emeralds, largest processor of cut and polished diamonds (90% of world market) and gold jewelry; largest number of post offices (153,423), largest number of university graduates every year (2.5 m); largest deposits of thorium, mica. Ayurveda (6000 BC) is the oldest medical system still in use, land of Sanskrit, the oldest Indo–European language. The Times of India is the world's largest circulated English broadsheet daily (over 2.144 million). State Bank of India has largest number of branches in the world, largest number of nuclear power plants (8) under construction (3960 MWe) in year 2002 (11 atomic power stations are producing electricity.)
SECOND	Second fatest growing economy in the world. Second largest population (1 billion plus), second largest producer of rice (86 m. tons), wheat (74.2 m. tons), ground nuts, cement (117 MT), sponge iron, natural silk, vegetables (80.8 m. tons) and two–wheelers; the second largest railway network (63,000

km. with a fleet of 7,000 passenger trains and 4000 goods trains, carrying over 4 billion passengers and 382 million tons freight per annum), the second largest technically trained manpower in the world, with 232 universities, over 150 medical colleges and over 50 dental collages. Hindi is the second largest spoken language of the world.

THIRD Third largest producer of cotton (16 m. bales of 170 kg. each), tobacco, pesticide industry, satellite and science & technology infra–structure, the third largest coal deposits (200 billion tons), the third largest printer of books in English, third largest road network (3.32 m km.); India has the third largest investor base in the world (Market capitalization of Bombay Stock Exchange was about US$ 400 billion in March, 2005). India is one of the first three countries to have indigenously manufactured super computers, apart from USA and Japan.

FOURTH Fourth largest economy on PPP basis (US$ 2913 billion GNP in 2001). G–20 member. Fourth largest producer of natural rubber (0.624 m tons), eggs (hen), nitrogen fertilizers and bauxite. The Indian Armed Forces are the fourth largest in the world, largely equipped with items made in India. GDP growth 6.1%(FY1999), 4.4%(FY2000), 5.6%(FY2001), 4% (FY2002); 8.5% (FY 2003–04) Indian economy is the 13th largest (US$ 477.4 billion: 2001) in the world (fixed parity basis). GDP (US$ 576 billion in 2003).

	GDP on PPP basis (US$ 2.86 trillion in 2003).
FIFTH	Fifth largest producer of coffee (.23 m tons), soybeans, iron ore, motor vehicles and computers including teraflop computers. India has the fifth largest hydropower potential at 84,000 MW at 60% load factor. Fifth in poultry stock.
SIXTH	India is one of the six countries having its own self–reliant nuclear capability and technology with 12 atomic power stations (2720 nuclear MWe), rockets and missiles, digital telemetry, satellites, launching of satellites into space; remote sensing satellites, managing steel, beryllium and titanium extraction. Sixth largest holder of FOREX (US$ 133 billion in Feb, 05).
SEVENTH	Seventh largest country area–wise in the world (3.29 million sq. km.). One of the seven countries with indigenous IRBM capability.
EIGHTH	Telecommunications (from being 14th in 1999) with 40 million telephones.

Richas & Shlokas with full Sanskrit Texts

Sl. No.	Richas/Shloka
1	RV (I.164.11)
2	RV (II.33.9)
3	RV (II.33.10)
4	RV (II.33.11)
5	RV (II.41.16)
6	RV (III.61.6)
7	RV (IV.5.11)
8	RV (IV.5.12)
9	RV (IV.57.8)
10	RV (IV.58.3)
11	RV (V.52.17)
12	RV (V.60.5)
13	RV (VI.45.31)
14	RV (VIII.43.11)
15	RV (X.18.12)
16	RV (X.18.7)
17	RV (X.18.8)
18	RV (X.31.11)
19	RV (X.40.2)
20	RV (X.40.8)
21	RV (X.75.5)
22	RV (X.75.6)
23	RV (X.85.42)
24	RV (X.85.46)
25	RV (X.90.9)
26	RV (X.90.11)
27	RV (X.90.12)
28	RV (X.90.14)
29	RV (X.91.14)

30	RV (X.93.9)
31	RV (X.125.5)
32	RV (X.191.2)
33	RV (X.191.3)
34	RV (X.191.4)
35	AV (III.30.1)
36	AV (III.30.5)
37	AV (III.30.6)
38	AV (III.30.7)
39	AV (VI.64.1)
40	AV (VI.64.2)
41	AV (VI.64.3)
42	AV (VI.64.4)
43	AV (VI.73.1)
44	AV (VI.73.2)
45	AV (VI.73.3)
46	AV (VI.74.1)
47	AV (VI.74.2)
48	AV (VI.74.3)
49	AV (VII.54.1)
50	AV (VII.54.2)
51	AV (XVIII.4.32)
52	Yaj (26.02)
53	Yaj (36.18)
54	Gita (V.18)
55	Gita (IX.32)
56	Gita (XVIII.41)
57	Gita (XVIII.42)
58	Gita (XVIII.43)
59	Gita (XVIII.44)
60	Gita (XVIII.68)
61	Gita (XVIII.69)
62	Gita (XVIII.71)
63	Mahabharata (I.V.4)
64	Valmiki Ramayana (1.1.98–100)
65	Manusmriti (IV.176)
66	ManuSmriti (X.65)

SELECT BIBLIOGRAPHY

I Books

Acharya, Pt. Shri Ram Sharma, *Rigveda* (Hindi), *Yajurveda* (Hindi), *Samaveda* (Hindi), *Atharvaveda* (Hindi), Sanskriti Sansthan, Khwaja Kutub, Barreilly'243003, India

Altekar, Dr AS, *The Position of Women In Hindu Civilization*, Motilal Banarasidass, Delhi (ISBN 81–208–0324–8)

Banerji, Sures Chandra, *Society in Ancient India* (ISBN 81–246–000–7)

Bhattacharjee, A.M., *Hindu Law and the Constitution*, Eastern Law House, New Delhi, India

Bloomfield, Maurice, *The Atharvaveda*, (1897) (www.sacred–texts.com)

Buhler, George, *The Laws of Manu*, (1886) (www.sacred–texts.com)

Buhler, George, *The Dharma Sutras*, (1879) (www.sacred–texts.com)

Chopra, Dr. Deepak, MD, *Perfect Health*, Harmony Books, New York, U.S.A. Dvivedi,

Dr. K.D., *Vedon men Ayurveda (Medical Sciences in the Vedas)*, Vishwabharati Anusandhan Parishad, Gyan Pur, Varanasi (India) (ISBN: 81–85246–36–X)

Engineer, Asghar Ali, *The Islamic State*, Vikas Publishing House, New Delhi

Frawley, David, *The Astrology of the Seers*, Motilal Banarasidass Publishers, New Delhi, India, (ISBN 81–208–1007–4)

Fyzee, Asaf A.A., *Outlines of Muhammadan Law*, Oxford University Press, India

Griffith, RTH & Arya, Dr. RP, *Yajurveda Samhita*, Parimal Publications, 27/28, Shakti Nagar, Delhi–110007, India (ISBN 81–7110–136–0)

Griffith, RTH & Arya, Dr. RP, *Samaveda Samhita*, Parimal Publications, 27/28, Shakti Nagar, Delhi–110007, India (ISBN 81–7110–113–1)

Griffith, Ralph T.H., *The Rigveda*, (1897) (www.sacred–texts.com)

Griffith, Ralph T.H., *The Samaveda*, (1895) (www.sacred–texts.com)

Grover, S., *A History of Development of Mathematics in India*, Atma Ram & Sons, Kashmere Gate, Delhi–110006, India (ISBN 81–7043–241–3 HB)

Hiro, Dilip, *War Without End*, Routledge, 11 New Fetter Lane, London EC4P 4EE, UK (ISBN : 81–7436–244–4)

Holy Bible (The Gideons International)

Hosain, Saiyid Safdar, *The Early History of Islam*, D.K. Publishers, 1 Ansari Road, New Delhi–110002, India (ISBN 81–86142–17–7)

Jois, Justice M. Rama, *Human Rights and Indus Values*, National Council for Teacher Education, New Delhi, India

Joshi, Dr. Bhramarlal, *Veda*, Gurjar Bharati, Ahmadabad, India

Kaushik, Ashok, *Srimad Bhagwadgita*, Star Publications, New Delhi–110002, India (ISBN 81–86264–64–7)

Keer, Dhananjay, *Dr. Ambedkar – Life and Mission*, Popular Prakashan, Bombay, India (ISBN 81–7154–237–9)

Keith, A.B., *The Yajur Veda*, (1914) (www.sacred–texts.com)

Kersten, Holger, *Jesus Lived in India*, Element Books Ltd (ISBN 1–85230–550–9)

Khan, Ansar Hussain, *The Rediscovery of India: A New Sub–continent*, Orient Longman Limited, Hyderabad 500 029 (AP), India (ISBN– 8125015957)

Khan, Maulana Wahiduddin, *Islam Rediscovered*, Goodword Books, New Delhi.

Khanam, Farida, *Life and teachings of the Prophet Muhammad*, Goodword Books.

Khosla Ishi, *The Cholesterol Facts*, Life Publications (India), Janakpuri, New Delhi, India

Lal, K.S., Muslim *Slave System in Medieval India*, Aditya Prakashan, New Delhi, India (ISBN: 81–85689–67–9)

Limaye, Madhu, *Indian National Movement, Its Ideological and Socio–Economic Dimensions*, ISBN–81–7027–133–9, Radiant Publishers, India

Macdonell, Arthur A., *A History of Sanskrit Literature*, Motilal Banarasidass Publishers, Delhi, India (ISBN 81–208–0095–8)

Machwe, Prabhakar, *Hinduism Its Contribution to Science and Civilization*, Machwe Prakashan, E–180, Greater Kailash II, New Delhi 110048, India

Majumdar, R.C., Raychaudhuri, H.C., Datta, Kalikinkar, *An Advanced History of India* (Fourth Edition), Macmillan India Limited.

Menezes, S.L. Lt. General (rtd), *Fidelity and Honour, The Indian Army*, ISBN 019 5650476, Oxford University Press, New Delhi.

Misra, Satya Swarup, *The Aryan Problem – A Linguistic Approach* (ISBN 81–215–0537–0)

Nahjul Balagha, Ansariyan Publications, Qum, Iran

Nehru, Jawahar Lal, *Glimpses of World History*, Oxford University Press (Fifth Impression 1988)

Nehru, Jawahar Lal, *The Discovery of India*, Oxford University Press (Seventh Impression 1988)

O'Flaherty, Dr. Wendy Doniger, *The Rigveda*, Penguin Books, India (1994)

Omvedt, Gail, *Dalits and the Democratic Revolution*, Sage Publications India Pvt. Ltd, M032, Greater Kailash, Market I, New Delhi, India

Ornish, Dr. Dean, *Reversing Heart Disease*, Ballantine Books, (ISBN 0–8041–1038–7)

Parpola, Asko, *Pre–Proto–Iranians of Afghanistan as initiators of Sakta tantrism: On the Schthian/Saka Affiliation of the Dasas, Nuristanis and Magadhans*, Iranica Antiqua 37 (Fs. C.C. Lamberg–Karlovsky), 2002

Parpola, Asko and Christian, Carpelan, *Emergence, Contacts and Dispersal of Proto–Indo–European, Proto–Uralic and Proto–Aryan in Archaeological Perspective*, Papers presented at an international symposium held at the Tvarminne Research Station of the University of Helsinki, January, 1999

Parpola, Asko, *From the dialects of Old Indo–Aryan to Proto–Aryan and Proto–Iranian*, The British Academy by Oxford University Press, 2002

Parpola, Asko, *Deciphering the Indus Script*, Press Şyndicate of the University of Cambridge, New York, U.S.A, 1994

Parpola, Asko, *The Religious background of the Savitri Legend*

Parpola, Asko, *Itanaih and Sita: On the Historical Background of the Sanskrit Epics.*

Parpola, Asko & Joshi, Jagat Pati, *Corpus of Indus Seals and Inscriptions* (1.Collections in India), (ISBN: 951 41 0555–9)

Payne, Robert, *The Life and Death of Mahatma Gandhi*, Smithmark Publishers Inc, New York, USA (ISBN 0–8317–5870–8)

Pickthall, Mohammed Marmaduke, *The Meaning of the Holy Qur'an*, UBS Publishers Ltd., New Delhi, India

Prasad, Dr. R.C., *Sri Ramacharitamanas*, Motilal Banarasidass Publishers, New Delhi, India (ISBN 81–208–0762–6)

Rodrigues, Valerian, *The Essential Writings of B.R. Ambedkar*, Oxford University Press (ISBN 0–19–565608–3)

Sarkar, Sir Jadunath, *Military History of India*, Orient Longmans, New Delhi

Saraswati, Swami Prakashanand, *The True History and the Religion of India*, Motilal Banarasidass Publishers, New Delhi, India (ISBN 81–208–1789–3)

Shastri, Acharya V.N., *Science in The Vedas*, Sarvadeshik Arya Pratinidhi Sabha, Ramlila Ground, New Delhi–110001, India

Sharma, Dr. Ganga Sahay, Ph.D, *Rigveda (Hindi)*, Sanskrit Sahitya Prakashan, M–12, Connaught Place, New Delhi–110001, India

Sharma, Dr. Surendra Kumar, *Hindu Itihas: Haron Ki Dastan (Hindu History: Story of Defeats)*; Vishwa Vijay (P) Ltd., M 12, Connaught Place, New Delhi

Shakir, M.H., *The Holy Qur'an*, Tahrike Tarsile Qur'an Inc, Elmhurst, New York 11373–1115, USA (ISBN 0–940368–56–0)

Sethna, K.D., *The Problems of Aryan Origins*, Aditya Prakashan, 24 Ansari Road, New Delhi, India

Singhal, D.P., Gypsies: *Indians in Exile*, Archana Publications, Meerut, India

Talageri, Shrikant G., *The Aryan Invasion Theory, A Reappraisal*, Aditya Prakashan, New Delhi, India

Talageri, Shrikant G., *The Rigveda, A Historical Analysis*, Aditya Prakashan, New Delhi, India

Ushanas, E. Richter, *The Indus Script and the Rigveda*, Motilal Banarasi Dass Publishers, New Delhi

Vidyalankar, Pt. Satyakam, *The Holy Vedas*, Clarion Books, Shahdara Delhi–110032, India

Whitney, WD & Joshi, K.L., *Atharvaveda Samhita*, Parimal Publications, 27/28, Shakti Nagar, Delhi–110007, India (ISBN 81–7110–172–0)

Wilson, HH; Arya & Joshi, *RG–Veda Samhita*, Parimal Publications, 27/28, Shakti Nagar, Delhi–110007, India (ISBN 81–7110–138–7)

Zakaria, Dr. Rafiq, "*The Man Who Divided India*"

II Articles on Internet

Abbas, Dr. Samar, *India's Parthian Colony* (www.iranchamber.com)

Agrawal, Prof. Dinesh, *Demise of Aryan Invasion/Race Theory* (www.itihas.com)

Agrawal, Sita, *Sati–Brahaman Annihilation of Widows* (www.dalitstan.com)

Agrawal, Vishal, *Vajrasuchika Upnishad* (http://vishalagrawal.bharatvani.org)

All About DHEA: (http://www.dreampharm.com/zDHEA.asp)

Amin, Hussein Abdulwaheed, *The Origins of the Sunni/Shia split in Islam*, (www.islamfortoday.com)

Amey, Rosemary A., *Animal Rights and the Dhammapada* (www.buddhismtoday.com)

April 2001 Document, *Combat Communalism* (http://www.sabrang.com/cc/archive/2001/april01/docu.htm)

Arthritis (www.drmcdougall.com/science/arthritis.html)

Astronomical Data and the Aryan Question (www.bharatvani.org/books/ait/ch23.htm)

Babari or Barabari, Indian Express, March 19, 1997

Bhosle, Varsha, *Hinduism' Corpse*, (http://cgi.rediff.com)

Bhelari, Kanhaiah, *Note of Dissent*, The Week (Jan. 31, 1999)

Bidwai, Praful, *Reality of Dalit Oppression*, (www.rediff.com) (Oct.22, 2002)

Bindra, Prerna Singh, *Heads I win*, The Week (Nov. 18, 2001)

Bovine Spongiform Encephalopathy Paper from Institute of Food Science & Technology, UK

Caste (http://21.1911encyclopedia.org)

Campbell, Jon, *Ten Reasons to Stop Eating Beef* (www.cqs.com/beef.html) *Caste and Conversion* (www.campus.fortunecity.com)

Comparative Study of Religions (www.global.globale.net/heritage/Source/0583.html)

Cow Slaughter in Hindu Scriptures (Haniff Inc) (http:// ehaniff.tripod.com/hinduism/slaughter.html)

Dani Interview; Full text (http://www.harappa.com/script/danitext.html)

Danino, Michel, *The Riddle of India's Ancient Past* (www.yrec.org/damino.html)

Dalit Muslims (www.truthindia.com) (Feb. 10, 2001)

Dean, Ward, M.D. & Fowkes, Steven Wm., *DHEA* (www.ceri.com/dhea.htm)

Difference Between Shi'ahs and Sunnis (www.brain.brain.net.pk/dsera/ qa105.htm)

Dr. Ambedkar & Caste, Harijan (www.mkgandhi–sarvodaya.org) (11.2.1933)

Dyslipidimia And Coronary Artery Disease ' Focus on Diet: Indian Medical Association, Kerala Branch (http://www.imakerala.org/cme/dyslipidimia.htm)

Elst, Dr. Koenraad, *The Politics of the Aryan Invasion Debate* (http://koenraadelst.bharatvani.org)

Frawley, David, *The Aryan–Dravidian Controversy* (www.hindunet. org)

Freiberger, Oliver, *Review of Buddhisten in Indian hente*, (http://jbe.gold.ac.uk)

Govindarajan Padman "India and Indus Valley Civilization" (http://www.hknet.org.nz/GP–IndiaandindusValley Civilization.html)

Green, Samuel, *The Different Arabic Versions of the Qur'an* (www.answering–islam.org/Green/seven.htm)

Gupta, Dipankar, *Killing Caste by Conversion*, The Hindu (November 13, 2001)

Gupta, Dr. Naresh K., *Saraswati' Legend or History* (www.hindunet.org/ araswati/resources/saraswati_ legend.htm)

Holy Cow! Do Indians eat a lot of Beef (Business Line, Sept. 04, 2001)

http://www.dialognow.org/node/view/740

http://www.zulunation.com/RELIGIONS.html

History of Vedic Saraswati River and projects to develop the Saraswati River Basin (www.hindunet.org/Saraswati/Vedic Saraswati1.html)

India, Hinduism and Religious Rebellion to 480 BCE, The Lost Civilization of Mohenjo–daro and Harappa (http://www.fsmitha.com/h1/ch05.htm)

Islam, Internet Sacred Texts Archive (www.sacred–texts.com/isl/index.htm)

Is Non– Vegetarian Food Permitted (www.allaahuakbar.net/jain/religious.htm)

Jayaram, V., Caste System is the biggest threat to Hinduism (www.hinduwebsite.com)

Klostermair, Klaus, Questioning the Aryan Invasion Theory and Revisiting Ancient Indian History (www.iskcon.com)

Know About Coronary Heart Disease & Hypertention (http://www.imakerala.org/healthtips/coronary.htm)

Mad Cow Disease, The BSE Epidemic in Great Britain (www.accessexcellence.org/WM/NM/madcow96.html)

Marxism and the Caste Struggle (http://campus.fortunecity.com)

Mirdamadi Ali, *Shia and Sunni: The Two Major Divisions of Islam*, (www.mctc.mnscu.edu)

Nagaswamy, Dr. R., *On Reading Vedic Texts*, (http://www.geocities.com/ifihhome/articles/m002.html)

Patrin : A *Brief History of the Roma* (www.geocities.com/Paris/5121/history.htm) (1996–2000)

Punj, Balbir K., *Cowboy Mentality*, The Pioneer (August 15, 2002)

Rajaram, N.S., A *Scientific Foundation for the Study of Ancient India* (www.vedanet.com)

Rajaram, N.S., *Origins of the Aryan Dravidian Divide* (www.swordoftruth.com)

Rajagopalan, Dr. M., *Aryan Nation* (www.viewsunplugged.com)

Rise and Fall of the Indus Civilization (A Review of papers/book of Prof. Asko Parpola) (http://sify.com/itihaas)

Robson, Rev. James, *Christ in Islam* (http://www.sacred–texts.com/isl/cii/cii.htm)

Sati (widow-Burning) (http://ehaniff.tripod.com)

Siddiqi, Mazheruddin & Morgan, Kenneth W., *Islam–The Straight Path: Islam Interpreted by Muslisms* (www.religion–online.org/cgi–bin/relsearchd.dll/showchapter? chapter_id= 1644) Sikand, Yoginder, The Badri–Vakili Controversy (http://www.dawoodi–bohras.com/perspective/badri_vakili.htm)

Sims, Hank, Shi'a-Sunni Schism, (www.internews.org/visavis/BTVPagesInews/ShiaSunni_ Schism.html)

Status of Widows (www.baharna.com)

Swamy, Dr. Subramanian, *Is the Dravidian Movement dying?* Frontline, June 07–20, 2003 (www.frontlineonnet.com)

The Caste System (www.atributetohinduism.com)

The Gypsies of Kosova: Their History and System: (www.chgs.umn.edu)

Thaper, Romila, *The Aryan Question Revisited* (Oct. 11, 1999) (http://members.tripod.com)

VanDoodewaard, William, *Islam United? A Comparision of Shi'ite and Sunni Belief and Practice* (1995) (www.rim.org/muslim/shiite.htm)

Witzel, Michael, *Westward Ho! The Incredible Wanderlust of the Rigvedic Tribes* (www.people.fas.harvard.edu)

Women in Hinduism (www.atributetohinduism.com)

www.dalitchristians.com

(i) Archbishop Arulappa's letter
(ii) Historic Evidence of Discrimination
(iii) Caste Church
(iv) Dalit Christian Issues, etc.

III Newspapers & Magazines

- Dainik Jagran, New Delhi, India
- Frontline, India
- Indian Express, New Delhi, India
- India Today, New Delhi, India
- Newsweek
- NDTV Website
- Observer, Jamaica
- The Gleaner, Jamaica
- Sarita, New Delhi, India
- The Hindu, India
- The Hindustan Times, New Delhi, India
- The International Herald Tribune
- The Pioneer, India
- The Statesman, India
- The Times of India, New Delhi, India
- The Week (India)
- The Outlook (India)

INDEX

A

Abu Bakr, Hazrat 118
Abdul Kalam, APJ 62
Abul–Fazl Allami 190
Agriculture 1, 18, 28, 47, 50, 54, 87, 226,
Ain–i–Akbari 190
Airship 4
Ajlaf 116
Akbar 191
Algebra 1, 6, 9
Ali, Hazrat 118, 119, 121
Allahabad 20, 227
Al–Mansur, Khalifa 6
Ambassador 33, 39, 97, 160, 169, 250, 257, 261, 266, 323
Ambedkar, B.R. 82, 89
Amritsar 191
Animal Fat 177, 181, 195, 196, 201
Animal Protein 196
Annihilation 84, 85, 109, 223
Anthropology 34, 263
Antiquity 3, 20, 22, 23, 26, 242, 262, 284
Anushtubha 7
Apastamba Dharmasutra 41
Apollonius 3
Arabic Numerals 6
Aravallis 20
Archimedes 3
Arithmetic 6
Arjikiya 236
Arya Samaj 77
Aryabhatta 7
Aryan Invasion Theory 177, 214, 215, 218, 230, 278
Aryas, Aryans 24, 210, 218, 232
Arzal 108, 116
Ashoka the Great 127
Ashraf 108, 116
Askini 236
Astrology 133, 275, 288
Astronomy 2, 6, 34, 263, 267, 275, 287
Atharvaveda 1, 2, 8, 11, 12, 13, 40, 52, 54, 55, 56, 58, 59
Atherogenicity 202
Attraction 4
Aurangzeb 37, 91
Aurovindo 213, 230
Avesta 124
Avian Flu 201
Axis 4
Ambedkar, Dr. B.R. 82, 89

B

Babur 37, 191
Baghdad 6, 95, 121, 241
Bakhtiyar 48, 89, 90
Bakrid 191, 193
Baluchistan 25, 211, 227, 278
Banerjee, R.D. 216

Bangladesh 36, 105
Basaveshwar 82
BBC 5, 124
Beef 168, 169, 173, 176
Bertrand Russel 44
Bhabha 5
Bhagwadgita 45, 63, 79, 86, 108, 111, 132, 165, 259, 268, 271
Bhattacharjee, A.M. 44
Bible 22, 23, 124, 127, 128, 132, 245
Bihar 43, 48, 89, 90, 94, 108, 152, 236, 238
Birmingham 95, 97
Black Hole 5
Boghaz–koi 123, 121
Bohra 120, 294, 121
Bopp, Franz 215
Bose, P.K. 29
Bovine Spongeform 196, 197
Brahama 47
Brahaman 63, 64, 65, 68, 74
Brahui 211, 241
Brhati 7
British 3, 5, 9, 37, 38, 42, 44, 49, 77, 78, 87, 91, 92, 93, 94, 95, 97, 98, 101, 124, 151, 164, 177, 178, 180, 220, 278, 297
Brockington 21, 111, 112, 246
Brotherhood Vedic 43, 62, 95
BSE 196, 197, 198, 199
Buddhism 85, 89, 90, 126, 106
Buhler, George 41, 42, 46, 74
Burial Sukta (RV:X.18) 158

C

Caldwell, Robert 210
Canal 28, 220
Cancer 26, 141, 147, 200
Canonical 40, 43, 76, 86, 167
Cappadocia 23
Cardiologists 201, 203, 272
Carey, George Dr. 124
Caste 37, 40, 44, 45, 48, 54, 110, 247
Casteism 54, 57, 78, 80, 82, 85, 86, 161, 136, 133, 132
Catholics 106, 124, 126, 129, 130
Census 35, 116
Chad 29
Chamberlain 5, 96
Chanakya 159
Charak 190
Charak Samhita 190
Cheddar Man 31
China 3, 38, 39, 99, 100, 101, 226
Cholesterol 196, 200, 201, 202, 306
Christ 123, 124, 125, 127, 128, 131, 137, 276
Christian 23, 36, 40, 43, 78, 86, 103, 106, 107, 112, 114, 123, 124, 127, 128, 130
Church 23, 78, 107, 128, 130, 132, 133, 135, 136, 137
Churhat 29
Circle 33, 106, 288, 263
Clinton, Bill 7
Clive, Robert 92, 98
Coconut Oil 202
Coli 200
Colin, Renfrew Prof. 217
Communism 62, 70
Conard, Dr. Nicholas J. 28
Conference 30, 34, 106, 261, 263, 264
Congress Party 168
Constitution of India 80, 81, 82, 100, 164, 168, 195
Conversion 77, 81, 84, 103, 104, 105, 106, 117, 113, 247, 254, 256, 258

Coronary Artery Disease (CAD) 202
Cosmology 2
Cosmos 5, 33
Council, Privy 42, 151
Creation Hymn 5
Creutzfeldt–Jacob Disease (CJD) 196
Crucifixion 123, 127, 128
Cunningham, Alexander 216

D

D'Souza, P.P. 33
Dales, G.F. Prof. 216
Dalits 45, 57, 83, 84, 106, 107, 110, 111
Dani, Ahmad Hassan 212
Danube 28
Das Kapital 70
Dasas 209, 218, 230, 232, 233, 234, 280
Dasyus 230, 231, 232, 233, 280
Daughter 10
David, Sir 97
Dayabhag 43
Dayanand, Swami 82, 246, 257
Dead Sea 127
Deobandi 123
Devanagari 1, 240
Devapi 52
Dhammapada 125
DHEA 138, 139, 140, 141
Dhimmis 88, 295
DIOXIN 200
Divine 1, 13, 16, 24, 125, 126, 146, 172, 176, 282, 289, 290
Dravida 53, 205, 206, 208, 210
Dravidian 54, 208, 210, 211, 212, 214
Dyumna Risi 51

E

Earth 4, 16, 20, 23, 31, 32, 33, 50, 71, 175, 176, 180, 206, 263, 281, 287, 288, 289
Eclipse 2, 25
Economy 101, 235, 283, 299, 300
Egypt 23, 99
Einstein, Albert 3, 290
Electricity 4, 281, 299
Electronics 4
Emancipation 67, 68, 81, 105, 110, 112
Emmelin Plunret 4
Emperor 128, 137, 160, 236
Empress 166, 236
Engels, Friedrich 70
Engineer 64, 253
England 107, 151
English 8, 9, 45, 69, 109, 112, 153, 154, 207, 215, 242, 268, 285, 293, 299
Equinox 26
Essene 98, 126, 127
Ethiopia 212, 230

F

Factor VIII 20
Family 2, 10, 52, 65, 72, 99, 112, 109, 120, 135, 143, 160, 163, 165, 166, 169, 182, 197, 212
Female 8, 10, 51, 87, 110, 142, 146, 147, 148, 228, 240, 255
Finlandisation 96
FOXP2 30, 262
France 29, 92, 95, 101, 134, 199

G

GASS 97, 100
Gajdusek Carleton 197
Gandhi, Mahatama 73, 82, 101, 177, 254
Gandhi, Indira 100
Gandhi, Rajiv 254
Gandhi, Sonia 104

Ganga/Ganges 52, 94, 191, 228, 236, 237, 239, 240
Gautam Dharmasutra 41
Gayatri Mantra 1, 12, 53, 284, 290, 291
GDP 100, 300
Geography 238
Geology 2
Geometry 216
Germany 28, 69, 101, 216
Ghazani, Mahmud 37, 241
Gita 4, 20, 27, 40, 45, 61, 63, 64, 65, 67, 68, 70, 76, 89, 109, 112, 124, 140, 164, 246, 247, 250
Glacier 19
Goldman 21
Gospel 76, 77, 103, 129, 131, 132, 137, 273
Grammar 2, 10, 216
Grassmann, H. 9
Gravitation 10, 287
Gray, Sir William 178
Greece 2, 245
Greek 2, 3, 6, 127, 132, 215
Griffith, RTH 147
Gupta, Mohan 24
Gurudwara 107
Guru, Sri Narayana 82

H

Habib, Irfan 89
Halal 169
Harappa 16, 17, 19, 21, 210, 216, 219, 227
Hardeo, Singhji Maharaj HH 113, 114
Hawking, Stephan 5
Hegelian 70
Heisenberg, W. 4
Helsinki 22, 25, 30, 34, 212, 250, 261, 264
Herbal 2, 12
Herbs 2, 172
High Commissioner 95, 97
Himalayan 17, 48
Hindsa 6
Hindu 1, 4, 8, 33, 36, 37, 40, 41, 42, 48, 49, 56
Hinduism 2, 40, 47, 67, 73, 75, 76, 77, 78, 82, 83, 84, 85, 86, 100, 105, 109, 111, 124, 143, 145, 146, 148, 212, 216, 224
Hittites 23
Hogben Lancelot 3
Homosapiens 30
Hanbali 122
Hyder Ali 93

I

India 3, 4, 6, 7, 18, 26, 31, 32, 35, 36, 38, 56, 62, 65, 81, 82, 89, 91, 92, 93, 94, 97, 98, 100, 101, 102, 104, 105
Indo–Aryan 3, 22, 23, 24, 27, 213, 234, 241
Indo–European 2, 3, 23, 30, 215, 216, 217, 234, 232, 299
Infidel 7
Inquisition 160, 161
Irrigation 25, 28
Ismailies 120, 121
Ivory 28, 29

J

Jacobi, Prof. 22
Jafaria Laws 120
Jagati 7
Jahnu 52, 240
Jai Prakash, Loknayak 82
Jambudvipe 31, 262
Jat 107

Jataveda Agni (Sacred Fire) 181, 188
Jehadi 37
Jehovah's Witnesses 129, 130
Jerusalem 137
Jews 99, 132, 133, 169, 294
Jeziya 90
Jha, D.N. Prof. 179
Jones, William Sir 44, 214
Jurassic Age 32

K

Kabul 88, 237, 240, 241, 250, 293
Kafir 77
Kalama 119, 135
Kali Era 27, 28
Kalibangan 17, 221, 226
Kamdhenu 175
Kane, P.V. 153, 164, 194, 195
Karna 126
Kashmir 17, 36, 37, 127, 214, 294
Kasi 9, 24
Kassites 23, 24
Kasturba 103, 104
Kenoyer, J. Mark 219
Kersten, Holger 127
Khan, Ansar Hussian 37, 90
Khan, Wahiduddin Maulana 116, 117, 125
Khanam Farida 117
Kikata 238
Kolff, Dirk 88
Kosher 169
Kravyad Agni (Funeral Fire) 181, 182, 185, 186, 187, 188
Krishna/Krisna 27, 63, 64, 67, 68, 71, 75, 76, 79, 165, 208, 248, 254, 272, 271, 273, 276, 280, 282, 290, 292, 295
Kulkarni, K.M. 19
Kunti 126, 165, 296
Kuru 197

L

La Place 3
Lal, B.B. 212
Lal, K.S. 88, 293
Lawrence, Stringer 92
LDL (Bad Cholesterol) 202
Lead Balls 8, 172
Limaye, Madhu 91, 94
Lion 229
Long Life 2, 191, 207
Lothal 17, 211, 225, 226
Lucy 30
Ludwig 9

M

MacDonell, Aurthor A. 2, 15, 42, 43, 156, 174, 185, 194, 230
Mackay, Earnest 220
Mad Cow Disease 196, 198, 200
Magic 2, 12
Mahabharata 21, 24, 28, 41, 53, 164, 165, 241, 278, 283
Mahathir 115, 116
Mahisha 182
Mahmood, Tahir 191
Maliki 122
Manchanda, Dr. S.C. 203
Mandal 9, 10
Manusmriti 8, 40, 41, 42, 43, 44
Marshall, Sir John 210
Marudvrdha 236
Marx, Karl 69, 83
Mary, Mother 126
Mathematics 3, 6, 289
Maulana Ansar Shah 193
Maulana, Madani Mehmood 193
Maulana, S.A.H. Dehlavi 192

Max Müller 21, 23, 178, 207, 209, 215, 216, 222
Medhatithi 43, 238
Medicine 2, 12, 190, 197
Mehrgarh 25, 221, 278
Menezes, Lt. Gen. S.L 91
Mesopotamia 221
Metaphors 9, 173, 176
Meteorology 2, 34, 263
Methyl Nitro–amines 200
Migration 15, 18, 210, 218, 236, 237, 241, 244
Mir Jaffar 92, 93
Mir Kasim 93
Misra, Satya Swarup 26
Missionary Religion 76, 273
Mitaksara 43
Mitanni 24, 244
Mitra, Abhas 5
Mohen–jo–daro 21, 211, 212, 216, 219, 220, 221, 224, 225
Moksha 67, 68, 69, 253, 286
Monotheism 145
Moon 4, 10, 173, 288
Mosque 119, 132
Motilal 23, 293
Mountbatten, Lord 98
Mufti Habibur Rahman 193
Mughal 38, 88 91, 116, 190, 191, 292, 249
Muhammadans 119
Multan 88

N

Nair R. 19
Narad Sutra 44
Narayan, Rishi 12
Nariman, Fali S. 104
Nasadiya Sukta 5
Navada, S.V. 19
Navya Shastra 257, 258
Nehru, Jawaharlal 6, 53, 82, 90, 98, 129, 160, 208, 231, 244
Nirankari, Mandal, 113
Nirukta 170, 238
Numerals 3, 6, 7

O

O'Flaherty, Wandy D. 154, 156, 158, 162, 174, 180, 185
Oldenberg, H. 9
Oldham, C.F. 18
Oldham, R.D. 18
Omar, Hazrat 18
Omvedt, Gail 84, 231
Ornish, Dean Dr. 202
Orthodox Russian Church 129
Otzi the Iceman 31

P

Pagans 23, 88, 249
Pakistan 17, 36, 89, 90, 101, 105, 123, 128, 191, 212, 219, 241
Panini 26, 178, 179
Parardhana 3
Parasar 43, 159, 164
Parpola, Asko 24, 25, 212, 213, 217, 221, 241, 261
Parthian 212, 309
Parusni 237
Pentecostals 106, 126, 129
Persians 3, 117
Philosophy 4, 6, 70, 105, 115, 126, 203, 251, 252, 255, 256, 269
Phonetics 2
Phule, Sant 82
Pig/Pork 193, 169, 201
Planet 281, 288
Plassey 92, 93

Plunret, Emmelin Politics 2, 57, 70, 78, 87, 256
Polycyclic 200
Poona Pact 101
Pope 44, 78, 129, 130, 131, 132, 133
POWs 101
PPP 101, 300, 301
Prakashanand Saraswati 177
Prion 197, 198
Prophet, Muhammad (saws) 105, 115, 117, 118, 124, 125
Protestants 129, 130
Proto–Siva 224, 225
Psychology 2
Purusha Sukta 320
Purna, Svami HH 246, 250, 251, 256

Q

Qasim 89, 90, 117
Qoraish Tribe
Quantum Mechanics 4
Qumran 127
Qur'an 108, 116, 117, 122, 123, 125, 138, 161, 192, 193, 295,
Qureshi, I.H. 89

R

Race 3, 54, 61, 65, 83, 84, 96, 207, 208, 210, 215, 230, 232, 274,
Radium 4
Rajnya 46, 47, 48, 49, 50, 61, 62, 87, 249
Rajput 88, 94, 117
Rama, Lord 7, 21, 23, 28, 72, 80, 208
Rao, SM 19, 145, 228
Rape 37, 88, 102, 173
Ravana 72, 285
Ravi, Shankar Sri 61, 69, 147
Reappraisal 37, 49, 154, 248, 261, Purusha Sukta 49, 248, 261
Rebellion 1857 177
Redacted 1, 41, 79, 208
Relatively 3, 199, 200, 204
Remarriages 161, 162, 247, 275
Resurrection 123, 130
Rheumatism 195
Rift Valley 29, 32
Rigveda 1, 2, 8, 11, 12, 13, 14, 22, 44, 47, 50, 52
Rishika 8, 53, 147, 148, 238, 247
River Sukta (X.75)
Roman 107, 129, 137, 161, 242, 243, 244
Rome 2, 40, 128, 133, 197
Rroma 241
Rudra 51, 139, 140, 170, 225
Rukum–al–Hindia 6

S

Sagan, Carl 33, 263, 288
Sahani, Dr. 216
Sahasra 2
Samdarsi 69
Samaveda 1, 11, 12, 14, 79, 149, 276, 285
Sanskrit 1, 2, 15, 23, 42, 76, 80, 109, 133, 136, 263, 264
Saraswati River 14, 15, 18, 25, 236, 237, 255
Sati 18, 151, 152, 153, 158, 164, 296
Saturated fat 202
Sayana 9, 157, 209, 238
Schrodinger 4
Scripture 1, 5, 11, 40, 76, 78, 195, 268, 272, 275, 280, 284
Scythians 3, 160, 245
Seilachar, Adolf 29
Sen, Mohit 83

Shafii 122
Shahadatah 119
Shankaracharya 251, 256, 260, 271, 290
Shantanu 52, 79
Shariat Law 120
Sharma, Ganga Sahay Dr., 14, 45, 61, 154, 163, 285, 291
Sharma, Shri Ram 11, 14, 48, 61, 154
Shankaracharya, Jyotirmath HH 251, 256
Shankaracharya, Kanchi HH 251, 256, 260
Shephard, E.W. 91
Shiite/Shia 115, 119, 120, 123
Shrimali, Radhakrishna 155, 156
Sicilian 7
Similes Sindhu 17, 237, 240, 267
Sita 226
Siva/Shiva 51, 79, 224, 225
Slave mentality 97, 99
Social Sciences 2
Software 7
Solar 2, 25, 281, 287
Somerset 31
Son 10, 24, 50, 64, 79, 103, 119, 121, 123, 126
Space Sciences 128, 131, 137, 138, 165, 213
Spain 6, 105, 134, 160, 241
Spherical 4
Suddhi 77
Sudra 147, 148, 296
Sumosa 237
Sun 4, 33, 126, 137, 144, 174, 176, 262, 263, 287, 288
Sunni 115, 117, 118, 119, 120, 122, 294
Supreme Court 104, 109, 157, 166, 191, 193, 292
Sutlej 15, 18, 20, 237
Suturdi 15, 236, 237
Swamy, Subramanian Dr. 212
Swara 1, 43
Swarit 1
Swastika 225, 226
Synagogue 132
Syria 24, 107, 127, 132, 234

T

Talageri, SG 27, 233, 236, 238, 239, 297
Talwar, KK Dr. 203
Tanzania 30, 32
Taranath 177, 178, 179
Taxila 128
Testament, New 125, 128
Testament, Old 23, 128, 132
Tethys Sea 32
Texas 5
Thapar, Romila Dr. 194, 207, 209, 232, 219
Thrombogenicity 202
Thromboxane 202
Thunderbolt 8, 13, 60, 172
Tiger 224, 229
Tipu 93
Toumai 29
Trinity 7, 123, 125, 130
Trishtubh 7
TSE 197
Tubingen 28
Tughlak 77
Turkey 23

U

Udatta 1
Unu–datta
Urine, Cow 142, 190
Usmani, M.S. Dr. 193

Uthman, Hazrat 118, 119

V

Vaishya 8, 46, 47, 48, 49, 50, 61, 63, 253
Vaisya 65, 66, 68, 73, 69
Vajpayee, AB 254
Valdiya 18
Valmiki Ramayan 21, 45, 72, 76, 285
Varanasi 9, 24, 238
Varkari 58, 82
Varuna 24
Vatican 130, 132, 133, 134, 161
Veda, Vedas 8, 14, 32, 41, 42, 250, 260, 274, 295, 297
Vedvyas 1, 79, 165, 194, 295
Venom 190
Victoria Cross 95
Vipasa 20, 237
Vishnu Smriti 43
Vishwamitra 52, 53, 291, 296
Vitasa 237
Vivekanand, Swami 82, 277

W

Wahhabi 122
War 2, 8, 12, 24, 25, 38, 65, 92, 93, 94, 95, 101, 182, 183, 235, 249
Weaponry 2
Weinberg, Steve 5
WHO
Widows/Widow 151, 153, 154, 155, 157, 158, 159, 162, 164, 247, 261, 296, 297
Wilcox, Wheeler 4, 218, 299
Wilhemy, Herbert 18
William Pitt 92
Wilson, HH 8, 9, 13, 14, 45, 45, 46, 47, 51, 148 154, 156, 158, 161, 162, 167, 180, 181, 183, 184, 186, 188, 237,
Witzel, Michael 219, 238, 240
Women 41, 53, 62, 68, 74, 69, 73, 85, 88, 123, 126, 135, 136, 143, 146, 147, 148, 158, 167, 204, 247, 250, 255, 256, 285, 290, 296, 296

X

X–mas 43, 137, 159, 194

Y

Yajnavalkya 43, 159, 194
Yajurveda 1, 2, 3, 11, 13, 14, 27, 47, 53, 54, 60, 61, 170, 187, 194, 285
Yamuna 15, 18, 20, 236, 239, 240
Yashpal 18
Yeravda Agreement 101
Yudhishthir 165
Yuz Asaf 128

Z

Zend Avesta 124
Zero 2, 3, 36, 267, 299
Zoroaster 207
Zoroastrian 124, 231, 233
Zulunation 212